The G20 Development Agenda

An Indian Perspective

EDITED BY
PARTHASARATHI SHOME

CAMBRIDGE
UNIVERSITY PRESS

CAMBRIDGE
UNIVERSITY PRESS

4843/24, 2nd Floor, Ansari Road, Daryaganj, Delhi - 110002, India

Cambridge University Press is part of the University of Cambridge.

It furthers the University's mission by disseminating knowledge in the pursuit of education, learning and research at the highest international levels of excellence.

www.cambridge.org
Information on this title: www.cambridge.org/9781107091528

First published 2015

Printed in India by Thomson Press India Ltd., New Delhi 110001

A catalogue record for this publication is available from the British Library

Library of Congress Cataloging-in-Publication Data

The G20 development agenda : an Indian perspective / edited by
Parthasarathi Shome.
pages cm
Includes bibliographical references and index.
Summary: "Analyses the evolution and broadening of the G20's agenda from
global financial sector matters to covering a vast development agenda"--
Provided by publisher.
ISBN 978-1-107-09152-8 (hardback)
1. Economic assistance--India. 2. India--Economic integration. 3.
Economic development projects--Management. 4. India--Economic
conditions--21st century. 5. Group of Twenty countries--Economic policy.
6. Economic policy--International cooperation. I. Shome, Parthasarathi,
1950- editor.
HC435.3.G2 2015
338.91--dc23
2014038364

ISBN 978-1-107-09152-8 Hardback

Contents

List of Tables and Figures

List of Tables

List of Figures

Preface

The Group of 20 nations (G20) continues to be the premier forum for global economic governance with its relative success in containing the deleterious aftermath of the global economic crisis of 2008–09. In 2010, there was an upturn experienced at a wider macro level if not at an individual economy level for which a more fundamental restructuring of the global economy would be required than was actually reached. The G20's achievement was, nevertheless, to bring together developed and emerging economies and initiate a series of macro-economic and financial sector reforms as the crisis originated from that sector, and be able to coordinate to an observable extent the policies that the members would take for cross-country stabilization.

As the global economy recovered in 2010, the G20 began expanding its brief to include a development agenda, in particular, achieving food security in an environment of commodity price volatility, recycling global savings to boost infrastructure investment, enhancing international burden sharing, and energy and environmental sustainability. Thus, the G20 embarked on a strategy to broaden its agenda that had included global macroeconomic coordination together with financial sector reforms and regulation and the reform of international financial institutions, to also include a list of development agenda pillars together with energy security and environmental sustainability. During the concerned period, India's position was that of a growing emerging economy of significant size that came off relatively unscathed by the crisis despite extensive opening up of its economy to international trade. It was well placed to influence the G20 in its functioning as a global steering entity.

A recent volume edited by Shome (2014)[1] has examined emerging economy concerns and perspectives on reforms of the financial sector and the international monetary system, with a focus on India, set in the context of G20 reform initiatives and impasses. With this backdrop, this new volume

[1] Shome, Parthasarathi (edited). 2014. *The G20 Macroeconomic Agenda: India and the Emerging Economies*, Cambridge University Press, New Delhi.

assesses the progress as well as unresolved concerns of the G20's development agenda, with a focus on India. The volume is a collection of essays covering important aspects of the G20's development agenda, with an introductory chapter that addresses the evolution of the G20 and its subsequent inclusion of a development agenda and brings together selected development concerns, touching upon component aspects.

The G20's concerns are varied and constantly changing, thus providing rich ground to present and analyse them. Section 2 addresses the issue of commodity market policy for food security and explores the role of financialization of commodities, both in the international and Indian context. The section also examines the matter of recycling global surpluses to finance infrastructure investment in emerging economies. Coexistence of a persistent gap in infrastructure investment in some countries *pari passu* with excessive savings elsewhere, represents a serious drawback in converting savings into investment at a global level. However, profitable recycling of global savings is inhibited by considerable maturity mismatch risks and several alternatives to effectively manage the mismatch risk are explored. Given the G20's development initiatives, India's role in international burden sharing is discussed. And the section also addresses the prevailing structural impediments to India's growth prospects.

This is followed by energy security and environmental sustainability that have been added to the G20's emerging agenda. Section 3 discusses global initiatives on climate change and adaptation financing in the context of equity and economic efficiency. It explores the cost and benefit of energy subsidies as the intent and impact vary substantially among G20 members. The OECD countries provide subsidies to ensure regional employment and energy-supply security, while emerging economies aim at managing the price of basic goods and services where energy is a key input, with the objective of reaching out to poor end-users. As India contemplates taking up membership in the International Energy Agency (IEA) for better energy security, this section also weighs the cost of membership and the loss of policy autonomy, against the fact that non-members, including India currently, enjoy the positive externalities of global oil stabilization measures taken by the IEA.

Undoubtedly, the G20 has proved its resilience in bringing to the table emerging issues proving to be of global concern, the most recent just having emerged being base erosion and profit shifting for tax minimization by multinational companies whose global tax contribution has fallen to negligible levels at a time when the need for funds to reduce fiscal deficits or fund much needed programmes is at its highest. Despite ever new challenges, the G20, somewhat surprisingly perhaps, appears to remain the most relevant international body to combat the continuing global recessionary environment while pursuing emerging development and structural challenges.

Appreciation for support received in the formulation of this volume authored by a wide array of authors is warranted. First, the Indian Ministry of Finance financed the research as a part of an overarching collaborative project on the G20 with the Indian Council for Research on International Economic Relations (ICRIER) where I was Director and Chief Executive when I headed the project. Francis Rathinam and Pooja Sharma managed the project on a day-to-day basis and Santosh Gupta provided secretarial help. It is hoped that the readership will find this work on the G20's development agenda a useful addition to the earlier work from the project on the G20's macroeconomic agenda, while the future calls for another volume on the G20's emerging concerns over depletion of tax revenues in the multinational context.

New Delhi — Parthasarathi Shome

Section 1
Introduction

1 Group of 20

The Development Agenda – An Indian Perspective

Parthasarathi Shome and Francis Xavier Rathinam

Introduction

The global financial crisis of 2008–09 originated in the United States, proceeded *pari passu* in European economies, spread to emerging economies through trade and finance channels, and led to a collapse of confidence. The fault lines comprised deep breaches in economic fundamentals including excessive bank credit, build-up of private consumption based on uncollateralized loans, and an inexorable rise in public debt (Shome, 2013). These elements possessed the potential to precipitate a global depression. Remittances slowed down, export demand weakened, export credit dried up and capital flows dwindled. The common consensus was to revive credit lines to restore confidence, curb protectionist tendencies, institute measures to stimulate and rebalance global demand in the medium term.

A group of leading global economies – the Group of 20 (G20) – was formed to frontally address the fault lines.[1] The G20 provided the critical mass needed for building global consensus for mobilizing resources to fend off the impending economic crisis associated with the 2008–09 financial crisis that acted as a precursor. It also imparted a sense of urgency, direction and action in the multilateral agencies for tackling the crisis. The G20 embarked on a strategy to formulate policies to address interconnected short-term and medium-term challenges with the objective of enhancing global economic governance i.e., re-regulating the financial sector, correcting macroeconomic and development imbalances, and providing for global public goods, in particular channeling global resources for financing development, energy and food security and environmental sustainability.

The G20 initiated a series of reforms in the financial sector which reflected the origin of crisis in this sector. Stimulus packages were formulated in the form of unprecedented bail-outs as well as the recapitalization of banks and financial institutions to loosen a severe liquidity crunch. The G20 also initiated a series of measures to identify and check global macroeconomic imbalances, introduced measures to check friction in global monetary arrangements, enhanced financial safety nets, and supported the use of capital controls under certain extenuating circumstances. Perhaps more importantly, it ensured that members opted for national policies that were not detrimental to the recovery of others, and agreed to avoid premature withdrawal of stimuli and exit from the programmes in a coordinated way. With these initiatives, the G20 is broadly perceived to have delivered on the immediate goal of preventing the crisis from deteriorating into a full-blown depression. The G20 leaders declared that their cooperation worked as the global economy fared better than expected in 2009 and recovered well in 2010 (WEO, 2010).

As the global economy recovered in 2010, the time appeared to be ripe for reorienting and expanding the G20 agenda to include developmental issues (Shome and Rathinam, 2011). Global developmental concerns were critical for some of the emerging economy members of the G20 themselves. The G20 also represented a gateway for them to reach out to other developing economies and gain credibility in the global governance arena if continuing cooperation was to be obtained from non-G20 economies. However, the G20 had to tread carefully as inclusion of development ran the danger of mission creep as several of the development agenda issues were already being dealt with elsewhere in multilateral organizations concerned with the development architecture. The job for the G20 was, therefore, to re-emphasize those issues by providing political critical mass and successfully leveraging the existing development architecture to deliver positive outcomes. Some commentators argued that the G20 should restrict itself to encouraging cooperation between international organizations, coordinating domestic policies of member countries and extending knowledge to non-members (Davies, 2013) rather than embarking on its own delivery framework. Nevertheless, the G20 expanded its brief to include a development agenda – in particular, achieving food security, controlling commodity price volatility, recycling global savings to boost infrastructure investment as well as enhancing energy and environmental sustainability. This volume relates to these issues.

The growing economic reach of emerging economies had a discernible impact on the global geopolitical balance and, hence, on their role in global governance and agenda. For example, Brazil, Russia, India, China and South Africa (BRICS), as members of the G20 were well placed to influence, support and even lead agenda on specific issues as well as contribute effectively to global economic discussion and policy setting. They found themselves as having a high stake in and possessing decisive power to contribute to, global recovery in the short run and to global governance in the longer run.

There are not yet too many scholarly treatises on the G20 with particular focus on emerging economy interests such as India's concerns and perspectives set in the context of G20 reform initiatives and challenges. The literature on the G20 from an emerging economy perspective is very recent. A volume edited by Shome (2014a) has examined emerging economy concerns and perspectives on reforms of the financial sector and the international monetary system set in the context of G20 reform initiatives and impasses, with the focus on India. It stopped short, however, of assessing the progress or any unresolved concerns of the G20's development agenda.

In the same vein, another attempt to provide a developing country perspective on the scope for cooperation among G20 members for better world economic outcomes may be found in Callaghan *et al.* (2014a). This volume focuses once again on key macroeconomic issues such as rebalancing in a multi-paced global growth scenario, balancing financial sector safety and development, reforming the international monetary system, and reinstating capital controls and austerity for optimal growth while considering the context of the Eurozone crisis. It discusses substantive structural and governance issues such as how best the G20 could become more inclusive at the same time remaining a manageably-sized leaders' forum. While the volume skilfully intertwines the likely impact of macroeconomic initiatives on India and other emerging economies, it does not directly address the barriers for further cooperation from a developing country perspective, in particular, regarding development issues.

In this backdrop, the current volume discusses the role India has played in the success of the G20 process with a focus on its development agenda. It delineates the possible barriers to India's enhanced involvement in the G20 and in global governance in general. It also explores what needs to be accomplished in the medium term for more inclusive global development. This volume follows a first volume (Shome, 2014a) cited above that was set in similar fashion while focusing on the G20's macroeconomic and financial sector agenda including the reform of multilateral institutions.

This second volume is organized in correspondence to the major development themes in the G20's focus areas, especially with respect to providing global public goods such as recycling global savings for development, and financing investment in global food and energy security, green growth and environmental sustainability.

Section 2 addresses the issue of recycling global savings to finance infrastructure investment in developing countries, and appropriate structural instruments in the context of India. Co-existence of a persistent gap in infrastructure investment in some countries, while excessive savings persist elsewhere, represents a serious drawback in converting savings into investment at the global level, underlying which is the need to rebalance the current accounts of deficit countries *vis-à-vis* surplus countries (Shome, 2012). If matching of demand and supply of savings could be achieved internationally, it would certainly provide an opportunity for removing structural impediments to growth in developing countries where the demand for investment lies thus boosting global production and growth. However, in practice, recycling of global savings is inhibited by considerable maturity mismatch risks. This section discusses potential impediments to growth in India, and explores alternatives to effectively recycle global savings and manage mismatch risks. Given the G20 development initiatives, India's role in international burden sharing is accordingly discussed. Finally, this section addresses commodity market policy for food security, and explores the role of financialization of commodities, both in the international and in the Indian context.

Section 3 first analyses the issue of energy security, and addresses the costs and benefits of energy subsidies as their intent and impact vary substantially across the G20 members. The Organization for Economic Co-operation and Development (OECD) countries provide subsidies to ensure regional employment and energy supply security, while the developing economies aim at managing the prices of basic goods and services in which energy is a key input, with the objective of reaching out to vulnerable end-users. As India contemplates taking up membership at the International Energy Agency (IEA) for better energy security, this section weighs the cost of membership and the loss of policy autonomy, against the fact that the non-members, including India, would enjoy the positive externalities of global oil stabilization measures taken by IEA if they were to take up membership.

Section 3 continues with the issue of environmental sustainability. It discusses global initiatives on climate change and adaptation financing in the context of global equity and economic efficiency. The G20 has been successful in bringing issues such as fossil fuel subsidy reform, climate change finance and energy efficiency into the mainstream debate that were earlier dealt with by specialized multilateral arrangements usually lacking adequate support. It has been able to fill the space and provide much needed political backing. This section explores new avenues for innovative revenue generation such as a global carbon emissions tax, air transport congestion tax, and other potential multi-source resource mobilization handles for financing global environmental objectives.

Purpose and Evolution of the G20 Development Agenda

The global developmental architecture (GDA), prior to the 2008–09 global financial crisis comprised a complex inter-linkage between the formal institutions of global development assistance – the United Nations and the Bretton Woods institutions – and informal groupings such as the Group of 7 (G7) and, later, the Group of 8 (G8). The GDA's main focus was coordinating macroeconomic management, fostering free international trade and development aid, while its non-core themes comprised energy, food security, environment, and countering terrorism.

The decade preceding the crisis witnessed significant geopolitical changes – the rise of new growth poles and a dwindling share of the G8 in both global GDP and trade. Consequently, the G8 by itself found itself unable to address newly emerging global challenges. The G8's outreach programme, named G8+O5, was to better integrate the emerging economic powers such as Brazil, China, India, Mexico and South Africa into the global governance process. While the outreach programme managed to include some issues pertaining to global economic development, the core governance issues remained unaddressed (Singh, 2009). With the advent of the G20 as a newly elevated premier forum for global governance, it became feasible to provide the necessary political impetus for both short term coordination and medium to long term development initiatives on a global scale.

In a joint paper issued at a G8 Summit organized in 2007, Brazil, China, India, Mexico and South Africa had indicated that the expanded network was able to look into pressing matters such as quota reforms in the Bretton Woods institutions, to conclude the Doha Development Agenda, to pursue differentiated climate change responsibility, and to help frame better energy and food security policies. However, by 2008–09, it had become clearer that such structural initiatives had not taken off too successfully. It was the G20 that subsequently provided the emerging economies a visible platform for steering the agenda to address seething development imbalances while, at the same time, managing to stem the crisis by 2010.

The promulgation of the G20 development agenda is generally attributed to the Seoul Summit. However, the G20 (1999) as a Finance Ministers' and Central Bank Governors' forum, had already recognized development as integral to global economic cooperation. Later, though the first Leaders' Summits were dominated by immediate concerns of the crisis, the Leaders also highlighted, for example, in Washington D.C., their development commitments through backing multilateral agencies' development mandates, recognizing member countries' own responsibilities for ensuring economic and social development, and urging other developing countries to undertake the Millennium Development Goals (MDG)[2] commitments consistent with their capacities (G20, 2008).

In the 2009 London Summit, the Leaders suggested that:

> growth, to be sustained, has to be shared; and that our global plan for recovery must have at its heart the needs and jobs of hard-working families not just in developed countries but in emerging markets and the poorest countries of the world too (G20, 2009a).

They promised more aid to sub-Saharan Africa for boosting trade and enhanced resources for lower income countries for better social protection and food security. Encouraged by global recovery, the Leaders endorsed a 'Framework for Strong, Sustainable and Balanced Growth' in Pittsburgh (G20, 2009b) and urged the World Bank and other multilateral agencies to emphasize agricultural productivity and food security, infrastructure investment, energy efficiency and climate resistance in developing countries.

In the Toronto Summit (G20, 2010a) the leaders reiterated their commitment to 'strengthen the focus on lifting the lives of the poor' and agreed to establish a Working Group on Development mandated to propose a development agenda and multi-year action plans to be discussed and adopted at the subsequent Seoul Summit (G20, 2010b). Primarily, however, until the Seoul Summit, developmental issues were mainly constrained to resisting protectionism and easing the supply of developmental finance for food security and infrastructure investment.

The Seoul Summit was the watershed moment in global development cooperation. The 'Seoul Development Consensus for Shared Growth' and 'Multi-Year Action Plan on Development' identified nine pillars for inclusive and sustainable development: infrastructure, human resource development, trade, private investment and job creation, food security, growth with resilience, financial inclusion, domestic resource mobilization and knowledge sharing. The action plan detailed the necessary action points for effectively removing the bottlenecks in achieving the endorsed development goals.

However, limited progress on several development pillars led, during the French presidency, to further streamlining of the agenda into the pillars that help promote growth and those that foster resilience (Davies, 2013). The 2011 Cannes Summit prioritized food security, infrastructure, and finance for development so as to 'overcome the most critical bottlenecks and constraints hampering growth in developing countries' (G20, 2011). They were picked over the other pillars, job creation, agricultural productivity, capacity building and knowledge sharing. While the Leaders returned to firefighting during the Mexican presidency of the G20, they reiterated that development remained one of the core objectives of the G20. In practice, the efforts were directed towards commodity price volatility, food security and infrastructure and newly introduced a key challenge inclusive of green growth into the agenda (G20, 2012).

The Russian presidency stated that the development agenda was among its priorities as infrastructure and access to basic amenities are fundamental prerequisites for spurring economic growth. Specifically, the stated priorities included food security, human resource development, financial inclusion, infrastructure and a post-2015 development agenda (G20, 2013). However, while the broad themes of Russian development priorities were consistent with previous development commitments, some commentators expressed the view that the Russian presidency's emphasis falls outside the purview of the Development Working Group (DWG) (Carin, 2013).

The Russian presidency also took forward the commitment on accountability made in the Leaders' Declaration at Los Cabos, Mexico to develop a mechanism for taking stock of the achievements, assessing the progress, drawing lessons and, in the process, streamlining and strengthening the G20 development agenda going forward (G20, 2013a). While lauding the G20 for delivering strong results on developmental issues, the St. Petersburg Development Outlook identifies several long-term objectives as key deliverables of the Russian Presidency. They include quality jobs and investment, trust and transparency, sustainability and resilience, and social inclusiveness (G20, 2013b). One of the welcome changes was to consult developing countries, particularly low income countries (LICs), and regional and sub-regional organizations, for refining the development agenda.

The Australian presidency's development focus is to link development to growth through better infrastructure investment by private sector, information sharing between tax authorities, access to financial services and reducing the cost of remittances into developing economies (G20, 2013c). Australia is well placed to 'mainstream' the development agenda into the

G20's core themes as it has been making considerable contributions to the development agenda through co-chairing the DWG.

India's Role in the G20 Development Agenda

In the new multi-polar world, India enjoys considerable attention reflective of its integration with the global economy through the current and capital accounts of its balance of payments (Shome, 2012; 2014b). However, its growing economic advances are not fully reflected in the prevailing global governance arrangements, beginning with the above-mentioned G8+O5 outreach programme, which did not represent India's interests adequately. Singh (2009) lamented that the outreach initiative was not cohesive, that the countries lacked a composite identity, and that the group did not participate fully in the proceedings and the preparations. Indian policy-makers repeatedly emphasized that India had 'a lot at stake and a lot to contribute' to global governance, and assured that 'India [would] seek its due place, play its destined role and share its assigned responsibility … guided by the principle of common but differentiated responsibility and respective capability'.

India is an avid supporter of including a development agenda in global economic governance arrangements. In its joint statement with Brazil, China, Mexico and South Africa during the G8 Summit in 2008 in Heiligendamm, Germany, it avowed:

> Development is a right, central to people's progress and critical to the eradication of poverty, fostering peace, stability and security of all nations... . We are committed to working with our partners to advance the development agenda and the eradication of poverty. We believe that eradication of poverty in the world is not only an issue of importance to developing countries, but also a matter of our collective global interest.

This book addresses India's concerns reflecting inadequate infrastructure, food and energy security, and green growth, how India has contributed to these G20 agenda issues, and how global coordination could result in better outcomes for India and other emerging economies.

Structural Impediments in Developing Economies and the G20

Underdevelopment is self-perpetuating. The literature on economic growth identifies accumulation of real and human capital and technological progress as fundamental to growth, and for progressing to a diversified economy based on manufacturing and services from a primarily agrarian economy.

Many impediments to growth could be successfully dealt with at a country level. For example, there are several instances where countries have transformed themselves from a developing to a developed status within a generation. However, there are other aspects of development that need international cooperation such as mobilizing resources for achieving MDG targets, mobilizing global savings for infrastructure investment in own countries, and ensuring free trade and trade finance, food and energy security, and knowledge sharing.

These are constraints that comprise not only national priorities for emerging economy G20 members but also represent growth constraints for developing countries more broadly. The G20 is well placed to address these constrains and igniting the forces of global growth. This section includes three papers that look into major structural impediments to growth in India, how the G20 could mobilize resources to finance development investment, and what role India could play in international burden sharing.

In his chapter, **Kirit Parikh** explores significant structural impediments to India's growth. The literature on total factor productivity growth (TFPG) in India reveals that capital accumulation, infrastructure development, human capital and technological progress, and energy, especially in the context of growing scarcity of natural resources, are fundamental constraints to growth in India. Shome (2011) has pointed to gross inadequacies in the formation of human capital and its conversion to a demographic dividend. Parikh, in this volume, addresses another infrastructure constraint. He identifies poor infrastructure, endemic power shortages, energy scarcity, and poor enrolment in primary and elementary schools as binding constraints on the Indian economy. Inefficiencies in power and transportation are argued to be critical. He estimates a 0.1 per cent negative growth elasticity for average energy deficit, and asserts that the differences in state level GDP between 2002–03 to 2009–10 could be explained by varying energy deficits among them.

D. K. Srivastava reviews how India and the G20 economies managed the crisis, the impact of the crisis on the developed countries' commitment to international burden sharing, and the role of emerging economies, especially India, in international burden sharing for own as well as global collateral benefits. He argues that although India lost about 1.5 to 2 percentage points in economic growth during the crisis *vis-a-vis* the average growth of 9 per cent during 2005–06 to 2007–08, India was considered to have weathered the crisis relatively successfully. Moreover, deceleration of growth could be partly attributed to inflation emanating from domestic supply-side shocks in the agricultural sector.

Highlighting the volatility and unpredictability of development aid in the form of Official Development Assistance (ODA) due to changes in donor priorities and budgetary procedures as well as administrative delays, Srivastava calls for exploring new sources and avenues for development assistance. Thus, emerging economies with surpluses could be a new source of development assistance. Further, many emerging economies, including India, could contribute to global efforts for achieving the Millennium Development Goals (MDGs) with both resources and knowledge based on local success stories, even while they themselves may require support from international initiatives to strengthen their past achievements. He argues that India would be better off by simultaneously contributing to, and receiving, international aid especially in fields such as health and education.

India's strategy for international burden sharing, Srivastava argues, should be consistent with its growth strategy focusing on the education and health sectors in the social sectors and also on physical infrastructure. The sharing should be in geographical areas where India sources its natural resources and, therefore, is obliged to contribute to the welfare of those economies. That would benefit both the recipient countries as well as India. He argues that the efforts should be concentrated on reducing negative externalities such as the spreading of Acquired Immunodeficiency Syndrome (AIDS) in the region, including Bangladesh, Nepal and Sri Lanka while reducing its incidence in India. He highlights the importance of prioritizing high quality and high impact interventions.

Contributions to development assistance should be appreciated in the light of the increasing presence of China in ODA. Srivastava discusses some innovative mechanisms with large revenue potential for financing such as a financial transactions tax or emissions trading. While these innovative financing mechanisms are not yet fully developed, according to him they should be made increasingly complementary to the traditional methods.

Against this backdrop, **Renu Kohli** discusses what the G20 could do to ease structural impediments such as inadequate infrastructure. In her chapter, she discusses historical incidents of recycling excess savings to invest in emerging economies and draws lessons for potential policy options for the G20 for recycling.

Export-led growth strategies of deficit emerging economies pose a challenge to them as global demand is slackening, even as surplus economies find it difficult to stimulate domestic demand. Developing a mechanism to intermediate surplus savings towards the countries where there is excess demand for investment would complement policies in place for reducing macro, trade and development imbalances. As infrastructure investment tends to be import intensive, such investment in emerging economies should help boost global demand. Further, targeted infrastructure investment should increase production capacities in receiving economies, create a favourable investment climate and encourage complementary domestic investment. Kohli argues that this is a win-win outcome for surplus and deficit countries alike and they can both contribute towards an international public good with dividends to both partners.

From the historical experience of Japan's capital-recycling savings programme of 1986, Kohli highlights the importance of low cost, long tenure financing, which is an essential prerequisite for the success of recycling. Based on analysis, she recommends setting up a special purpose vehicle (SPV) that would be named Emerging Markets' Infrastructure Financing Facility (EMIFF), and suggests India should offer to support the setting up of the facility. She also draws attention to the political viability and advantages of choosing the SPV option. As it is aligned with the interests of the G20's surplus (source) as well as receiving (host) countries which extends to non-members, the G20 is well placed to broker such a model that could deliver low cost, long-gestation financing. The SPV would not only channel savings but would coordinate that function with appropriate macroeconomic policies that could help reduce the twin macro and development imbalances. Further, the G20 should structure the management of the SPV to best reflect the prevailing geopolitical conditions and represent the interests of major economies essential for successful buy-in.

Food and Energy Security and Commodity Price Volatility

Food and energy security are fundamental to India's development agenda. Indian policy makers have repeatedly emphasized the need for food and energy security and how to address the increasing financialization of the commodities markets that is perceived as a source of volatility. The G20 Leaders at the 2010 Seoul Summit sought to understand national, regional and global food stocks and associated forecasts, to access to humanitarian supplies to maintain nutrition levels, and to manage price volatility without distorting market behaviour (G20, 2010b). Further, the 2011 Cannes Summit managed to create an Agricultural Market Information System (AMIS) for collecting better data on food stocks, improve production and price forecasts, and realistically assess food scarcity and the need for wider access to non-commercial humanitarian food supplies. While India has always supported humanitarian assistance and freer trade, it has felt compelled to give priority to food security at home.

On commodity price volatility, researchers identified demand and supply imbalances and export restrictions as the factors that explain recent price fluctuations, especially for major energy commodities such as crude oil and natural gas, and staple foods such as corn, rice and wheat. India, however, remained cautious about excessive financialization of major food and energy commodities, especially regarding large financial interventions in the market.

In their chapter, **Rajesh Chakrabarti, Francis Xavier Rathinam and Vijay Kumar Varadi** suggest that excessive importance placed on the primacy of commodity derivatives is misplaced and, instead, the G20 as well as the Indian government should concentrate on freer trade and better policy certainty. Using monthly data from the Indian commodity markets, the authors show that commodity prices in India could be explained by market fundamentals and macroeconomic factors in general, while financial factors such as lagged changes in spot prices do not help explain all of the commodity movements. This indicates a lack of concrete proof of any powerful negative impact of financialization on commodity prices in India. Similarly, causality tests indicate a bidirectional flow of information, thereby indicating no obvious unidirectional effects of futures markets on spot prices.

Based on their empirical analysis, the authors suggest two broad classes of possible policy options for the G20, first pertains to free trade of food and commodities and the second pertains to the regulation of commodity derivatives market. Maintaining export continuity and reduction of tariff levels of commodities for a wider and freer trade in foodgrains and commodities would help ensure deeper, long term benefits to both producer and consumer countries. On the derivatives, the G20 should strive for policy continuity since an 'on-now off-again' approach would lead to uncertainty in the markets and hurt market participation as well as the quality of price signals.

The G20 energy agenda includes stemming of price volatility, gradually eliminating fossil fuel subsidies, and promoting clean and efficient energy. The Leaders committed at the 2009 Pittsburgh Summit to phase out fossil fuel subsidies in the medium term, and create an environment for clean energy. They reaffirmed their resolve in 2010 at Seoul. India maintained in various fora that phasing out subsidy was a priority but that it should be adapted to the local context while keeping the interest of the poorest in mind.

In their chapter on fossil fuel subsidization in India, **Meeta Keswani Mehra** and **Divya Datt** discuss the rationale for energy subsidies in general, and for providing access to energy and reducing energy poverty in the context of developing countries. Using three National Sample Survey Organisation (NSSO) survey rounds on consumer expenditure and energy use, they attempt to assess the impact of price on the use of important fuels such as fuel wood, kerosene, liquefied petroleum gas (LPG) and electricity, and estimate price elasticity of demand for each fuel in rural and urban settings. While the efficiency principle of taxation would mean that the tax (or subsidy) reforms should be directed towards fuels with least elastic demand, the equity principle would ask for examining which group of consumers use a particular fuel and for what purpose. Thus, any reform should balance equity and efficiency objectives.

Based on their analysis, the authors suggest that subsidies should be targeted towards maintaining the prices of basic goods and services of only lifeline consumers. This should also be complemented with production, transportation and distributional reforms in the fuel production chain. First, as LPG and petrol are used by relatively richer segments of the population, the prices of LPG and petrol should be reformed to increasingly reflect international prices while, kerosene, which is mainly used by lifeline consumers below the poverty line, may continue to be subsidized. They find no compelling reason to subsidize diesel which is used mainly for transportation. It is indicated that Government may gain from reforming the delivery mechanism i.e., using IT enabled smart cards to best target the subsidized population. They highlight that, while coal can afford to suffer little price escalation, there are considerable avenues for reform of investment in the sector, as well as in the handling and transport networks, with the objective of gradually freeing the pricing of coal. The current subsidy structure makes average electricity tariffs in India one of the lowest and uneconomic in the world. While there is little doubt that, in the future, electricity tariffs have to be revised upwards, cross-subsidization of agriculture should be directed away from the richer farmers as well as from water-intensive crops to achieve better equity and resource conservation.

On India's energy security and on whether India should join the IEA, **Prodipto Ghosh** asks for carefully weighing the pros and cons of IEA membership and the prospects for a potential governance reform at the IEA that would truly reflect the current international energy usage structure, with options outside a formal membership. The costs of membership seem to be the cost of strategic petroleum reserves and the sacrifice of an independent national petroleum policy. Oil stabilization measures comprise a global public good that would benefit both members as well as non-members. Hence, non-members may benefit from IEA's oil stabilization measures without losing control over national petroleum policy. He argues that the potential cost of joining the IEA outweighs the benefits from IEA's global oil stabilization measures, unless serious governance reforms are undertaken at the IEA. India should, of course, collaborate with the IEA and participate in its non-core activities to build mutual confidence.

Green Growth and Environmental Sustainability

Climate change is both a national as well as a transnational issue. While many of the climate adaptation and mitigation initiatives are national or at best regional in nature, there are several cross-national issues with a wider reach, such as climate financing, standard setting, emission control, carbon tax or technology transfer. The transnational aspects of climate change make environmental sustainability and green growth a quintessential matter for the G20. While several of them such as fossil fuel subsidy reform, climate change finance and energy efficiency are dealt with through existing multilateral arrangements, the inclusion of a green growth agenda into the G20 has provided political impetus to global environmental cooperation. The G20, in turn, has expanded the traditional domain to include reduction of energy price volatility and developing a new subject-related database. This section includes two chapters that attempt to chart out solutions to selected environmental challenges and explore avenues for innovative financing, cooperation and problem-solving.

Parthasarathi Shome and Amrita Goldar, in their chapter, provide a comprehensive overview of the G20's energy and environment agenda focusing on fossil fuel subsidies, energy efficiency, climate change finance and oil price volatility and cast this entire area of concern and action as an integral part of global governance. In the backdrop of the G20's opportunities, initiatives, and success on climate change issues, they attempt to weave these disparate pieces together for providing a new 'greener' agenda for the G20. They compare market based incentives and taxes against the cap and trade system in the context of global emission reduction to suggest that, while both provide incentives to the private sector to innovate and minimize negative externalities, care should be taken to ensure that the vulnerable are adequately protected. They call for including a broadened emphasis on climate change and infrastructure in the G20 agenda that would effectively improve the coping and adapting capabilities of individual economies. Investment in green infrastructure, it is argued, could be financed through a global carbon tax and is rewarding both for the exchequer and for the economy's sustainable growth. Another area in need of greater international cooperation is in funding, capacity building and knowledge sharing in science, technology and innovation. Research consortia comprise one avenue to ensure adequate scale and knowledge sharing.

The crux of the 'greener' G20 agenda depends critically on the feasibility of generating global revenue for financing these global objectives. The authors propose a global carbon emissions tax and an air transport congestion tax that may provide needed revenue and, at the same time, ensure optimal use of energy and the environment. These global taxes could fund global objectives within the development agenda.

On a similar theme of finding innovative revenue sources for addressing climate change, **A. Damodaran** explores existing environmental financing avenues, potential new sources, and the delivery and management of financial resources. The existing arrangements fall grossly short as they are not adequate, equitable or predictable. Public investment and private funding are inadequate, multilateral sources are small and proposed solutions are, on the whole, uncertain in terms of fruition. Exploring options for public investment, private direct investment and using carbon markets for adaptation and mitigation, he argues that a likely global consensus could be found in public funding with support from stakeholders in both developed and developing countries. This could then be complemented by the use of carbon markets. The G20, he argues, is capable of effecting such a win-win solution reflecting the existing nexus within the Group and its observed ability to strike consensus among its members.

The following chapters elaborate on the various themes as described in the above narrative.

Endnotes

1 The countries were Argentina, Australia, Brazil, Canada, China, France, Germany, India, Indonesia, Italy, Japan, Republic of Korea, Mexico, Russian Federation, Saudi Arabia,

South Africa, Turkey, United Kingdom, United States and the European Union (EU) that represented the bulk of global GDP and international trade, and already played a key role in fashioning the rules and regulations for international economic and financial flows.

2 Download MDG details from the Net.

References

Callaghan, M., C. Ghate, S. Pickford and F. X. Rathinam, eds. 2014. *Global Cooperation among G20 Countries: Responding to the Crisis and Restoring Growth*. New Delhi: Springer.

Carin, B. 2013. 'Development in the G20: White Elephant or Cornerstone?', CIGI. Available at: http://www.cigionline.org/publications/2013/7/development-g20-white-elephant-or-cornerstone. Accessed in July 2013.

Davies, R. August, 2013. 'What Plot? Rationalising the G20's Development Agenda', *G20 Monitor* 5: 6–18, Sydney.

G8. 2007. Joint position paper issued by Brazil, China, India, Mexico and South Africa participating in the G8 Summit, 8 June, Heiligendamm, Germany.

G20. 1999. *Communiqué*. G20 Finance Ministers and Central Bank Governors Meeting, 15–16 December, Berlin, Germany.

G20. 2008. *Declaration of the Summit on Financial Markets and the World Economy*. 15 November, Washington DC.

________. 2009a. *Global Plan for Recovery and Reform*. Statement Issued by the G20 Leaders, 2 April, London.

________. 2009b. *G20 Leaders Statement*. Pittsburgh Summit, 24–25 September, Pittsburgh.

________. 2010a. *Summit Declaration*. 27 June, Toronto.

________. 2010b. *Leaders' Declaration*. 12 November, Seoul.

________. 2011. *Final Declaration – Building Our Common Future: Renewed Collective Action for the Benefit of All*. 4 November, Cannes.

________. 2012. 'Discussion Paper', *Mexico's Presidency of the G20*. January, Los Cabos.

________. 2013a. *Leaders' Declaration*. 6 September, St Petersburg.

________. 2013b. *Accountability Report on G20 Development Commitments*. 15 October, St. Petersburg.

________. 2013c. *Overview of Australia's Presidency*. 1 December, Brisbane.

Shome, P. 2011. 'Issues in Utilizing India's Demographic Transition', Thought leadership paper in *India, a New Dawn*. New Delhi: Ernst & Young.

________. 2012. 'Rebalancing and Structural Policies—An Indian Perspective', *Oxford Review of Economic Policy* 28(3): 587–602.

________. 2013. 'Political Economy of Debt Accumulation and Fiscal Adjustment in a Financial Crisis', in *Monetary Policy, Sovereign Debt and Financial Stability: The New Trilemma*, edited by Deepak Mohanty, 255–274. India: Cambridge University Press.

________. 2014a. *The G20 Macroeconomic Agenda: India and the Emerging Economies*. New Delhi: Cambridge University Press.

________. 2014b. 'Government Taxes and Expenditures: Experience and Reform', in *Oxford Handbook of the Indian Economy in the 21st Century*, edited by Ashima Goyal. India: Oxford University Press.

Shome, P. and F. Rathinam. 2011. 'India's Expectations from G20', in *Global Financial Stability: A Dialogue on Regulation and Cooperation*, edited by M. Metzgar, 99–116. Deutsche Gesellschaft für Internationale Zusammenarbeit (GIZ).

Singh, M. 7 July 2009. 'PM's Vision of How the World is Governed in the 21st Century', Press Release. New Delhi: Government of India.

WEO. April, 2010. 'Rebalancing Growth', *World Economic Outlook*. IMF, Washington DC.

Section 2
The Development Agenda

2 Commodity Market Policy for Food Security – The Road Ahead for G20

Rajesh Chakrabarti, Francis Xavier Rathinam and Vijay Kumar Varadi

The persistence of widespread hunger is one of the most appalling features of the modern world. Amartya Sen and Jean Dreze, 'Hunger and Public Action'

...we will prioritize action under the Seoul Consensus on addressing critical bottlenecks, including infrastructure deficits, food market volatility, and exclusion from financial services G20 Seoul Declaration

Introduction

By most indications, the world seems to be facing another round of severe food shortage, if not a full-blown crisis, in the coming months and years. After abating from record highs in the 2008, food prices spiked again in late 2010 and early 2011, and are still close to their all-time peak (see Figure 2.1). Further, the volatility in food prices has become more pronounced in recent months (Figure 2.2).

Figure 2.1: Price indices – food and agricultural commodities

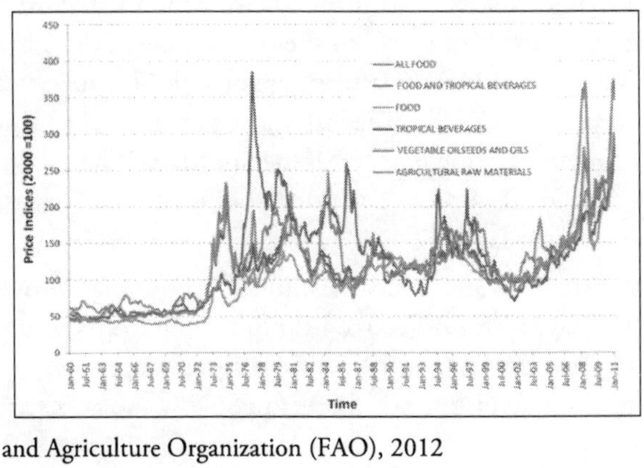

Source: Food and Agriculture Organization (FAO), 2012

Figure 2.2: Price index volatility – food and agricultural commodities

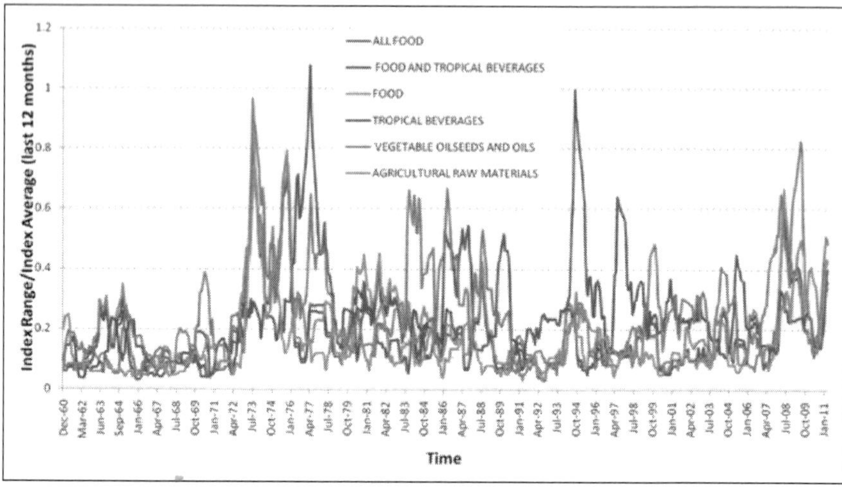

Source: FAO, 2012

At nearly a billion according to FAO estimates (Ortiz *et al.*, 2011), the number of undernourished people in late 2010 remained higher than it was before the recent crises, higher than what it was 40 years ago and in 1996 when the World Food Summit adopted the hunger-reduction target. A majority of the undernourished live in the developing countries with just seven countries – Bangladesh, China, The Democratic Republic of the Congo, Ethiopia, India, Indonesia and Pakistan – accounting for two-thirds of them. Between them China and India account for over 40 per cent of the world's undernourished, roughly in line with their population share in the world.

What should be the G20's role in food security? Clearly with China, India and Indonesia being members of the G20, the food insecurity problem is very much a crisis of some of the G20 members themselves. However, given that the purpose of G20 is in ensuring global stability, its objective in this area should also be to ensure food security at a global level and not just from a narrower members' national interest perspective. Therefore, the policy objective that should drive G20's actions should be the provision of food security to humanity at large.

This chapter tries to address the question of optimum commodity market policy for the G20 with this objective in mind. It attempts to provide policy recommendations for the G20 in the commodity markets space so as to ensure food security to the maximum number of people without discrimination in terms of nationality.

There are, of course, multiple channels through which governments can approach the issue of food insecurity. These include macroeconomic incentives towards greater food production, technological improvements in food storage and distribution, prevention of protracted political crises that have often formed the background of severe food insecurity. The scope of this chapter does not extend to all these areas. It would remain focused on only the policy initiatives concerning the agricultural commodities markets. These include the spot and derivatives (futures) markets as well as the national and global markets. The attempt made in this chapter would be to review and collate various market related interventions that have been made in the past and assess their impact on food security so as to come up with a set of clear policy recommendations that may drive the G20's approach towards alleviating food insecurity through market based policies. Needless to say, these policies can and perhaps should be supplemented by complementary policy action addressed in this volume.

This chapter looks at some of the past food crises with special attention paid to the latest one that occurred in 2008 and reviews various policy steps that were taken to manage them, particularly in the area of commodity markets. It also describes broad policy measures available for intervention in the case of food crisis, some or all of which have been used in the past. The following section provides an assessment of these policy decisions as well as a general introduction to the concept of futures for agricultural commodities and describes its trading around the world. Next, the chapter goes on to describe the size of Indian futures markets, the trading systems involved as well as the current policy debates. The final section draws upon the preceding analysis to list some policy recommendations for G20.

The Global Food Situation

While the food crisis of 2008 was one of the most severe ones in recent history, the more worrisome fact is that current food prices in global markets are more or less near the past peak with staggering rises in 2010. Ortiz *et al.* (2011) point out that after a year-and-a-half long stability following the 2008 spike, FAO's food price index rose sharply by over 30 per cent between June and December 2010. The rise has been even more dramatic for cereals at a scary 57 per cent. Worse, local food prices have not even relented from the peak levels even when the global prices have stabilized. Across 58 countries local food prices fell by less than 10 per cent since their September 2008 peak and remained 55 per cent higher than in mid-2007 before the crisis set in. Between May and November 2010 local food prices rose by over seven per cent, but for countries with rising price levels the rise ranged from about 10 per cent in the Democratic Republic of Congo to over 40 per cent in Belarus. Among large countries, India registered a 25 per cent change. Eight countries experienced higher local food inflation. The distribution of the price change is problematic as well. The rise has been more marked in low-income countries than in middle-income economies as well as in vulnerable geographic areas than in urban centers.

Current estimates of the undernourished population in the world range from 925 million (FAO) to 1.3 billion (Brinkman *et al.*, 2010). Given high food prices, the undernourished and borderline population is already running out of coping mechanisms like eating cheaper and less nutritious foods, eating less per meal and skipping meals. Even avenues for extra income like working greater number of hours in the informal sector and getting more family members (including children) to work appear to be exhausted. As a result, the current price rise looks more ominous in terms of its human impact. MDG 1 (reducing to half the population suffering from hunger) is under threat as are the goals of child and maternal mortality. Provision of food security is not just a key policy imperative – right now it is a most urgent necessity.

Policy Reactions to Previous Crises

Policy reactions across the world to previous food crises can be broadly classified into three categories – (1) supporting consumers through better distribution and access; (2) supporting producers through giving a boost to agriculture; and (3) managing and regulating food markets. Without disputing the importance of the first two categories, it is the last category that is of direct concern to this chapter.

Policy initiatives in the market management and regulation area in turn can be largely seen as government involvement in two broad areas: the linkage between local and global markets and that between spot and derivative markets. The former have included measures of broadly two kinds: lowering tariffs to boost food imports and banning or restricting exports to make more food stocks available in the producing country. The latter typically involves restricting and banning of futures markets and hoarding in the hope of raising current supplies and avoiding speculative price runs. Figure 2.3 summarizes the broad policy choices.

Figure 2.3: Broad policy reactions to food crises

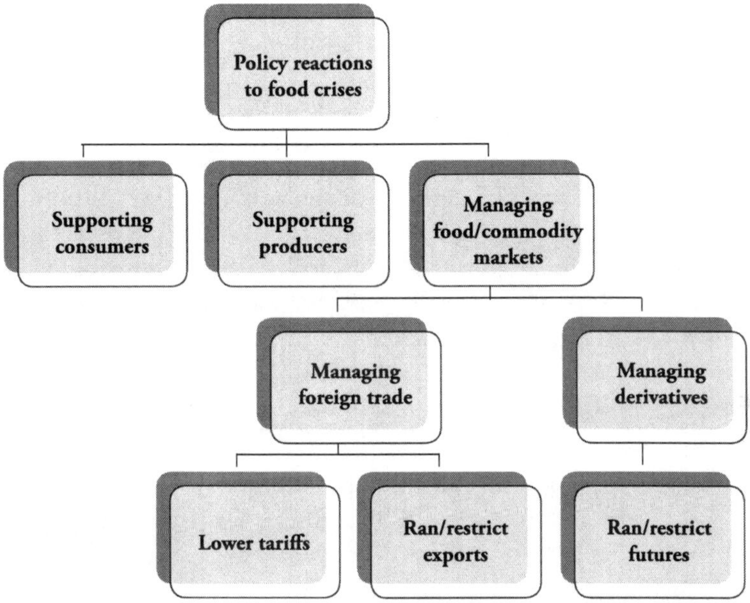

Source: Authors' calculation

A disclaimer is in order here. The categorization of policy reactions presented above is less water tight than it may seem at first glance. Consider, for instance, an action like releasing more stocks to the market from national food reserves. It may be viewed both as a step to support consumers by providing greater access to food grains, as well as a direct and quantitative intervention in the food market. Similarly for reduction of a particular tax on food grains, that would affect prices by working through market forces. If one chooses to categorize such an action as a consumer support rather than market based policy action, the same question can be raised for tariffs. Import and export of food grains by public agencies fall in the same gray area. Therefore, at some level, this classification is not completely free from arbitrariness, but the authors follow the extant policy literature in the area to focus on policy initiatives that seek primarily to influence the local-global connect and/or the spot-derivative connect as market-based policies.

An Assessment of Past Policy Measures

Responses directed at international trade

Many countries including Bangladesh, Egypt, India, Mexico, Pakistan and Turkey, have used reduction or elimination of food tariffs or taxes as a response to the 2008 food crisis. Tariffs have anyway been on a secular decline because of multilateral and bilateral trade agreements in recent years but some tariff drops have been substantial (130 per cent to 2.5 per cent for wheat in Morocco; 100 per cent to 2.7 per cent for rice in Nigeria; 130 per cent to 8 per cent on wheat and elimination of a 100 per cent tariff on barley in Turkey as well as the removal of a 36 per cent tariff on wheat flour for India) (Ortiz *et al.*, 2011). In many cases, tariff reduction has also been accompanied by reduction of elimination of domestic taxes to reduce food prices.

The counterpart of tariff reduction has been export bans or restrictions. Large producers like Argentina, China, India and Russia among others, have all restricted exports to increase domestic availability of food grains. Sometimes the measure has come in the form of raised export taxes (as in Argentina) while in other cases (like in India) quantitative blocks have been put in place.

Broadly speaking, food crises appear to have pushed several countries away from a more global market paradigm of the Washington consensus leading to attempts at isolation of domestic prices from world prices for exporters; adoption of food self-sufficiency rather than food security as an explicit policy goal; greater shift towards market interventions with price controls and anti-hoarding laws and even diversification by buying land abroad or entering into regional bilateral trade agreements that bypass the global markets.

While the measures may have arguably eased the pressures on local prices in the producer countries or averted further rises, from a global perspective the effects of export restrictions have been nothing short of disastrous. Figure 2.4 shows the impact of export restrictions on global prices for rice to illustrate the point.

Figure 2.4: Rice price behaviour

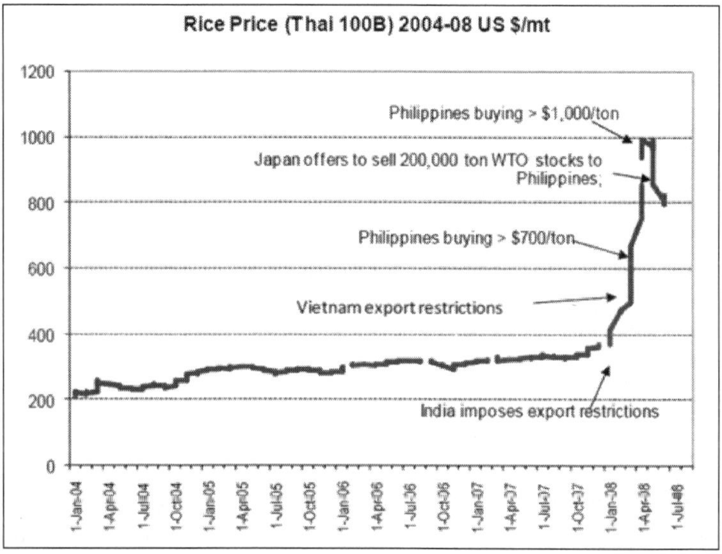

Source: Brahmbhatt and Christiansen (2008)

Furthermore, export restrictions are cascading in long run, introducing uncertainty in global food markets and forcing importing countries to move towards goals of food self-sufficiency rather than reliance on global food markets. Current WTO rules allow export restrictions and the move by Japan in 2008 to make the option more difficult failed to get traction. However, recently, in January 2011, the WTO Director-General Pascal Lamy pointed out that export restrictions have in fact played a causal role in generating food crises (creating a 7 per cent drop in trade in rice between 2007 and 2008 for instance) and implored member countries to consider other options to shore up their domestic supply of food grains.

Policy responses related to commodity derivatives

Commodity derivatives, particularly commodity futures, have been a prime suspect each time a country has witnessed a significant price rise. Restrictions and outright bans on futures trading in the face of rising prices have been common in many countries including India for agricultural commodities. The link, however, has been tenuous at best and the issue has been the subject of academic investigation in multiple countries at various points in time. Despite the lack of conclusive evidence of the role of futures in aggravating price rises in all of these investigative attempts, the suspicion has not completely vanished. So it is well worth re-looking at the arguments and evidence on this issue.

The root of the argument that commodity futures may have a significant causal role in aggravating price rises lies in the belief that a sudden large long (buy) position in the futures market will lead to an upward pressure in spot prices for the commodity in question (Bose, 2009). In particular hedge funds, investment banks and large institutional investors are thought to be the prime sources of such market imbalances. While the fear is easy to find flaws with – it is not clear why the demand should be systematically one-sided, in other words why market pressures will not lead to a equilibrium otherwise mandated by spot market demand and supply, and why in the medium to long run such higher prices will not motivate greater supply – it seems difficult to vanquish it from the public mind as well as the minds of some policy-makers. It is true that at times all markets – spot and derivatives – can become vulnerable to sustained one-sided movements or bubbles whether for rational reasons like informational cascades or behavioural biases. That itself cannot be held against futures markets. If anything, futures prices actually have a lower chance of deviating too much from the underlying value as they have the visible anchor of spot prices to hold them back. The real fear stems from the fact that since the margin requirements in futures markets are much lower than in spot markets it is the preferred market for speculative trading. However, the market for futures comprises hedgers as well and unless the market can be manipulated or cornered by a small group of people, it is virtually impossible for the feared situation to arise.

Nevertheless, in the wake of the 2008 commodity crisis, the US Commodity Futures Trading Commission (CFTC) was asked to investigate the effects of commodity futures market on commodity prices. Using its data on Large Trader Reporting System under which major traders file daily reports with the CFTC, the investigation revealed a few interesting insights (CFTC, 2008). Prices have risen sharply for commodities irrespective of the existence of developed futures markets or large institutional traders. Index trading, often blamed for the increase in prices, has actually been associated with declining prices. Speculators are on both sides of the trade and typically follow price trends rather than cause them. Using additional information from a broader group of traders the CFTC concluded that between January 2003 and June 2008 daily position changes of no trader group systematically preceded price changes. There was also no directional pattern among traders who exceeded position limits.

The conclusion of the CFTC study was that while the increased action in futures market did reflect beliefs of rising prices, and signaled the same to producers, there was no evidence that any trading actually manipulated prices or caused the higher prices.

The accompanying argument that is often made out in emerging markets is that findings of market efficiency in advanced markets do not apply to these countries. Even this is put to rest by a recent study on the effects of futures trading on inflation by the Expert Committee on Futures Trading (ECFT) led by professor Abhijit Sen. Methodology of the study here was a comparison of price trends and volatility before and after introduction of futures. While the agricultural commodities did show a higher price rise than general inflation, the committee found no significant evidence of futures contributing to price rises (ECFT, 2008).

It also found that price volatility actually fell significantly often by half or more on introduction of futures. For potatoes, a perishable crop, the decline was more than two-thirds.

Nevertheless, the Indian government suspended futures trading in soy oil, potato, rubber and chickpea in May 2007. Perhaps unsurprisingly, the price trends never softened. Despite repeated evidence to the contrary, futures trading has always come under attack in times of sustained price rise. It appears to be the most common error made by policymakers and politicians in interfering with markets.

Commodities Futures – The Concept and Trading around the World

Financial markets help transfer risk from some agents to other. One is hard pressed to think of a business venture more risk-prone than agriculture. The quantity of the produce is uncertain and so is the price. Throughout the life of a crop, therefore, the growers as well as the potential customers have to make decisions that are inherently risky given the uncertainty associated with agriculture. It is hardly a surprise then, that commodity futures have been among the earliest derivatives thought of by man and the daily trading volume of agricultural commodity futures worldwide runs into several billion dollars.

Futures and options constitute the most active derivatives trading markets round the world. The volume of agricultural commodity derivatives trading around the world in 2010 amounted to 1.3 billion contracts, up over 40 per cent from the corresponding figure in 2009. Apart from foreign exchange contracts which grew at an outstanding rate of 140 per cent, agricultural derivatives showed the highest growth among the different categories of derivative products.[1] In terms of volume, agricultural commodities came after equity indices and individual equity, interest rate and foreign currency, ahead of energy, and metals (precious and non-precious metals combined). Table 2.1 shows trading volume in the most active agricultural derivatives markets in the world. The Chicago Board of Trade (CBOT) houses several of the actively traded contracts. But the Dalian Commodity Exchange (DCE) and the Zhengzhou Commodity Exchange (ZCE) have helped China edge out the US as the largest commodity trading venue. Outside the US and China, India's National Commodity and Derivatives Exchange (NCDEX) is the sole entrant in the league with its guar seed contract.

Table 2.1: Top 20 agricultural futures and options worldwide ranked by number of contracts traded in 2010

Rank	Contract	Contract size	Jan–Dec 2009	Jan–Dec 2010	% change
1	White Sugar Futures, ZCE	10 tonnes	146,063,344	305,303,131	109.0%
2	Rubber Futures, Shanghai Futures Exchange (SHFE)	5 tonnes	89,035,959	167,414,912	88.0%
3	Soy Meal Futures, DCE	10 tonnes	155,404,029	125,581,888	–19.2%
4	Soy Oil Futures, DCE	10 tonnes	94,836,881	91,406,238	–3.6%
5	Cotton No. 1 Futures, DCE	5 tonnes	8,534,688	86,955,310	918.8%
6	Corn Futures, CBOT	5,000 bushels	50,948,804	69,841,420	37.1%
7	Palm Oil Futures, DCE	10 tonnes	44,426,498	41,799,813	–5.9%
8	No. 1 Soybean Futures, DCE	10 tonnes	42,507,076	37,393,600	–12.0%
9	Soybean Futures, CBOT	5,000 bushels	35,758,855	36,933,960	3.3%

Rank	Contract	Contract size	Jan–Dec 2009	Jan–Dec 2010	% change
10	Corn Futures, DCE	10 tonnes	16,744,088	35,999,573	115.0%
11	Sugar #11 Futures, ICE Futures, US (Intercontinental Exchange)	50 long tonnes	27,300,259	29,052,539	6.4%
12	Early Rice Futures, ZCE *	10 tonnes	1,950,083	26,854,086	1277.1%
13	Wheat Futures, CBOT	5,000 bushels	17,677,547	23,090,255	30.6%
14	Corn Options on Futures, CBOT	5,000 bushels	14,435,687	20,810,260	44.2%
15	Soybean Oil Futures, CBOT	60,000 pounds	17,132,082	20,791,164	21.4%
16	Soybean Meal Futures, CBOT	100 short tons	12,880,767	14,052,845	9.1%
17	Live Cattle Futures, CME (Chicago Mercantile Exchange)	40,000 pounds	8,797,033	11,332,739	28.8%
18	Guar Seed Futures, NCDEX	10 tonnes	9,029,772	10,937,797	21.1%
19	Soybean Options on Futures, CBOT	5,000 bushels	9,555,840	10,046,345	5.1%
20	Rapeseed Oil Futures, ZCE	10,956,863	10,956,863	9,527,915	-13.0%

* Began trading in April 2009

Source: Annual Volume Survey, 2010 (www.futuresindustry.com)

The idea of trading futures may be traced to forward contracts as far as back to around 2000 BC in China. In essence, a future is a contract to deliver a specified amount of a certain commodity at a particular date for a specified price. Table 2.2 in the appendix explains the fundamentals of a future contract. A forerunner and close relative of the future contract was the forward contract.

The beginnings of the modern worldwide futures markets can be traced to Chicago that had emerged as an important agricultural commodity trading centre in the early 1800s. In 1848, eleven years after Chicago became a city, the CBOT was founded as a commodity exchange. Forward contracts were traded along with 'spot' commodities in the initial years, but their lack of standardization was soon proving to be a hindrance to their liquidity and trading. So in 1865, the CBOT came up with a futures contract that standardized quality, quantity and other features of the forward contracts. The futures market received a major boost over a century later, in the early 1970's, not from any major innovation in the agricultural/commodity sector but because of the increased volatility in exchange rates as the Bretton Woods system broke down and in interest rates during the rocky 1970s. As risk in financial markets increased, there was an acute need for hedging instruments and a panoply of financial futures were designed and started trading heavily in the USA as well as in other developed countries.

Though commodity futures, which lie at the root of the development of the futures market worldwide, may have been created primarily out of the hedging needs of the buyers and sellers, over 95 per cent of the trading volume in futures comprise speculative trades. This is because the nature of future trading lends itself easily to speculative motives and allows speculators, who are willing to take on risks in expectation of profits, take on large positions for very little investment. In other words, future markets allow for highly leveraged trading, because of a feature of the futures markets known as *marking to market* that changes the settlement price on the futures contract being traded every day.

The most important economic function that agricultural commodity futures markets serve is that they enable farmers as well as buyers to hedge price risk. Interestingly enough, the exact mechanism of hedging with futures does not even necessitate delivering on the futures contract.

Speculative trading in futures markets have received a boost in recent years with managed funds focusing specifically on futures contracts. Like in any other market, however, speculation has its risks in the futures markets as well and given its high leverage a wrong bet has the potential of having devastating effect on the speculators' fortune.

The Indian Context

Commodity markets in India and determinants of commodity prices

Accounting for a quarter of nation's gross domestic product (GDP) and providing employment to about two-thirds of its labour force, agriculture's importance to the Indian economy cannot be overemphasized. Also, compared to many other activities, agriculture continues to be a risky occupation in India. In spite of the role of government agencies to act as a buffer and help stabilize market prices, agricultural prices in India continue to be volatile and the output heavily dependent on weather conditions.

In spite of critical importance of agriculture in India, till recently there was no nationwide commodity market. Commodity trading has traditionally been dispersed and fragmented across the country where regional commodity markets and local *mandis* accounting for all trading and largely functioned in isolation. The reason for this is not difficult to find. Lack of adequate physical warehousing, transportation and information hindered the development of a national market. As a result, agricultural prices varied greatly across the country with some parts of the nation burdened with excess supply of the same produce that was in severe need in some other parts. Clearly, the distributional benefits of a market system remained untapped because of such fragmented trading in agricultural produce. Market fragmentation paved the way for acute foodgrain shortages and poverty among the growers of the same crops to exist simultaneously.

The telecommunication revolution that swept through the country in the 90s, including the advent of internet, reduced information problem and set the stage for establishment of national-level commodity markets in India. The physical encumbrances to storing and moving bulky and perishable agricultural commodities persist and their removal would lead to further strengthening of the national markets.

Determinants of commodity prices

Commodity prices are inherently volatile as they are susceptible to unexpected supply and demand shocks, and also macroeconomic policy shocks. Commodity booms, especially food crisis in 2008 and more recently in 2011 have increased the urgency in understanding the determinants of commodity boom and bust cycle and the factors that drive the cycle.

The fundamentals, demand and supply shocks, play a vital role in influencing the commodity prices. Mostly they are individual commodity specific or at times specific to a group of commodities. Over and above these fundamental factors, overall macroeconomic variables such as money supply, real interest rate, inflation and exchange rate at global level do affect the commodity prices. The recent boom also triggered a debate on the role of financial markets, especially the derivatives and instruments such as index futures on commodity booms.

Around the same time of global commodity boom in 2008, Indian commodity prices also increased considerably. However, in the event of global financial crisis, global commodity prices have cooled down in mid-2008 before picking up again in 2009. Whereas Indian commodity prices especially food prices have been consistently on the rise.

Recent literature examining commodity boom at the global level have identified three main sources of boom and bust cycles: demand and supply factors especially high demand from China and India, macroeconomic factors such as real interest rate, global money supply and general inflation, and financial sector factors such as size and volume of open interest in the futures market.

In this section,the authors seek to explore the impact of these three groups of factors on the Indian commodity price rise in the recent time. In the Indian case, also robust demand boosted by buoyant economic growth, easy monetary policy especially manifested in negative real interest rates and recently financial derivatives argued to have played a significant role.

Determinants of commodity prices: Directions from the literature

Commodities demand mainly arises from food, feed and industrial inputs. The economy wide determinant of commodity demand is economic activity. GDP is typically used in the literature as a measure of economic activity (Frankel, 2003). However, for want of a more frequent indicator the authors use a deseasonalized index of industrial production. Increased industrial activity should positively affect commodity prices.

Commodities are also storehouses of value i.e., an asset class themselves. Thus, any demand for inventories would have implications on commodity prices. However, data on inventories are notoriously difficult to obtain. Further, the decision to leave the commodities in the ground, on the trees or even unaccounted hording which would determine the inventories, is impossible to measure. Thus, any inventory data is necessarily incomplete. The information contained the futures market prices has been used to find a proxy for inventories or rather the value of inventories which would matter for determining spot prices. As spot-future spread is a measure of speculative return of holding inventories, it could be used as a proxy for demand for inventories. On the other hand, spot-future spread is generally used as a proxy for risk premium. As a proxy for the demand for inventories, one expects the spread to be positively associated with commodity prices but as a proxy for risk premium, one expects a negative relationship. Thus, it is an empirical matter as to which of the forces is dominant as the theoretical relationship is ambiguous.

Volatility of spot prices is an important determinant of inventory holdings thus would have impact on the commodity prices. The demand for holding inventories was expected to go up in the time of volatile prices as to insure timely supply of inputs and also to take advantage of unexpected spikes in prices.

Commodities derivatives, though theoretically expected to be beneficial in optimal risk sharing and price discovery, are considered to be the cause of recent global commodity boom. Uninformed trading, which generally follows trend or passively track a commodity index rather than commodity market fundamentals, is argued to be the cause of price rise. To test the role of commodity derivatives two indicators were used: (1) the size of open interest in the markets; and (2) lagged spot index was used as a measure of herd behaviour which may produce self-confirming bubbles or busts i.e. the bandwagon effect. For individual commodities the authors also tested for the implications of the existence of vibrant futures market measured by net open interest on the spot prices.

Macroeconomic factors that influence commodity prices include real interest rate, total money supply in the economy, general inflation and exchange rate. Real interest rates are said be negatively correlated with commodity prices as more money would flow into commodities as yield from financial assets would be lower. When commodity prices approach their long-term equilibrium values, when the future expectation of price rise would be lower, the reversal would set in. Thus, one may expect real interest rate to be negatively correlated with commodity prices. Excessive money supply, which depresses real interest rates, is used an alternative measure to test the implications of easy monetary policy. Money supply in the economy is measured by M2.

General inflation is expected to have negative influence on commodity prices. As discussed earlier, commodities are also asset classes. Thus, they would be used as a hedge against general price level. Core Wholesale Price Index (WPI), which excludes food and oil prices to measure general price level, was used. As domestic prices are influenced by international prices through international trade exchange rate has been included. Dollar exchange rate has been used rather than composite multi commodity real interest rate as almost 80 per cent of Indian foreign trade is invoiced in dollar. Further, international oil prices also have been included.

Indian commodity markets: Data, results and interpretation

Figures 2.5 and 2.6 show the time plot of real spot prices in Multi-Commodity Exchange (MCX) commodity markets using commodity price index. This has been deflated using core WPI. Figure 2.7 shows the real economic activity measured by Index of Industrial Production (IIP). IIP has been de-seasonalized. Financial factors i.e., Spot-Futures spread, spott-1 and volatility are plotted in Figure 2.8. Spott-1 is natural logarithm of first difference of spot values. Volatility of spot returns is a computed using Generalized AutoRegressive Conditional Heteroskedasticity or GARCH (1,1) model. Macroeconomic factors such as M2, real interest rate and inflation are plotted in Figure 2.9. International oil prices and rainfall, used as control factors in the regressions, are plotted in Figures 2.10 and 2.11 respectively. Spot and futures commodity prices are provided by MCX Commodity Exchange; money supply, interest rate, and IIP are obtained from Business Beacon; WPI and exchange rates are collected from Reserve Bank of India (RBI), and international oil prices are from DATASTREAM. For all variables, the sample period is June 2005–June 2011 (monthly). They have converted daily spot and futures prices into monthly series.

Figure 2.5: Real commodity prices

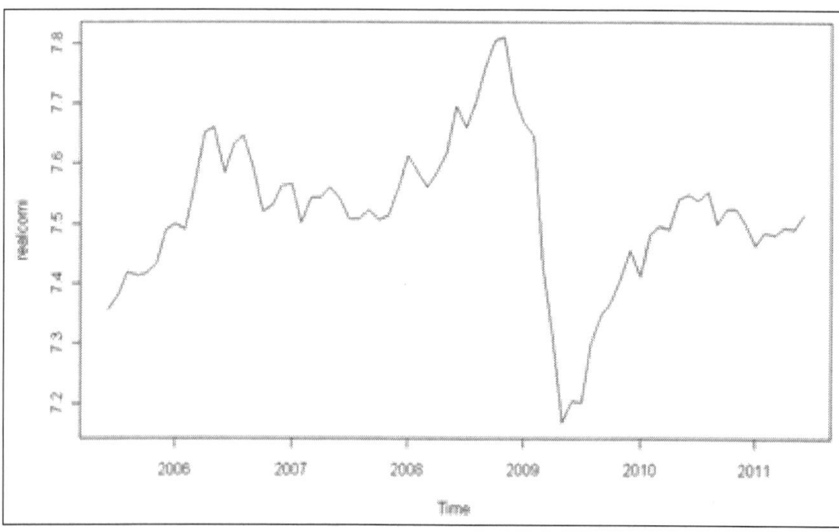

Source: MCX Commodity markets, 2012

Figure 2.6: Spot prices of soy oil, mentha oil, crude oil and natural gas

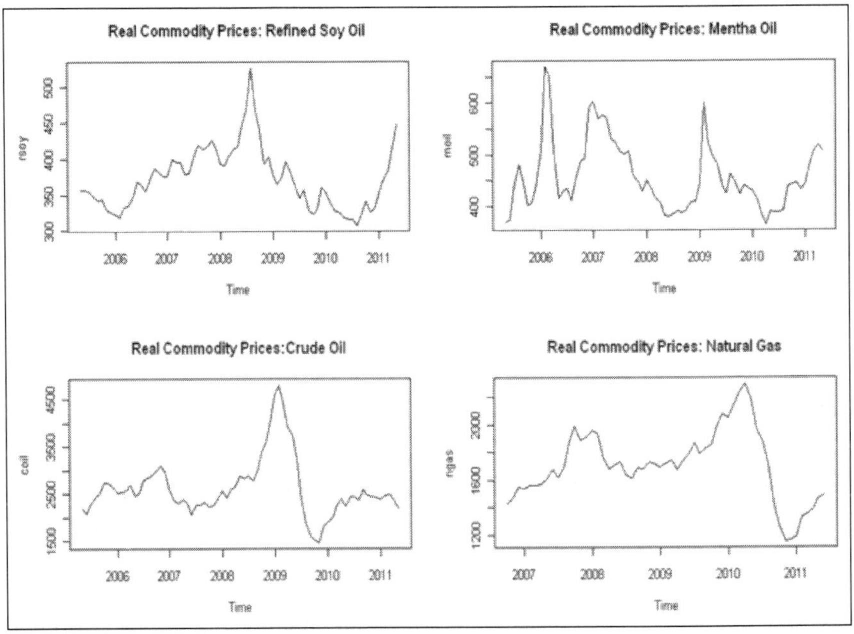

Source: MCX Commodity markets, 2012

Figure 2.7: Real economic activity

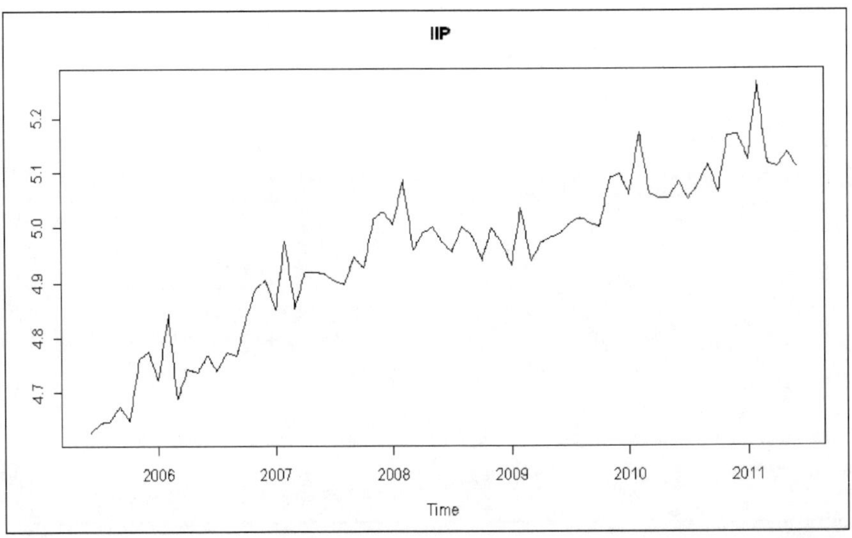

Source: Business Beacon, 2012

Figure 2.8: Financial factors

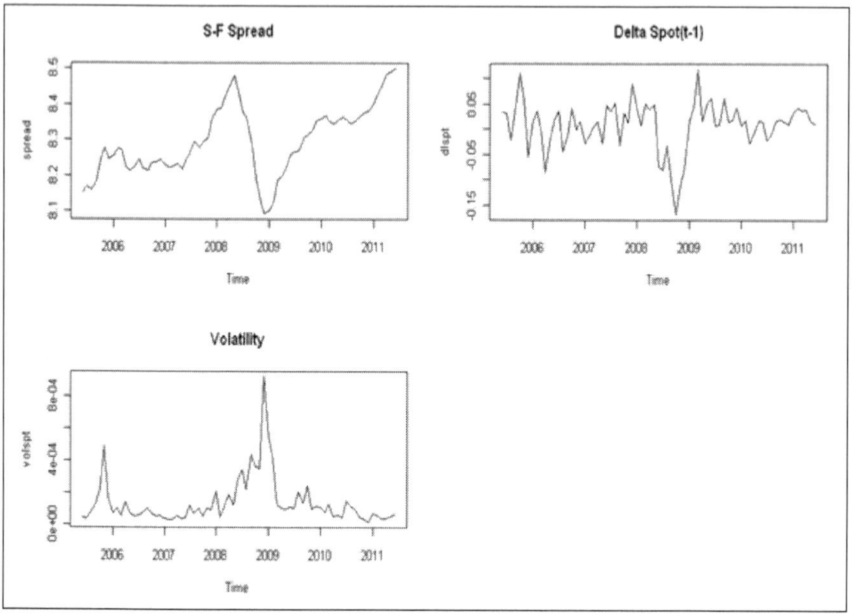

Source: Authors' calculation

Figure 2.9: Macroeconomic factors

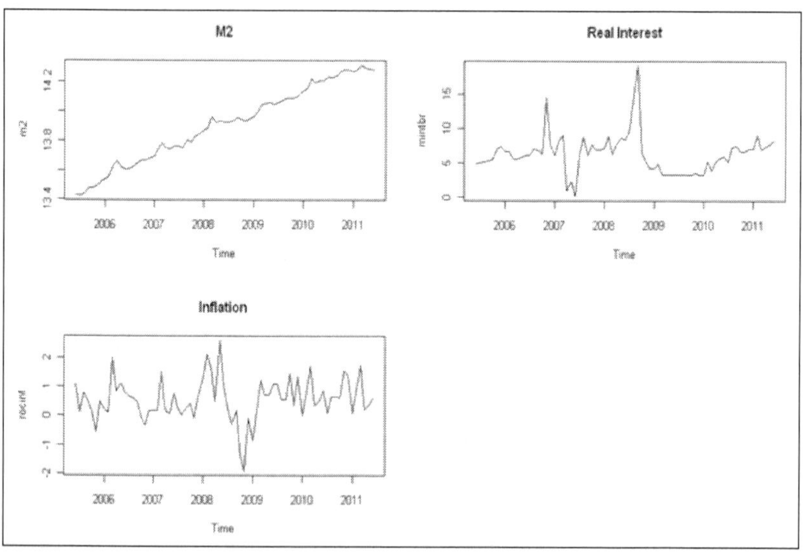

Source: Business Beacon, 2012

Figure 2.10: International oil prices and exchange rate (US$ vs ₹)

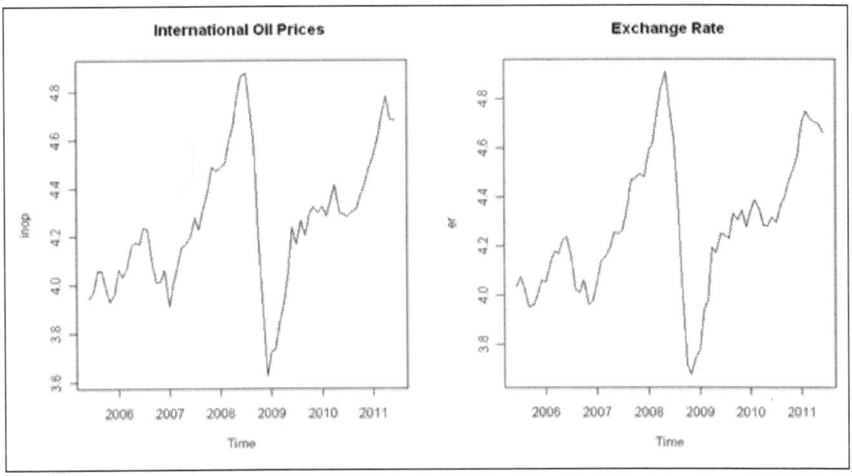

Source: RBI, 2012 and DATASTREAM, 2012

Figure 2.11: Rainfall

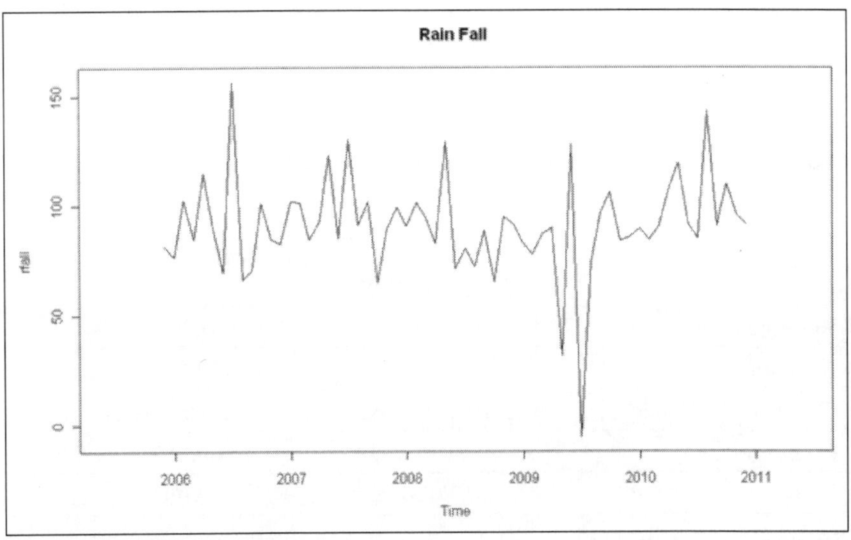

Source: Business Beacon, 2012

The regression results show that the demand factor measured by IIP though has the right sign is not statistically significant (Table 2.2). More importantly, the financial factors variables volatility and change in lagged spot values are significant. Rate of change of lagged spot values ($\Delta Spot_{t-1}$), an indicator of bandwagon effect, is significant indicating the persistence of spot prices due to trend spotting and passively tracking indices by the investors especially at the aggregate level.

However, Spot-Futures spread, a measure of demand of inventories, though positive, is not significant indicating lack of support in the data for the theoretical prediction of information contained in the futures prices on the value of inventories i.e., expectations on the convenience yield affect spot prices.

Two indicators have been used for measuring the impact of monetary policy. The real interest rate measured by Mumbai interbank rate is not statistically significant, whereas M2 is positive and significant indicating a strong influence of monetary policy. General inflation, measured by core WPI is not significant. Exchange rate is negative and significant as expected. Appreciating the Indian National Rupee would make imports cheaper and export costlier, thus increasing domestic availability of commodities and put a downward pressure on prices.

Table 2.2: Determinants of real spot index prices

	Model A	**Model B**
Intercept	–10.755 (8.028)	3.392 (4.254)
IIP	0.247 (0.340)	0.169 (0.350)
Spot-Futures spread	0.586 (0.502)	0.425 (0.512)
$\Delta Spot_{t-1}$	–0.662 (0.355)*	–0.774 (0.355)**
Volatility	343.278 (84.163)***	296.244 (81.375)***
M2	0.941 (0.506)*	–
Real interest	–	0.007 (0.004)
Inflation	–0.031 (0.025)	–0.015 (0.020)
Oil prices	0.101 (0.126)	0.043 (0.143)
Exchange rate	–0.181 (0.095)*	–0.082 (0.121)
Trend	–0.015 (0.006)**	–0.003 (0.002)

Source: Author's estimations
Note: Sample period is June 2005–June 2011. All dates are on log. * 10 per cent level, ** 5 per cent level and *** 1per cent level of significance

Analysis based on individual commodities confirms a substantial role of domestic monetary conditions. For soy oil, though IIP has a right sign, it is not significant (see Table 2.3). The Spot-Futures spread is significant indicating the information content in the futures price on the demand for inventories and its positive impact on the current real spot prices of soy oil. Though the authors do not find any significant bandwagon effect, the size of net open position does affect the spot prices of soy oil. As expected, the monetary indicators, both M2 as well as real interest rate are statistically significant and have right sign implying the monetary policy in commodity price discovery. The size of impact of M2 is significantly higher than that of real interest. Interestingly when inflation is introduced in the model, it is not significant with M2 but not with real interest rate implying the larger influence of monetary policy and the limited information content of real interest rate.

Table 2.3: Determinants of real spot prices – refined soy oil

	Model A	**Model B**
Intercept	–2.463 (1.374)*	5.227 (0.359)***
IIP	0.038 (0.087)	0.008 (0.075)
Spot-Futures spread	1.569 (0.079)***	1.675 (0.074)***
$\Delta Spot_{t-1}$	–0.036 (0.066)	0.012 (0.062)
Volatility	0.531 (17.337)	–9.929 (16.745)
Open Interest	0.014 (0.007)*	0.011 (0.006)*
M2	–0.166 (0.093)*	–
Real Interest	–	–0.004 (0.001)***
Inflation	–0.004 (0.003)	–0.007 (0.003)**
Rain Fall	–0.001 (0.002)	0.001 (0.001)
Trend	–0.002 (0.001)*	–0.004 (0.000)***

Source: Author's estimations

Note: Sample period is June 2005–June 2011. All dates are on log. * 10 per cent level, ** 5 per cent level and *** 1 per cent level of significance; values in parenthesis are hetroscadasticity and autocorrelation consistent (HAC) standard errors.

Table 2.4: Determinants of real spot prices – mentha oil

	Model A	**Model B**
Intercept	–2.152 (1.224)*	–5.685 (0.388)***
IIP	–0.010 (0.061)	0.011 (0.064)
Spot-Futures spread	1.807 (0.032)***	1.742 (0.035)***

	Model A	Model B
$\Delta Spot_{t-1}$	–0.029 (0.023)	–0.002 (0.022)
Volatility	–1.196 (0.562)**	–1.631 (0.703)**
Open interest	0.005 (0.004)	0.002 (0.004)
M2	–0.290 (0.093)***	–
Real interest	–	–0.002 (0.000)***
Inflation	0.005 (0.002)*	0.000 (0.002)
Rain fall	–0.000 (0.002)	0.001 (0.001)
Trend	–0.001 (0.001)	–0.005 (0.000)***

Source: Author's estimations
Note: Sample period is June 2005–June 2011. All dates are on log. * 10 per cent level, ** 5 per cent level and *** 1 per cent level of significance; values in parenthesis are HAC standard errors.

Table 2.5: Determinants of real spot prices – crude oil

	Model A	Model B
Intercept	–5.990 (0.910)***	–5.642 (0.226)***
IIP	0.076 (0.039)*	0.075 (0.040)*
Spot-Futures spread	1.566 (0.013)***	1.566 (0.013)***
$\Delta Spot_{t-1}$	–0.069 (0.020)***	–0.069 (0.020)***
Volatility	–8.720 (3.361)**	–9.391 (3.458)***
Open interest	0.008 (0.002)***	0.008 (0.002)***
M2	0.025 (0.062)	–
Real interest	–	–0.000 (0.000)
Inflation	0.004 (0.002)	0.004 (0.002)*
Oil prices	–0.043 (0.008)***	–0.041 (0.009)***
Exchange rate	0.011 (0.010)	0.010 (0.011)
Trend	–0.005 (0.000)***	–0.005 (0.000)***

Source: Author's estimations

Note: Sample period is June 2005–June 2011. All dates are on log. * 10 per cent level, ** 5 per cent level and *** 1 per cent level of significance; values in parenthesis are HAC standard errors.

Table 2.6: Determinants of real spot prices – natural gas

	Model A	Model B
Intercept	–4.552 (1.602)***	–6.290 (0.677)***
IIP	–0.029 (0.135)*	–0.042 (0.139)
Spot-Futures spread	1.738 (0.028)***	1.737 (0.030)***
$\Delta Spot_{t-1}$	0.016 (0.033)	0.023 (0.033)
Volatility	–19.295 (8.096)**	–19.705 (8.158)**
Open interest	0.000 (0.003)	0.002 (0.002)
M2	–0.134 (0.109)	–
Real interest	–	0.001 (0.001)
Inflation	0.010 (0.004)**	0.008 (0.003)**
Oil prices	–0.082 (0.013)***	–0.095 (0.018)***
Exchange rate	0.036 (0.012)***	0.040 (0.016)**
Trend	–0.004 (0.002)**	–0.005 (0.001)***

Source: Author's estimations

Note: Sample period is October 2006–June 2011. All dates are on log. * 10 per cent level, ** 5 per cent level and *** 1 per cent level of significance; values in parenthesis are HAC standard errors.

Whereas for mentha oil, $\Delta Spot_{t-1}$ and net open interest are not significant while the monetary factors are highly significant (see Table 2.4). In case of crude oil, it is observed that all the financial sector variables are significant. Especially significant bandwagon effect and the role of futures market in spot price discovery (see Table 2.5) is also observed. Surprisingly crude oil spot prices in India are negatively related to international oil prices. This could be due to weak pass through of international prices due to significant government presence. Domestic monetary factors play little role, as expected. Similar results were observed for natural gas as well with respect to monetary factors while the results show little implications of financial factors on natural gap spot prices (see Table 2.6).

Findings

In this section, the authors have modeled commodity prices as a function of conventional 'fundamental' factors, macroeconomic factors and financial factors. The literature predicts that the fundamental factors and real interest through affecting cost of carry lead to circumstances whereby the demand for inventories would affect the spot prices. However, recent studies have shown that both macroeconomic factors such as inflation, exchange rate and financial factors such as derivatives do play a vital role.

In sum, the monetary factors are most influential for over all commodity index, soy oil and mentha oil, whereas financial factors and international factors such as international oil prices and dollar exchange rate are important for crude oil and natural gas. They have mixed results for financial factors as ΔSpott-1 affects only the index and crude oil while the net open interest is significant in explaining variations in only crude oil spot prices. There are several other fundamental factors such as transportation, storage, and supply-enhancing policies that are key to explaining domestic food prices. However, measurement issues and lack of availability of monthly data on these factors dictate the final list of control variables used.

Commodity futures markets in India

Commodity derivatives are not new to India. In fact forward trading in commodities existed in India from ancient times (it is mentioned in Kautilya's *Arthashastra*) and the first modern futures market was established in 1875 for cotton contracts by the Bombay Cotton Trade Association, just a decade after CBOT traded its first future. Oilseed and food grain futures followed and before the Second World War, futures were being traded on commodities like wheat, rice, sugar, groundnut, groundnut oil, raw jute, jute products and castor seed as well as precious metals. During World War II futures trading was prohibited to contain runaway speculation and illegal hoarding.

After independence, the Forward Contracts (Regulation) Act was enacted in 1952 to regulate the trading in forward and futures trading. The Forward Markets Commission, which oversees forward trading, was instituted as regulatory body the following year. The Act applied to all contracts whereby the delivery of goods occurs after a period longer than 11 days. Futures contracts were viewed as a subset of standardized forward contracts and were never formally defined in the Act. The task of the Commission is to monitor and regulate the trading of forward contracts since manipulation in these markets is likely to create severe imbalances with adverse welfare effects.

Nevertheless, Indian markets did not really blossom over the following four decades. Regulators viewed markets in general with suspicion and derivatives markets as the terrain of unscrupulous speculation. Price control was also a central feature of economic policy during much of this period. This overly regulated nature of the economy did not bode well for the development of these markets. In 1966, futures trade was altogether banned to give effective powers of governmental price control. A few select commodities saw a reintroduction of futures in 1980 following the Khusro Committee report.

All began to change with liberalization in the early 1990s. In 1993 the Kabra Committee was appointed to look into forward markets. The committee recommended in 1994 that all futures banned in 1966 be reintroduced as well as many others added. Six years later, the National Agricultural Policy, 2000 envisioned removal of price controls in agricultural markets and widespread use of futures contracts. Since its establishment in 1995, the Department of Consumer Affairs, set up within the Ministry of Consumer Affairs, Food and Public Distribution, has been working at the promotion of futures trading. Its efforts included reforming and strengthening the existing commodity exchanges.

In recent years, several derivatives exchanges have sprung across the country facilitating trading in agricultural commodities, as well as commodity futures. Table 8 in the appendix provides a list of exchanges of commodities included in the FCRA and the exchanges where commodity futures are traded. Of these exchanges, the four national level commodity exchanges are the most important. They have been granted the 'nationwide multi-commodity' status and they are rapidly emerging as the major centers of commodity futures trading.

A Glimpse of future trading practices in India

The futures contract: Commodity futures contracts vary depending upon the exchange and the commodity in question. The exact design of a contract is driven by the rules and byelaws of the exchange where it is traded. The futures contract specifies several aspects of the contract. The standardized unit of trading and delivery eases price quoting, and facilitates trading. Specification of different quality parameters is essential in the case of commodities when the underlying asset is inherently heterogeneous. The contract also specifies the range of variation in quantity that can be within the acceptable range. If a seller delivers a product that falls below the acceptable quality or quantity ranges, the buyer can refuse the settlement of the contract. Delivery centres are specified as well to take into account possible issues with transportation costs.

Several other elements mentioned in the contract relate to the trading rules for the specific contracts in the relevant exchange. The tick size and price bands address market micro-structure issues and prevent excessive price volatility and market manipulation. Individual and broker position limits prevent market manipulation by a single buyer or broker. Table 2.2 also provides a calendar for trading of contracts and specifies the number of contracts that are active at a point in time.

Futures contracts on the same commodity may vary in specifications across exchanges. The tick size, price bands and trading rules are likely to be different. Needless to say, the specifications vary to a great extent across commodities.

Trading systems in exchanges: As Thomas and Varma (2010) point out, traditional foodgrain markets in India were the local *mandis* spread throughout the country doing spot transactions, while futures trading is restricted to exchanges. Till recently, all trading in commodity futures took place just the way the physical commodities themselves have always traded, through an 'open outcry' system. Of late, however, there is a distinct move towards 'de-materialization' or online electronic trading. Three of the four major national-level exchanges use screen-based electronic trading. In most of the other regional exchanges, trading takes place primarily through an open outcry system.

Apart from the trading that goes on in the exchanges, there is a significant gray market outside the exchanges where futures change hands. According to some estimates, trading in the gray market may account for as much as 25–30 per cent of the total futures trading in India. But in the three main exchanges – National Multi-Commodity Exchange (NMCE), NCDEX and MCX – the order book is accessible to all market participants, a feature that has added substantial transparency in commodity trading for both spot and futures trading.

A complex and potentially problematic part of futures trading is the settlement of futures contracts. It must be borne in mind, that a relatively small fraction of the futures traded actually come up for delivery – most are 'squared off' before maturity. For those sellers who intend to deliver on their contracts exchanges follow more or less the same system. Usually about a week before the maturity of the futures contract, the sellers and buyers have to notify the exchange whether they want to deliver/take delivery on the contract or 'square it off' on maturity, i.e., pay/accept cash. The exchange then matches up the buyers and sellers intending on making delivery. The actual delivery almost always takes the form of warehousing receipts. A warehousing receipt is a receipt issued by a government recognized warehouse, certifying that a certain quantity of an agricultural commodity is kept in storage there. The receipt itself is negotiable and is acceptable as settlement of claims.

Margins in India typically fall in the 5–10 per cent range and one can start trading in commodities with as low a balance as ₹ 5,000. In addition there are brokerage and other fees. Brokerage charges usually range from 0.10–0.25 per cent of the contract value and generally higher for a contract resulting in delivery. There are also transaction charges of approximately ₹ 6 to ₹ 10 per contract. The brokerage varies from commodity to commodity and is below maximum limits set by the relevant exchange.

The organization and governance of futures exchanges

In India, futures exchanges, like other financial exchanges have been traditionally run as self-regulating associations of traders and brokers under the overall guidance of the Forward Market Commission rules and regulations. Most regional exchanges still retain that form of organizational structure. They are managed by a board of directors comprising largely the members of the trading association, supplemented by independent public representatives. The four national-level exchanges, however, have external promoters and shareholders, with the majority stake often coming from public sector financial institutions. This is also reflected in their board composition. The board appoints a management team that runs the day-to-day affairs of the exchange.

In most cases, the exchanges have different committees to look into the various functions like floor trading, setting of settlement price for the day, settlement and delivery of contracts etc. Clearing houses associated with the different futures exchanges play a crucial role in the futures market. They take the counterparty position in futures contracts thus guaranteeing against the counter-party default risk. Presently, many exchanges have their internal clearing houses. However, there are recommendations (as, for instance, in the World Bank report of Frida Youssef (2000)) to set up a national-level clearing house facility whose services could be availed by all futures exchanges.

The direction of causality and volatility spillovers in the Indian commodity markets: A time series analysis

Commodity prices are inherently volatile due to unexpected demand and supply shocks. Due to this volatility, producers and consumers who have exposure to commodities often seek to hedge the price risk. Instruments such as futures and forward contracts and other derivatives are created to help hedge the risk in spot prices. Future price is the contracted price to be paid upon delivery of a pre-specified quantity in acceptable quality in a future date whereas the spot price is the cash price in the physical market for immediate purchase. Non-arbitrage theory states that the future price should be equal to the spot price plus the per-unit cost of storage and risk free interest rate for the period (Pindyck, 2001). On the other hand, asset pricing theory states that spot and future prices are linked by the expected risk premium.

The futures markets are generally considered to perform two major roles in commodity markets, a risk-transfer role and price discovery role. The risk-transfer role results from the fact that a futures market is a place where risks are reallocated between hedgers (producers) and speculators. Producers are then willing to compensate speculators for sharing the risks inherent in their productive activity. Futures prices also transmit information to all economic agents, especially to uninformed producers who, in turn, may base their supply decisions on the futures price. It can also be argued that physical traders use futures prices as a reference to price their commodities due to the greater transparency and (often) greater liquidity of commodity futures over physical commodities.

The essence of the price discovery function of futures markets hinges on whether new information is reflected first in changes of futures prices or in changes of cash prices. In other words, price discovery means whether price changes in futures markets lead price changes in cash markets more often than the reverse. The share of price discovery originating in the futures markets has important implications for hedgers and arbitrageurs who use these markets.

However this assumes that the market participants are well-informed stakeholders in physical commodities and use the derivatives to hedge their risk based on their information on market fundamentals. However, lack of extensive physical production, inventory and trading data, and noise in market information, market participants may follow market sentiment during a prolonged bubble or bust. While noise in information is amplified due to development of index investing and correlation among asset markets, uninformed trading would take place when the participants would resort to mimic the performance of market 'leaders' and/or relay on momentum trading and statistical techniques rather than market fundamentals. Also 'weight-of-money' effects i.e., the impact of a large position taken by large traders in the absence of matching counterparty liquidity, would also affect the efficiency of the market.

Thus, identifying the direction of information flows between spot and futures prices appears to be an empirical issue. A considerable amount of empirical research has been directed towards examining the relationship between futures and the underlying spot prices in different commodity and financial futures markets. In particular, the focus of attention has been on the lead-lag relationship between futures returns and the underlying spot returns; for the futures prices to fulfill their price discovery role they must lead the underlying spot prices. Overall, the findings of these studies indicate that causality between spot and futures prices can run in one (futures to spot) or both (futures/spot feedback) directions, depending on the market under investigation, and in all the cases futures prices contribute to the discovery of new information regarding the future level of spot prices.

In most empirical studies the lead-lag relation between different markets is examined by estimating a Granger-Sims causality regression where the returns in one market are explained by lagged, contemporaneous and lead returns in the other market (e.g. Kawaller *et al.*, 1987; Chan. 1990; Stephan and Whaley, 1990; Stoll and Whaley, 1990; Chan *et al.*, 1993). Empirical research aimed at testing the lead-lag relationship between the index futures and the underlying spot market produced mixed results. Empirical evidence indicates that, (1) future prices tend to influence spot prices (Abhyankar, 1998), (2) spot prices tend to lead futures prices (Subrahmanyam, 1991; Chan, 1992), and (3) a bi-directional feedback relationship exists between spot and futures prices (Abhyankar, 1998; Silvapulle and Moosa, 1999).

Thus, this chapter explores the causal relationship between spot and future prices in the Indian commodity markets for selected commodities (mentha oil, crude oil, refined soy oil and natural gas) and indices from MCX commodity exchange.

Data: The spot data used in the analysis are daily (six trading days in a week) prices obtained from the Multi Commodity Exchange (MCX). Commodities that are liquid and traded for considerably long time such as mentha oil, crude oil, refined soy oil and natural gas are considered. The sample data differs for commodities according to availability. Index (7 June 2005 to 9 June 2011), crude oil (9 February 2005 to 15 April 2011), natural gas (7 October 2006 to 30 June 2011), refined soy oil (23 September 2004 to 11 July 2011) and mentha oil (26 April 2014 to 12 July 2011). All prices are in INR. The futures data are closing prices of futures contracts traded each day. The authors have considered the far month contracts for the analysis as they are most liquid. The futures data were provided by MCX commodity exchange.

Figure 2.12 shows the evolution, in real terms, of spot and futures prices for the indices and four commodities during the entire sample period. As predicted by non-arbitrage theory both spot and future prices move together with significant fluctuations in the sample period. While they observe crude oil and mentha oil showing contango relationship, the other series show normal backwardation (see Figures 2.12 and 2.13). The futures market seems to dominate the spot market or in other words changes in spot prices echo changes in futures prices for the indices and all the commodities considered except crude oil.

Figure 2.12: Levels of spot and futures (index, crude oil, natural gas, refined soy oil and mentha oil)

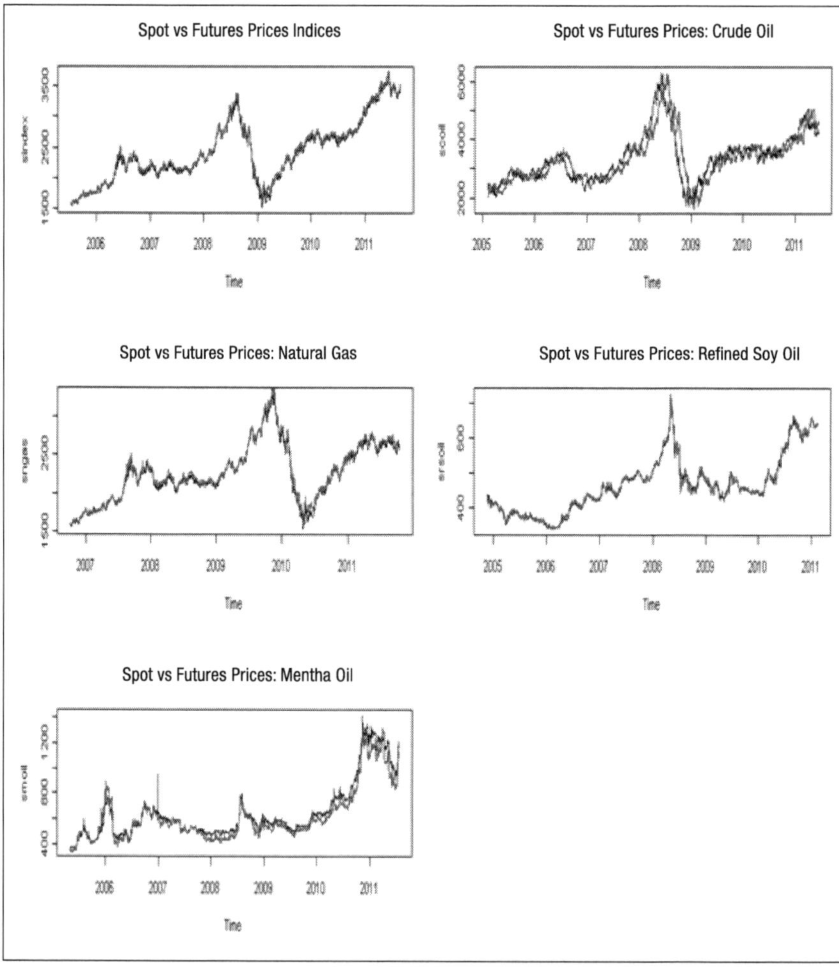

Source: Author's estimations

Figure 2.13: Relationship between spot and futures

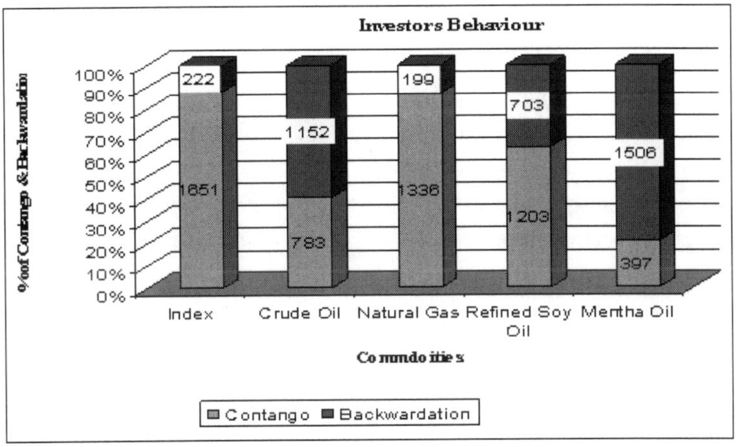

Source: Author's estimations

Causality between spot and futures: Causality tests are used to examine whether changes in futures price lead changes in spot prices, whether changes in spot prices lead changes in futures prices, or both. The authors use Granger causality tests to analyse the dynamic relationship between spot and futures prices, which would help explain the direction of information flows between spot and futures markets. Spot and futures returns have been used instead of levels data as all the selected commodities were found to be non-stationary (see Table 2.7).

Table 2.7: Augmented Dickey-Fuller (ADF) test for unit root

Variable	Index	Refined soy oil	Mentha oil	Crude oil	Natural gas
Spot levels	–1.778	–2.3998	–1.6749	–2.1191	–2.0297
Futures levels	–1.8504	–2.3876	–2.2286	–2.0686	–2.0856
Spot returns	–11.609***	–11.1336***	–10.8186***	–12.9985***	–10.8474***
Futures returns	–11.3345***	–11.814***	–11.4867***	–12.1196***	–10.5491***
Spot volatility	–6.4613***	–11.0593***	–11.8069***	–7.407***	–5.8952***
Futures volatility	–7.4996***	–11.8339***	–12.6644***	–8.6844***	–7.0495***

Source: Authors' estimations.

Notes: The spot (futures) returns is the series are calculated based on $\left(\frac{x_t - x_{t-1}}{x}\right)$. The spot (futures) volatility is estimated through GARCH (1,1). The ADF test includes an intercept. The appropriate lag lengths were selected based on Schwartz Bayesian Criterion (SBC).

*** 1% significance Levels. ADF t-statistic is reported.

The linear Granger causality [based on Vector Auto-Regression (VAR)] examines whether past values of spot prices can help explain current values of futures prices, conditional on past values of the futures prices. Intuitively, it determines whether past values of the spot contain additional information on the current value of the futures that is not contained in past values of the latter.

In this case, the authors evaluate whether futures returns Granger-cause spot returns (that is, whether the return in the spot market at time *t* is related to past returns in the futures market, conditional on past spot returns), whether spot returns Granger-cause futures returns, or both. Similarly, it is evaluated whether volatility in the futures market Granger-cause volatility in the spot market, or otherwise.

Granger causality results for spot and futures returns for the index and for all four agricultural commodities for the whole sample period are presented in Tables 2.8a and 2.8b. The upper section of the table reports F-statistic for the null hypothesis that spot returns and volatilities does not Granger-cause futures returns and volatilities; the lower section reports the F-statistic for the null hypothesis that cause futures returns and volatilities returns does not Granger-cause spot returns and volatilities.

Tables 2.8a and 2.8b: Granger causality – returns and volatility

Granger causality H0: Spot returns do not Granger-cause futures returns and Granger causality H0: Spot volatility does not Granger-cause futures volatility

	Returns		**Volatility**	
	F-statistic	**P-values**	**F-statistic**	**P-values**
Index	1.0003	0.4232	3.9288	0.0006422
Refined soy oil	30.4071	< 2.2e-16	583.8576	< 2.2e-16
Natural gas	0.7286	0.6266	3.2624	0.003364
Mentha oil	14.1289	5.551e-16	0.0906	0.9973
Crude oil	2.2068	0.0396	4.7162	8.585e-05

Granger causality H0: Futures returns do not Granger-cause spot returns and Granger causality H0: Futures volatility does not Granger-cause spot volatility

	Returns		Volatility	
	F-statistic	**P-values**	**F-statistic**	**P-values**
Index	204.5198	< 2.2e-16	26.6374	< 2.2e-16
Refined soy oil	14.7671	< 2.2e-16	68.147	< 2.2e-16
Natural gas	158.9376	< 2.2e-16	18.8725	< 2.2e-16
Mentha oil	21.6719	< 2.2e-16	0.0842	0.9978
Crude oil	0.8273	0.5485	7.1802	0.007371

Source: Author's estimations
Notes: SBC suggested lag structure of 6; H0 = Null Hypothesis

Table 2.8c: Summary of causality results

	Spot does not cause futures		Futures does not cause spot	
	Returns	**Volatility**	**Returns**	**Volatility**
Index	No	Yes	Yes	Yes
Refined soy oil	Yes	Yes	Yes	Yes
Natural gas	No	Yes	Yes	Yes
Mentha oil	Yes	No	Yes	No
Crude oil	Yes	Yes	No	Yes

Source: Author's estimations

The summary of causality results given in Table 2.8c shows that index and natural gas futures cause the spot returns and volatility, while mentha oil and refined soy oil returns show bi-directional causality. All the series except mentha oil show bi-directional causality in volatility. The results show that in the Indian context there is no strong one way causality from futures to spot or spot to futures rather, the authors observe significant bi-directional causality.

Findings: In this section the authors have explored the time series properties of the commodities market indices and a few individual commodities that are heavily traded in the Indian commodity exchanges. They have utilized Granger causality test and vector error correction models to assess the nature of information flow in the commodity markets.

As discussed in World Economic Outlook (2008), they also observe a unidirectional causal relationship. As is popularly debated during the recent global food crisis, speculation in the futures markets does not lead the spot markets in the Indian case. Instead, they find a strong two-way causal relationship between spot and futures which corroborates the theory. Further, volatility spillover analysis confirms the findings from causality tests as they observe the existence of strong volatility spillover between spot and futures markets from both the directions.

Thus, the time series analysis does not bear the contention that the vibrant derivatives markets may be a cause of spot price increase in the recent times. In the next section, they explore the role of the whole gamut of determinants of including the fundamental demand and supply factors, macroeconomic factors such as real interest rate and inflation and also the futures markets in explaining the recent commodity price rise in India.

Policy issues

Policy issues in commodity trading in India

While organized exchange-based trading in foodgrains have increased manifold over the past decade, several key policy issues relating to these markets remain in a limbo. For instance the Forward Contracts (Regulation) Amendment (FCRA) Bill seeks to change, *inter alia*, the status of the Forward Markets Commission and to give it the powers of an apex regulator comparable to those enjoyed by SEBI in the case of securities markets as well as to increase its regulatory bandwidth. The absence of regulatory powers and the ability to penalize offending market participants hold back an improvement in the quality of commodity markets in India.

With high inflation being the most important challenge for policy makers in India in recent years and with significantly higher food inflation, the issue of food prices has been in the limelight in India constantly in recent years. Policy response has proceeded along expected lines with trade restrictions and now-on-now-off restrictions of futures trading. See Table 2.12 in the Appendix for a partial list of policy actions in India in the area of foodgrains in recent years.

Effects of bans on export and futures trading

A recent working paper of the Finance Ministry (Dasgupta *et al.*, 2011) has argued that while export ban on wheat from February 2007 has been largely ineffective, the ban on futures between February 2007 and May 2009 has helped drive a 'wedge' between international and domestic wheat prices and held back inflation. This finding is at significant odds with much of the literature and needs to be probed closely.

Figure 2.3 shows the domestic and international wheat prices with the period of the futures ban shaded. It is clear from the graph itself that the main driver of the result in Dasgupta *et al.* (2011) is the spike in 2008 in international prices that the Indian wheat prices avoided. Given that at that time both bans were in place and that the spike itself was, in the greater scheme of things, an aberration, the conclusion needs to be re-examined. In terms of econometrics too, the specifications of the regressions used in the study can benefit from reconsideration. In the main text, the coefficient of the futures ban term is insignificant at 5 per cent level. Hence its value is statistically indistinguishable from zero. Besides it is based on a sample of just 45 quarters and the inclusion of the futures ban variable does not improve the explanatory power much. The fact that wheat futures were only introduced as late as July 2004 further reduces the data available for the test.

Further analysis using co-integration type adjustment apparently validates the negative effect of the ban on the domestic price. Nevertheless, the issues about the regression specification stay and it is not clear whether the Auto-Regressive Distributed Lag (ARDL) approach addresses all the econometric problems with the original specification.

Finally, regardless of the regression estimates, there is the question of causality. Given the overlap in the windows of export ban and futures trading ban in wheat, it is difficult to attribute the observed patterns in prices to one of the two policy effects or other policy measures around that time. What is undeniable is that prices in India saw a much smaller rise as compared to international prices. Once again, that spike itself was a one-time phenomenon given its near-complete reversal. Hence drawing general conclusions like banning futures trading can give a 26 per cent discount in prices need further investigation.

Better market infrastructure

Notwithstanding the doubt about efficacy of banning futures trading, there can be no doubt about the need for efficient and transparent markets in commodity futures. An early passage of the FCRA is a *sine qua non* in this matter. While comparing with the post-SEBI growth of financial security markets may not be an appropriate, there is no doubt that giving regulatory powers to the FMC can improve the quality of the players and bring about more transparent and informed trading in the area. This is likely to contribute to the information content of prices – both spot and future – and bring about significant improvement in the area of commodity trading and trading in commodity derivatives.

Conclusions and Policy Recommendations for the G20

In an era of rising commodity prices, steps to ensure global food security should include market-based measures that include the spot and futures markets in commodities. The case of India, a major producer and consumer of agricultural produce provides one certain directions in carrying out optimum market-based measures. The empirical analysis carried out in this chapter provides some important pointers in this direction, particularly in light of periodic bans on foreign trade and suspension of trading of commodity futures in India.

The findings may be summarized as follows. For spot trading, while monetary factors are most influential for over all commodity index, and certain specific commodities like soy oil and mentha oil, financial factors and international factors such as international oil prices and dollar exchange rate are important, particularly for crude oil and natural gas. The authors have mixed results for financial factors as $\Delta Spot_{t-1}$ affects only the index and crude oil while the net open interest is significant in explaining variations in only crude oil spot prices.

As for futures markets, the commodities index and natural gas futures cause the spot returns and volatility, while mentha oil and refined soy oil returns show bi-directional causality. All the series except mentha oil show bi-directional causality in volatility. The results indicate that in the Indian context there is no strong one way causality from futures to spot or spot to futures. Rather, the authors observe significant bi-directional causality. This raises considerable doubts about the wisdom of suspending futures trading in an attempt to contain rising prices.

The lessons from recent policy experiments with commodity market regulation discussed above as well as the findings of research studies all point to certain policy prescriptions for the G20 in the commodity markets sphere so as to help improve food security in the world. Consistent with the categorization of policy measures used before, these recommendations fall in two broad classes – those affecting international trade and those dealing with commodity derivatives. The recommendations are listed below:

1. Ensure free trade standards for agricultural commodities. Most of the WTO regulations deal with opening up import markets and relatively less with ensuring export continuity. In the case of food trade, it is the export bans that create the maximum damage. So a mechanism needs to be developed whereby WTO member-countries are committed to maintaining export continuity and let the global market price, rather than national policy restraints determine the international allocation of food grains.

2. Together with ensuring export continuity, the G20 should work towards helping countries reduce their domestic tariff levels of commodities to move towards greater free trade in food grains.

3. In the case of commodity futures, it is best to leave them alone. Restricting or banning futures trade does not help matters at all, so it is best not to interfere in their operations. Futures actually contribute towards sending appropriate signals to commodity producers and serve a positive role in reducing price volatility both in the short term and the long term. There is no evidence of strong unidirectional causality running from futures to the spot market; the relationship appears to be bi-directional. Re-introduction of suspended or banned futures would in fact be steps in the right direction.

4. The G20 governments should eliminate policy uncertainty in this matter. The 'on-now-off-again' approach to allowing and suspending futures trading introduces significant policy uncertainty in these markets, reduces market participation and seriously compromises the quality of the prices as signals of information and beliefs.

5. However, ensuring proper trading processes and transparency in both future and spot markets is a must. While futures markets by themselves cannot create too much trouble, faulty processes and narrowness of futures and spot markets together can conceivably contribute to possible cornering of select commodities and even cause short-term runs in these commodities. The G20 governments must therefore focus on ensuring that commodity exchanges are equipped with proper disclosure standards and trading processes and daily position reporting so as to avoid such situations. Failure to do so would be costly since it would only take a small number of such cases to move the policy debate in this area back by several years.

Appendix

Table 2.9: NCDEX soy bean – specifications of a futures contract

(Applicable for contracts expiring in September, October, November, December and January)

Name of commodity	**Soy bean**
Ticker symbol	SYBEANIDR
Trading System	NCDEX trading system
Basis	Ex-warehouse Indore exclusive of sales taxes
Unit of trading	10 MT
Delivery unit	10 MT
Quotation/base value	₹ per quintal
Tick size	50 paisa
Quality specification	
Moisture	10 %
Foreign Matters	2 %
Damaged	2 %
Green Seed	7 %
Quantity variation	+/- 2%
Delivery center	Indore (within a radius of 50 km from the municipal limits)
Additional delivery center	Akola, Nagpur (Maharashtra); Itarsi, Sagar (MP); and Kota (Rajasthan) Location premium/discount as notified by the exchange from time to time.
Trading hours	As per directions of the Forward Markets Commission from time to time, currently -
Mondays through Fridays	10:00 AM to 05:00 PM
Saturdays	10.00 AM to 2.00 PM
The exchange may vary the above timing with due notice	
Due date/expiry date	20th day of the delivery month. If 20th happens to be a holiday, a Saturday or a Sunday then the due date shall be the immediately preceding trading day of the exchange, which is not a Saturday.

Delivery specification	The sellers would be required to give their intention to give delivery at least five days before the maturity of the contract. If a buyer with an outstanding position at maturity or a seller, who has given an intention to deliver, fails to meet their respective obligations, the penalty structure will be
As per circular number	NCDEX/TRADING-091/2007/235 dated October 4, 2007. The operators giving the intention for delivery shall not be allowed to square off their position
Delivery logic	Seller's option
Closing of contract	On the expiry of the contract, all outstanding positions not resulting in giving/taking of physical delivery of the commodity shall be closed out at the final settlement price announced by the exchange
Opening of contracts	Trading in any contract month will open on the 10th day of the month. If the 10th day happens to be a non-trading day, contracts would open on next trading day
Number of active contracts as per launch calendar	
Price limit	Daily price fluctuation limit is (+/–) 3per cent. If the trade hits the prescribed daily price limit there will be a cooling off period for 15 minutes. Trade will be allowed during this cooling off period within the price band. Thereafter the price band would be raised by (+/–) 1per cent and trade will be resumed. If the price hits the revised price band (4 per cent) again during the day, trade will only be allowed within the revised price band. No trade / order shall be permitted during the day beyond the revised limit of (+ / –) 4 per cent
Position limits	
Member level	150,000 MT or 15 per cent of market open interest, whichever is higher
Client level	30,000 MT
The above limits will not apply to bona fide hedgers. For bona fide hedgers, the exchange will, on a case to case basis, decide the hedge limits.	

Near month limit (applicable from 28 days prior to expiry date):	
Member level	40,000 MT or 15% of market wide near month open position whichever is higher
Client level	8,000 MT
Quality Allowance(for Delivery)	Quality delivery with variation shall be acceptable with discount as under:
Moisture: From 10–12% accepted at 1:1, above 12% rejected Foreign Matter: From 2–4 per cent accepted at 1:1. Above 4 per cent rejected (The term 'foreign matter' would, in general, mean anything other than soy bean e.g., sand, silica, pebbles, stalks and other seeds) Damaged Seed: From 2–5 per cent accepted at 2:1, above 5 per cent rejected Green Seed: Above 7 per cent rejected Free from non-edible seeds such as mahua, castor and neem and any toxic substances, should be free from any foul odour.	
Special Margin: In case of additional volatility, a special margin at such other percentage, as deemed fit, will be imposed in respect of outstanding positions, which will remain in force as long as the volatility exists, after which the special margin may be relaxed. **Final Settlement Price:** The Final Settlement Price (FSP) shall be arrived at by taking the average of the last three days' spot prices. The last spot price for the day as polled by the Exchange during the last three days shall be taken for arriving at the FSP. In the event of unavailability of the spot prices during any one of the last three days excluding the expiry day (i.e., on E – 1 or E – 2), the spot price of the previous day (E – 3) shall be considered for the average of the last three days. In case spot prices are not available during the three day period prior to the expiry date, the last spot price of the expiry day shall be considered for arriving at the FSP.	

Source: NCDEX website (www.ncdex.com)

Table 2.10: List of exchanges

Sl. No.	Name of the exchanges
A.	**National multi commodity exchanges**
1	National Multi Commodity Exchange of India Ltd., Ahmedabad (NMCE)
2	Multi Commodity Exchange of India Ltd., Mumbai (MCX)
3	National Commodity & Derivatives Exchange Ltd., Mumbai (NCDEX)
4	Indian Commodity Exchange Ltd., Mumbai (ICEX)

Sl. No.	Name of the exchanges
B.	**Commodity specific regional exchanges**
5	Ahmedabad Commodity Exchange Ltd, Ahmedabad
6	Bikaner Commodity Exchange Ltd, Bikaner
7	Bombay Commodity Exchange Ltd, Mumbai
8	Central India Commercial Exchange Ltd, Gwalior
9	Cotton Association of India, Mumbai
10	The Chamber of Commerce, Hapur
11	East India Jute & Hessian Exchange Ltd., Kolkata
12	First Commodity Exchange of India Ltd, Kochi
13	Haryana Commodities Ltd., Sirsa
14	India Pepper & Spice Trade Association, Kochi
15	The Meerut Agro Commodities Exchange Company Ltd, Meerut
16	National Board of Trade, Indore
17	Rajkot Commodity Exchange Ltd., Rajkot
18	Spices & Oilseeds Exchange Ltd, Sangli
19	Surendranagar Cotton Oil & Oilseeds Association Ltd, Surendranagar
20	The Rajdhani Oil & Oilseeds Exchange Ltd, Delhi
21	Vijai Beopar Chamber Ltd., Muzaffarnagar

Source: Annual Report, 2009–10, Forward Market Commission

Table 2.11: Recent policy actions in India – foodgrains (cereals, pulses, sugar)[2]

Date	Group	Commodity	Policy actions
28 June 2005	Cereals	Maize	The current Exim Policy has no restrictions on exports and a quota of four lakh tonnes of import on actual-user basis has been fixed at a duty of 15 per cent. A duty of 60 per cent is levied on imports above four lakh tonnes.
April 2003	Futures markets	Futures markets	India allows futures trade in commodities.

Date	Group	Commodity	Policy actions
March 2006	Cereals	Wheat	India abolishes 60 per cent import tax on overseas purchases of wheat by official agencies, and decides to buy wheat after a gap of six years. The import tax for private players is cut to five per cent.
May 2006	Cereals	Wheat	State-run Food Corp of India buys only 9.2 million tonnes of wheat from local farmers against a target of 16.2 million tonnes.
June 2006	Pulses	Pulses	The export ban was imposed in June 2006 to augment the domestic supply and check prices.
July 2006	Cereals	Wheat	Government wheat stocks fall to 8.2 million tonnes, nearly nine million tonnes below target.
July 2006	Cereals	Wheat	The government estimates India's 2006 wheat production at 69.4 million tonnes against an initial estimate of 73.0 million tonnes.
14 September 2006	Pulses	Pulses	The central government has directed the state governments to impose stock limits in pulses on individual wholesale dealers under the Essential Commodities Act.
14 September 2006	Pulses	Pulses	Maharashtra government took the lead and imposed stock limit on urad, tur and chana with immediate effect which would be applicable for six months.
December 2006	Cereals	Wheat	India's wheat imports totaled 5.5 million tonnes in 2006.
17 January 2007	Futures markets	Futures markets	Government bans futures trade in pigeon peas and black matpe, for alleged role in stoking prices in physical market.
25 January 2007	Cereals	Maize	In another attempt to rein in the rising prices of essential commodities, government allowed import of maize freely up to 31 December 2007.
February 2007	Cereals	Wheat	India bans wheat exports.
February 2007	Cereals	Wheat	India bans wheat futures trade.

Date	Group	Commodity	Policy actions
18 February 2007	Futures markets	Futures markets	Government suspends rice and wheat futures – constitutes Abhijit Sen Committee to study link between futures and spot prices.
May 2007	Cereals	Wheat	Food Corp of India, which buys grain from farmers on behalf of the government, purchased 11 million tonnes of wheat in the season, up from 9.2 million tonnes a year earlier.
December 2007	Cereals	Wheat	India imports 1.8 million tonnes of wheat.
December 2007	Cereals	Wheat	India axes 36 per cent import tax on wheat flour.
April 2008	Futures markets	Futures markets	Sen Committee submits report saying there was no conclusive evidence showing a link between futures trade and stoking of physical market prices.
May 2008	Cereals	Wheat	Food Corp of India buys 22.7 million tonnes of wheat from domestic farmers during the season.
7 May 2008	Futures markets	Futures markets	Futures in soy oil, rubber, chickpea, and potato suspended on demand from the government's leftist allies.
July 2008	Cereals	Wheat	The government estimates 2008 harvests at 78.5 million tonnes.
3 July 2008	Cereals	Maize	Government had banned export of maize in July up to 15 October in the backdrop of runaway inflation.
15 October 2008	Cereals	Maize	The ban on maize exports lapsed on 15 October 2008 with the government deciding against extending it any further
3 December 2008	Futures markets	Futures markets	Government restores futures trade in soy oil, rubber, chickpea, and potato.
17 Februrary 2009	Sweetener	Sugar	The government allows mills to import duty-free raw sugar on condition that an equal quantity of white sugar would be exported within three years. (Compiled by Ratnajyoti Dutta in New Delhi; editing by Krittivas Mukherjee)

Date	Group	Commodity	Policy actions
17 Februrary 2009	Sweetener	Sugar	The government allows mills to import duty-free raw sugar on condition that an equal quantity of white sugar would be exported within three years.
23 Februrary 2009	Sweetener	Sugar	India imposes stock limits on the quantity of sugar that can be held by traders until 9 July to tame prices.
23 Februrary 2009	Sweetener	Sugar	India imposes stock limits on sugar until 9 July to tame prices.
19 March 2009	Pulses	Pulses	The ban on export of pulses extended for one more year
19 March 2009	Pulses	Pulses	Pulses import at zero duty extended for one more year till 31 March 2010.
10 April 2009	Sweetener	Sugar	India allows duty-free imports of white sugar and asks three state-run trading firms and a farmer cooperative to import up to 1 million tonnes of tax-free white sugar before 1 August. It exempts mills importing raws until 31 July from an obligation to export white sugar.
10 April 2009	Sweetener	Sugar	The country allows duty-free imports of white sugar and asks three state-run trading firms and a farmer cooperative to import up to one million tonnes of tax-free white sugar before 1 August. It exempts mills importing raws until 31 July from an obligation to export whites.
May 2009	Cereals	Wheat	Food Corp of India buys a record 25 million tonnes of wheat from local farmers.
May 2009	Cereals	Wheat	India allows wheat futures trade to resume.
21 May 2009	Futures markets	Futures markets	Ban on wheat futures lifted.
May 2009	Futures markets	Futures markets	India's commodities market regulator bars launch of new sugar futures contracts until the end of 2009.
26 May 2009	Sweetener	Sugar	India's commodities market regulator bars the launch of new sugar futures contract until the end of 2009 to check speculation and price rizes.

Date	Group	Commodity	Policy actions
26 May 2009	Sweetener	Sugar	India's commodities market regulator bars the launch of new sugar futures contract until the end of 2009 to check speculation and price rises.
19 June 2009	Sweetener	Sugar	The government extends sugar stocks limit until 8 January, 2010. In February, India had imposed limits on the quantity of sugar that can be held by traders for six months. The limit was to expire on 9 July.
19 June 2009	Sweetener	Sugar	The government extends a sugar stocks limit until 8 January 2010, to ensure adequate supplies in the local market.
25 June 2009	Sweetener	Sugar	India raises the minimum price that mills must pay to farmers for sugarcane by a third to a record high of 107.76 rupees per 100 kg to encourage farmers to plant more.
July 2009	Cereals	Wheat	The government sees 2009 wheat output at a record 80.7 million tonnes.
July 2009	Cereals	Wheat	The government lifts a ban on wheat exports, but re-imposes the restriction within 10 days on concern food prices may rize as the seasonal monsoon rains fail.
July 2009	Cereals	Wheat	India allows exports of 650,000 tonnes of wheat products until March.
31 July 2009	Sweetener	Sugar	India extends duty-free imports of raw and refined sugar.
25 August 2009	Sweetener	Sugar	The government asks large consumers to keep sugar stocks at levels that meet 15 days of demand, down from 30. 31 July – India extends duty-free imports of raw sugar until March 2010 and white sugar imports up to November 2009.
25 August 2009	Sweetener	Sugar	The government asks large consumers to keep sugar stocks at levels that meet 15 days of demand, down from 30.
17 September 2009	All	All	Centre asked states to regulate stocks of sugar, pulses, paddy, rice and edible oilseeds that traders can keep till September-end 2010.

Date	Group	Commodity	Policy actions
17 September 2009	Sweetener	Sugar	
29 October 2009	Sweetener	Sugar	The government fixes a 'fair and remunerative' price of rupees 129.84 ($2.80) per 100 kg of 2009–10 cane crop.
13 November 2009	Cereals	Maize	Deve Gowda demands support price for maize at ₹ 1,200 per quintal.
13 November 2009	Sweetener	Sugar	India issues formal orders extending tax-free imports of raw sugar until 31 December 2010 and white sugar until 31 March 2010.
19 November 2009	Sweetener	Sugar	The ruling Congress party says Prime Minister Manmohan Singh will consider changes in fixing cane prices after farmer leaders disrupt parliament demanding higher returns on cane.
December 2009	Futures markets	Futures markets	Government maintains status quo on sugar futures. Regulator to decide on relisting in September 2010.
13 January 2010	Sweetener	Sugar	India's cabinet panel allows duty-free imports of refined sugar up to 31 December 2010.
February 2010	Cereals	Wheat	India allows 50,000 tonnes of wheat exports to neighbouring Nepal.
February 2010	Cereals	Wheat	India produces 80.8 million tonnes of wheat in 2010.
5 February 2010	Sweetener	Sugar	The government bars large sugar consumers from stocking sugar of more than 10 days of consumption. The limit would be applicable for six months from 20 February.
March 2010	Cereals	Wheat	Farm Minister Sharad Pawar said a panel of ministers would consider lifting ban on wheat exports.
9 March 2010	Sweetener	Sugar	The Indian Sugar Mills Association, the top body of private producers, raised 2009/10 output forecast by five per cent to 16.8 million tonnes.
10 March 2010	Sweetener	Sugar	Indian sugar mills abandon deals as sugar prices tumble.

Date	Group	Commodity	Policy actions
13 May 2010	Sweetener	Sugar	The farm minister says India's sugar output in 2010/11 is likely to rise to 24 million–25 million tonnes from 18.5 million tonnes in the current year.
5 July 2010	Sweetener	Sugar	Pawar says India may tax sugar imports in the new season that starts in October.
9 July 2010	Sweetener	Sugar	Farm Minister Sharad Pawar invites sugar millers for discussions on reforms in the sugar sector.
19 August 2010	Sweetener	Sugar	Big users like soft drink makers and confectioners can hold stocks to meet three months of requirements, up from 15 days earlier, a limit itself raised from 10 days originally set in February. The new restriction will apply for six months. 5 July – Farm Minister Sharad Pawar says India may tax sugar imports – duty-free until the end of 2010 – in the new season that starts in October. So far, no decision has been made. 17 January – Four state-run firms are allowed to import tax free white sugar with a cap of 1 million tonnes. Some of this sugar remains in ports because of transport problems.
19 August 2010	Sweetener	Sugar	Big users like soft drink and confectionery makers can keep stocks to meet their requirement for three months, up from the earlier limit of 15 days. This new limit will be valid for six months.
September 2010	Futures markets	Futures markets	Government says it will allow futures trade in sugar from October onwards.
15 September 2010	Sweetener	Sugar	India lifts ban on sugar futures from 1 October.
27 October 2010	Sweetener	Sugar	India puts sugar output estimate for the current year from October at 25 million tonnes, up from 18.8 million in 2009–10.
2 November 2010	Sweetener	Sugar	Top cane producing state, Uttar Pradesh, hikes the minimum price sugar mills to be paid to farmers by 23.5 per cent, or 40 rupees per 100 kg, to 210 rupees ($4.7).

Date	Group	Commodity	Policy actions
4 November 2010	Sweetener	Sugar	India to allow 930,000 tonnes of extra sugar for export from mid-November, government sources say.
15 December 2010	Sweetener	Sugar	Farm minister Sharad Pawar announced 500,000 tonnes of sugar for exports under Open General Licence (OGL).
27 December 2010	Futures markets	Futures markets	Futures trading in sugar resumes
1 January 2011	Sweetener	Sugar	India imposes a 60 per cent import tax on sugar after expire on 31 December as output outlook improved. The tax was imposed in 2009 to overcome an acute domestic shortage.
3 January 2011	Sweetener	Sugar	India asks sugar mills to register for OGL or unrestricted exports.
10 January 2011	Sweetener	Sugar	India, the world's top consumer of sugar, dropped a 60 per cent import tax, reserving the rule that was slapped from 1 Jan.
11 January 2011	Sweetener	Sugar	Decision to allow half a million tonnes of exports under OGL referred to a panel ministers for a review as the government adopted a cautious approach amid high food prices.
March 2011	Cereals	Wheat	Junior farm minister Arun Yadav said a decision on the four year old ban on wheat exports could come as early as in April.
15 March 2011	Sweetener	Sugar	India hiked the price sugar mills must pay to cane growers by 4.2 per cent to rupees 145 ($3.2) per 100 kilograms for 2011/12.
24 March 2011	Pulses	Pulses	DGFT extends ban on pulses export till next March 2012. The prohibition will not apply to the export of kabuli chana and 10,000 tonnes of organic pulses during 2011–12, Directorate General of Foreign Trade (DGFT).

Date	Group	Commodity	Policy actions
24 March 2011	Pulses	Pulses	To augment the domestic availability of pulses, the Government has permitted imports at zero duty up to 31 March 2012.
April 2011	Cereals	Wheat	April 2011 – India forecasts 2011 wheat harvest at 84.3 million tonnes, higher than the previous forecast of 81.5 million tonnes and last year's output of 80.8 million tonnes.

Endnotes

[1] Futures Industry (www.futuresindustry.org).

[2] Many thanks to MCX for providing this table.

References

Abhyankar, A. 1998. 'Linear and Nonlinear Granger Causality: Evidence from the U.K. Stock Index Futures Market', *The Journal of Futures Markets* 18(5): 519–540.

Bose, S. March, 2009. 'Role of Future Market in Aggravating Commodity Price Inflation and the Future of commodity futures in India', *Money & Finance* 3(ICRA bulletin): 1–28.

Bosworth, B. P. and S. M. Collins. 2003. 'The Empirics of Growth: An Update', *Brookings Papers on Economic Activity* 2: 113–206.

Brahmbhatt, M. and L. Christiaensen. 2008. 'The Run on Rice', *World Policy Journal* 25 (2): 29–37.

Brahmbhatt, B. and L. Christiaensen. 2008. *Rising Food Prices in East Asia: Challenges and Policy Options*. Available at: http://siteresources.worldbank.org/EASTASIAPACIFICEXT/Resources/EA_Rising_Food_Prices050508.pdf. Accessed on 1 March 2014.

Brinkman, H., S. Pee, I. Sanogo, L. Subran and M. Bloem. 2009. 'High Food Prices and the Global Financial Crisis Have Reduced Access to Nutritious Food and Worsened Nutritional Status and Health', *Journal of Nutrition* 140(25 November): 153S–61S. Doi: 10.3945/jn.109.110767.

CFTC. September 2008. *Staff Report on Commodity Swap Dealers & Index Traders with Commission Recommendations*.

Chan, K. 1992. 'A Further Analysis of the Lead-lag Relationship between the Cash Market and Stock Index Futures Market', *Review of Financial Studies* 5:123–152.

Chan, K., P. Chung and H. Johnson. 1993. 'Why Option Prices Lag Stock Prices: A Trading-based Explanation', *Journal of Finance* 48(5): 1957–68.

Dasgupta, D., R. N. Dubey and R. Sathish. 2011. 'Domestic Wheat Price Formation and Food Inflation in India: International Prices, Domestic Drivers (Stocks, Weather, Public Policy), and the Efficacy of Public Policy Interventions in Wheat Markets, Ministry of Finance', *Working Paper No.2/2011-DEA*.

Demeke, M., G. Pangrazio and M. Maetz. 2009. 'Country Responses to the Food Security Crisis: Nature and Preliminary Implications of the Policies Pursued', *FAO's Initiative on Soaring Food Prices*. Rome: FAO.

Dreze, J. and A. Sen. 1989. *Hunger and Public Action*. Oxford: Clarendon Press.

ECFT. 2008. *Report of the Expert Committee to Study the Impact of Futures Trading on Agricultural Commodity Prices*. New Delhi: Ministry of Consumer Affairs, Food and Public Distribution, Government of India. Available at: http://www.indiaenvironmentportal.org.in/files/file/Abhijit%20Sen%20Report.pdf.

FAO, World Food Programme (WFP) and IFAD. 2012. *The State of Food Insecurity in the World 2012: Economic Growth is Necessary but Not Sufficient to Accelerate Reduction of Hunger and Malnutrition*. Rome: FAO.

G20 Seoul Summit Leaders Statement. 2010. Available at: http://media.seoulsummit.kr/contents/dlobo/E1._Seoul_Summit_Leaders_Declaration.pdf. Accessed on 1 March 2014.

Kawaller, I., P. Koch and T. Koch. 1987. 'The Temporal Relationship Between S&P 500 Futures and the S&P 500 Index', *Journal of Finance* 42: 1309–29.

Mousseau, F. 2010. 'The High Food Price Challenge: A Review of Responses to Combat Hunger'. Oakland: The Oakland Institute. Available at: www.oaklandinstitute.org/pdfs/high_food_prices_web_final.pdf. Accessed on 1 March 2014.

Ortiz, I., Chai, J. and M. Cummins. 11 February 2011. 'Escalating Food Prices: The Threat to Poor Households and Policies to Safeguard a Recovery for All', *UNICEF Working Paper*. Available at SSRN: http://ssrn.com/abstract=1760162. Accessed on 1 March 2014.

Pindyck, R. 2001. 'The Dynamics of Commodity Spot and Futures Markets: A Premier', *The Energy Journal* 22(3).

Silvapulle, P. and A. Moosa. 1999. 'The Relationship between Spot and Futures Prices: Evidence from the Cruide Oil Market', *The Journal of Futures Markets* 19: 175–193.

Stephan, J. and W. Robert. 1990. 'Intraday Price Change and Trading Volume Relations in the Stock and Stock Options Markets', *Journal of Finance* 45: 191–220.

Subrahmanyam, A. 1991. 'Risk Aversion, Market Liquidity, and Price Efficiency', *Review of Financial Studies* 4: 417–441.

Thomas, S. and J. R. Varma. 2010. 'Derivatives Markets', in *Capital Markets in India*, edited by Rajesh Chakrabarti and Sankar De. New Delhi: Sage Publications.

World Economic Outlook. 2008. *Financial Stress, Downturns, and Recoveries*. Available at: http://www.imf.org/external/pubs/ft/weo/2008/02/pdf/text.pdf. Accessed on 1 March 2014.

3 Recycling Global Surpluses for Infrastructure Investment in Emerging Market Economies

Renu Kohli

Global imbalances have mounted in the world eccnomy since 1996, in the form of surpluses in some countries with large deficits in other nations, chiefly the United States. Starting around the mid-90s, growing surpluses mounted in countries like China, Japan and Germany, offset by a widening current account deficit in the United States. Combined global reserve holdings grew more than 20 per cent annually from 2001–02, falling steeply to nearly half the rate in 2008 in reflection of the sharp contraction in world trade and cross-border investments. The imbalances however, started rising again in 2010. According to McKinsey Global Institute (2011), central bank foreign reserves were the fastest growing components of global foreign investment assets in 2010, reaching US$ 8.7 trillion; nearly 9 per cent of the world's financial stock was invested in government bonds and other low-risk securities.

Several factors explain the accumulation of these world imbalances. For one, the United States followed an increasingly lax monetary policy to counter its recession from 2000 onwards. Two, China pursued an aggressive, export-led growth strategy throughout the 90s and up to the 2008 crisis through an undervalued exchange rate leading to substantial accumulation of reserves. In the same period, commodity-exporting countries also accumulated surpluses to smooth terms-of-trade shocks and prevent setting in of 'Dutch Disease', i.e., a real appreciation-driven, expansion in domestic demand from rising export incomes that erodes productivity of the manufacturing sector, eventually resulting in falling exports as imports become more competitive.

Another factor prompting reserves' accumulation is the increased capital mobility since the 90s that challenged most developing economies as capital controls began losing their grip while the frequency and intensity of financial crises rose. This triggered a wave of precautionary reserves' accumulation as affected countries sought to 'self-insure' against future liquidity shocks

(Eichengreen, 2004). After the East Asian Crisis of 1997–98, perceptions of an unfair international financial architecture rose too, adding further momentum as Asian nations created sizeable liquidity buffers and regional reserve pools. Effectively, by the end of 90s, exchange rate regimes across the world polarized into 'free floaters' and 'intermediate' (Fischer, 2001), the pace of reserves' accumulation accelerated and global imbalances built up.

It was against this backdrop that the Indian Prime Minister, Dr Manmohan Singh, proposed at the G20's Seoul summit in 2010 that some of the surplus savings could be recycled towards infrastructure investments in emerging market countries. So far, policy efforts had largely focused upon the major countries, especially China and the United States, to resolve the global imbalances' build-up through respective economic and exchange rate policy changes. The Indian prime minister's proposal to recycle a portion of the surpluses complemented the G20's macroeconomic cooperation efforts in this regard and cast a spotlight on evolving intermediation mechanisms to channel savings from surplus nations towards those with deficits, or excess demand. Recycling capital surpluses in this manner was valuable from a time perspective too – political convenience of structural reforms to raise domestic expenditures in surplus countries was unlikely to be quick following a large shock, while such reforms, when instituted, would bear fruit with a lag. In the medium-term therefore, some recycling of surpluses would help bridge a gap in infrastructure financing in the emerging market economies, help prop global demand and contribute to boosting global productivity over longer periods.

Besides imparting a countercyclical demand boost to offset recessionary conditions in the advanced economies, such an exercise would generate other externalities normally associated with public investments.[1] Additional benefits perceived were the restraining impact upon asset prices through some diversion of surplus resources towards real, rather than purely financial investments. Finally, this was also justifiable as a contribution of the surplus countries towards maintenance of international financial stability, an international public good, from which they themselves would gain too.

Much water has flown under the bridge in the three years since. Does this mean the proposal to recycle surpluses is no longer valid? A perusal of major global trends in this regard suggest otherwise. Post-crisis, the picture on global imbalances is somewhat mixed: Some of the pre-crisis factors underlying these have diluted; others remain in place, perhaps even intensified. The maximum amount of change has been in the shift in China's exchange rate policy towards gradual appreciation of its currency; economic policy changes to rebalance the growth pattern, reorienting it towards domestic, consumption-based demand; and slowdown to more moderate levels relative to its pre-crisis, high growth rate. A reversing commodity cycle has contributed to lower surpluses in exporting countries. In addition, moderating consumption with improving savings in the United States has contributed to shrink its current account deficit.

These trends are offset by other developments. Global liquidity rose significantly from the strong balance sheet expansion of advanced countries' central banks. In particular, the US monetary policy was extraordinary loose to combat the crisis shock and ensuing recession with three rounds of large-scale asset purchases, or quantitative easing. Global capital flow cycles have been more volatile too, with shorter frequencies and duration (IMF, 2011). And international cooperation efforts at the G20 to reform the international monetary system have barely progressed. The combined outcome of these developments is a return to reserve accumulation by most emerging and developing countries, seeking to preserve macro financial stability and competitiveness vis-à-vis other currencies, especially the dollar, losing their value.

Reflecting these trends, global reserve holdings resumed their upward climb by 2010, although at half the pre-crisis rate, or 10 per cent annually. The argument for recycling surplus savings into infrastructure requirements in developing countries remains as forceful therefore. The G20 could be a platform for pursuing such a proposal as the group has focused considerably upon infrastructure issues. The institution of a High Level Panel on Infrastructure Investment by the G20 and which submitted its report to the leaders in October 2011, reflects the forum's interest in the subject. However, the context guiding the panel's report was somewhat different from this chapter's focus as the former examined how investment flows from the private sector could be channeled towards infrastructure projects in low-income group of countries, and how the G20 could, in cooperation with Multilateral Development Banks (MDB), identify areas where such investment could be fostered. The G20 Working Group on Infrastructure also made a submission in June 2011 on supporting infrastructure in developing countries.

Against this background, this article expands upon the surplus-recycling proposal made in 2010. It addresses four key questions: What are the infrastructure requirements of developing countries, including Asia? What are the historical precedents, if any, of recycling surpluses? What are the relevant issues in this context? What are the different policy options? It concludes with the possibility of creating a special fund for infrastructure financing at multilateral institutions like the World Bank or Asian Development Bank (ADB), through mutually agreed capital contributions, perhaps under the aegis of the G20. It argues that two attributes – security and low costs – are an essential prerequisite for the success and viability of the proposed structure.

Infrastructural Needs of Developing Countries

The developing countries face a significant infrastructure deficit as a group. As such, their financing needs are vast. Against this, most of these countries are fiscally constrained. They also face a challenging growth and financing environment, domestic as well as external. Bhattacharya *et al.* (2012) argue '… many emerging markets and all low-income countries require a major step increase in infrastructure investment to alleviate growth constraints, respond to urbanization pressures and meet their crucial development, inclusion and environmental goals.' They estimate the incremental investment spending across emerging markets and developing countries is around one trillion dollars a year more than what is currently spent; the bulk of spending needs are in electricity, water and transport. Crude estimates of the Multilateral Development Bank (MDB) Working Group on Infrastructure at its submission to the G20 (June 2011) also showed that in the next one decade, an average of 7 per cent of developing country GDP would be required to be invested in infrastructure for meeting basic needs like electricity, drinking water, all-weather roads etc.

To meet this large infrastructure development need, annual infrastructure spending would have to be more than double by 2020, according to Bhattacharya *et al.* (2012). Spending on infrastructure in developing countries, according to them, was approximately \$0.8–0.9 trillion per year, and the majority of this came from domestic budgetary financing (\$500–600 billion); the balance annual financing was provided by a mix of private sector institutions (20–30 per cent or approximately \$150–250 billion), ODA from developed countries and various MDBs (5-8 per cent, or \$40–60 billion) and more recently, by emerging countries like the BRICS (about 3 per cent, or under \$20 billion). While domestic budgetary financing would still be important, macroeconomic considerations like debt sustainability and affordability limit the additional financing strains. The existing architecture, e.g. role of MDBs, is deficient in providing financing on the scale as well as other characteristics required.

Investment and maintenance expenditure requirements arising from income increases-linked demand are especially large, especially in the low-income countries. Fay *et al.* (2011) estimated that required investments in 2013 would be between $1.25–1.5 trillion per year (at 2008 constant prices) in order to sustain economic growth. This translates into about 5–6 per cent of developing countries' GDP; assuming annual GDP growth of 4 per cent over 2013–20, Fay *et als* (2011) steady-state forecasts indicate that such investments could amount to $1.6–2.0 trillion annually by 2020. These estimates suggest that infrastructure investment needs would rise from around 3 per cent of GDP at present to 6–8 per cent of GDP by then. The implications for total financing requirement for fulfilling infrastructure needs is an escalation of about 1 trillion dollars more per year than being currently spent.

For the energy sector alone, the IEA (IEA, 2010) calculates a requirement of $33 trillion of investment over the next 25 years; of this amount, 64 per cent or about $21 trillion, is expected for investment in the developing and emerging countries. The additional investment need for this group of countries then is $845. Bhattacharya *et als* (2012) calculations showed that 45–60 per cent of the investment requirement will be in the electricity sector, including generation capacity, transmission and distribution networks; the remainder is split almost equally between the transport, telecoms and water sectors. They add that were maintenance requirements of existing infrastructures to be included, the transport sector's share would be even more as existing stocks are relatively high in this sphere, although the energy sector would continue to be leading source of maintenance needs.

Projections of infrastructure financing needs by region are equally compelling. For the South Asian Region, the World Bank (2010) estimates infrastructure investment needs between 7.6 and 11 per cent of the region's GDP. The ADB Institute (2010) calculated a sum of $748 billion for total Asia over 2010–20, or at 6.5 per cent of estimated GDP. Foster and Briceno-Garmendia (2010) estimated total annual expenditure needs of about 15 per cent of GDP for the African region. Fay *et al* (2011) judge that such estimates are conservative – if there is need of a step increase in developing countries, infrastructure spending could be far higher. Bhattacharya *et al.* (2012) projected that the majority of their estimated investments, 35–50 per cent, were required in East Asia, with lower sums needed in other regions; around 85 per cent of the total amount projected is expected to be required in low and lower-middle income countries. Similarly, the MDB Working Group for the G20 calculated that countries that grew rapidly, e.g. China, Japan and Korea, invested upwards of 9 per cent of GDP each year for several decades; actual total needs could therefore, be much higher and would correspond to growth rates achieved by respective countries.

Cross-country regional infrastructure needs are vast too. The MDB Working Group on Infrastructure for the G20 (June 2011) for instance pointed out that Asia alone would need to invest $26 billion annually in regional infrastructure projects over a decade to develop its regional transport infrastructures, given the substantial rise in intra-regional trade in the past 20 years. This was in addition to the combined national infrastructure needs of the region ($750 billion per year). Likewise, Africa would require annual investments of $19 billion, in addition to its total national infrastructure requirement of $93 billion, for transformative regional projects.

The requirements also need placing in a broader perspective wherein traditional sources other than direct budgetary financing are either static or on the decline. The MDB Working Group on Infrastructure, for instance, notes that external assistance for infrastructure investments reached nearly $90 billion in 2009, as ODA rose from pre-crisis level of $10 billion to $20 billion thereafter due to substantial efforts of the multilateral and bilateral agencies to help cope with the crisis shock. It is instructive that ODA is largely concentrated in the low-income countries and besides, will expectedly revert the trend. Multilateral lending for infrastructure, which was on a a steady increase over last half decade, rising from $24 billion in 2004 to about $70 billion in 2010, is also expected to decrease over the next five years as the various institutions shrink back lending to more ordinary levels.

In summary, these assessments make it abundantly clear that the infrastructure-financing gap in the developing world currently coexists with surplus global savings, which continues to grow albeit at a slower pace than in the pre-crisis period. It is possible to redirect and invest some of these excess savings more productively into financing the unmet infrastructure needs in developing and emerging countries. How to recycle these is the challenge. The next section delves into history for guidance on the issue.

Historical Experience with Recycling Surpluses

History offers an insight from the capital-recycling programme of Japan in 1986, which sought to redirect excess savings from Japan to developing countries. High levels of trade surpluses accumulated by Japan in the 1980s raised similar questions. The subsequent revaluation of its currency, the Yen, following the Plaza Accord in 1985, did not significantly contribute to a sizeable reduction in Japan's current account surplus. The Japanese government then considered the alternative of absorbing these surpluses into the world economy, while simultaneously strengthening its absorption channel through policies to raise domestic expenditure. Through a number of extensive plans, Japan made major contributions – totaling $30 billion over 1986 and 1987 – to increase both bilateral and multilateral flows to developing countries. At the same time, Japan also raised its own level of official development assistance on concessional terms.[2]

In September 1986, a plan to recycle approximately $10 billion in capital was announced at the joint International Monetary Fund (IMF)-World Bank annual meeting. At the time, Japan's current account surplus was approaching $100 billion per year. The key elements of the $10 billion recycling programme were:

1. Setting up of a *Japan Special Fund* ($2 billion) to recycle domestic private capital to developing countries through the World Bank – under the programme, Japan would allow the World Bank to raise 300 billion of yen-denominated funds beyond the established quota between 1987 and 1990.
2. *Loans to the IMF* ($3.6 billion) to build up its financial base, enhancing its ability to aid debtor nations with balance of payments deficits.
3. *Contributions to international development financing institutions* ($3.9 billion). The International Development Association (IDA) was pledged $2.6 billion, while $1.6 billion was committed to the Asian Development Fund to increase their capital bases.

A $20 billion capital-recycling programme was unfolded in May 1987 as a set of 'emergency economic measures'. This consisted of direct, untied funds to international developing financing institutions as well as the mobilization of the Export-Import Bank of Japan, the OECF (Overseas Economic Cooperation Fund)[3] and private capital. Specifically, it consisted of the following:

1. *Contribution to international development financing institutions and cooperation through private capital* ($8 billion) to establish new, and expand existing special funds through contributions to MDBs like the World Bank, Asian Development Bank, Inter-America Development Bank, etc. and encourage such institutions to issue bonds on the Tokyo capital market to recycle private capital.
2. *Expansion of syndicate loans made with World Bank and other international development financing institutions through the OECF, Export-Import Bank of Japan, commercial banks, etc* ($9 billion or more). Specifically,

syndicate loans were to be made available to developing countries for instituting structural adjustment policies through the MDBs, while supplementary yen loans were offered independently through the OECF on a bilateral basis.

3. *Expansion of direct finance for developing countries through Export-Import Bank untied loans* ($3 billion).

Japan also established an 'ASEAN/Japan Development Fund in December 1987 as part of the capital-recycling programme. This granted a total of $2 billion to ASEAN nations over a three-year period to foster development of private enterprises, over and above the existing bilateral aid programmes.

What Are the Issues at Stake?

A number of issues arise in recycling current account surpluses. This applies to the contributing, i.e., surplus, nations as well as recipient countries. For the former, the obvious consideration is a tradeoff between recycling the excess savings into real investments abroad *vis-à-vis* foreign assets held abroad. Yet another choice is the relative weights each country may assign to the capital account channel, i.e., foreign currency not spent on imports but saved in foreign assets held abroad, and the absorption channel, i.e., foreign currency spent to finance domestic consumption and investment through increased imports of goods and services, towards reconciling its own savings-investment balance. For the recipients too, there are a number of issues at stake, which this section attempts to identify.

The size of the corpus, i.e., amount of surplus capital, is a starting point. Several questions arise in this regard. For example, what should be the extent of capital contribution by each country? Should it be a fraction of the existing stock of respective international reserves or should it be limited to incremental reserves to limit further buildup? Alternatively, should the ratio of current account balances to GDP be the reference point? Should the recycling be a one-time offering or an annual plan for a specific duration? Should cases of persistent surpluses reflect in extended duration? On the other hand, should the reference point be an estimate of the infrastructure-financing gap in emerging market countries? What form should the contributions take, i.e., capital contribution into a trust fund, or through loans raised in respective local capital markets? Several international policy cooperation issues arise in this context.

The nature of the capital support is an important consideration for recipients. The extent to which capital can be recycled into infrastructure investments on favorable terms is an important aspect of such channeling.

The loans for infrastructure must be attractive, in terms of both costs and conditions. A key issue here is the rate of return currently earned on international reserves by the surplus countries.[4] The role of guarantees may therefore assume relevance to offset the increased risk from investments in infrastructure projects abroad. An important determinant of success is the extent to which capital can be recycled at rates of interest lower than the market rates. Likewise, the terms of conditions attached to usage of capital funds, e.g., project-tied, tenure, expansion of export markets and the internationalization of financial markets and currencies of surplus nations, foreign policy considerations, etc. are important factors to consider while devising a viable and successful recycling plan.

The public-private composition of recycled capital is another issue. The choice between direct capital support by governments or private capital that MDBs may mobilize from local capital markets is likely to arise in devising a recycling plan. The public-private distribution may also depend upon the source of generation of current account surpluses in respective countries. If a hybrid plan, i.e., a mix of direct capital contribution and private financing, it is important that the plan be transparent and well understood so that excessive expectations are not generated. For example, mobilizing funds from local capital markets has a bearing upon the total amount of capital made available as this could mean just a shift from one financial market to another without an overall increase in funding for infrastructure investments. Further, given bonds issued by the World Bank bonds are assigned AAA rating, this could also be an extremely attractive portfolio investment for private investors, leaving the question of real beneficiaries from additional purchases of MDB bonds hanging over the projects so financed.

Policy Options

The proposal to recycle the surpluses should possess the two broad features of security and subsidy. In view of the long gestation period of infrastructure financing, a reasonable security of capital, i.e., long tenure, is an essential prerequisite. Moreover, some concession might have to be included to allow capital raised in the markets from private savers to be channeled to emerging economies that can absorb these funds only at below-market rates – despite high social rates of return – to prevent a rapid buildup of commercial debt. In this context, as international financial stability is a public good, the financial contributions by current account surplus countries may be regarded as a component for the resolution of financial crises, because these countries are not importing significantly enough of the goods and services produced abroad. The target should be a socially acceptable rate of return rather than purely commercial ventures.

Several recycling options exist, assuming that the recycling proposal finds acceptance by the surplus nations. As the issues flagged above indicate, a key choice is whether the recycling plan should be commercial or concessional in nature. Given the nature of investments, viz. infrastructure, that typically have very long gestation periods, market-based resources may not be appropriate or sufficient despite the intermediation through MDBs. Therefore, longer-term resources, with longer grace periods at below-market costs could be envisioned as an essential prerequisite.

Addition to the capital base of MDBs could be an option for recycling funds. Under this route, surplus countries could contribute by augmenting the capital base of chosen MDBs, such as World Bank or the ADB. The surplus capital resources could be provided either on soft-loan terms or on grant terms to the MDB. In the former case, the intermediation of resources by the MDBs would be on the same lines as they intermediate market funds while in the case of a grant, capital resources could be re-lent by the MDBs as low-cost, longer-term credits to borrowers on a revolving basis. Given that security of tenure and below-market costs of capital are necessary for the viability and success of any such venture, an addition to the capital base of international development financing institutions like the IDA, The Asian Development Fund (AsDF), etc. would be the best possible route of providing concessional, long-term resources under this option.

Another option is to create a new intermediary as an special purpose vehicle (SPV). The facility – housed at an MDB like the World Bank, which has the technical expertise to intermediate such funds – could be a separate, contribution-based trust fund with capital contributions from the surplus member countries. The mandate would be to provide concessional lending for infrastructure investments to emerging markets. The creation of a special fund would distinguish the recycled capital from ordinary capital resources and allow these to be managed distinctly. For instance, it would permit concessions and incentives either by subsidizing the interest rate on loans to countries or by providing some collateral to private savings institutions which could mobilize private capital as a multiple of the resource available from the fund. Moreover, an SPV would make it possible to incorporate a role for the private sector through the creation of public-private partnerships. Equity support from governments in the form of equity participation, concessions on land or water supply, dedicated revenue streams for loan repayment, and a transparent regulatory framework could be elicited with relative ease in such a structure. The advantage of a new entity is that it offers a blank canvas for evolving rules, operating procedures, governance, management, etc. based upon recipients' goals and market requirements. On the other hand, a new entity would take time to create and establish itself.

A variant of an international infrastructure financing SPV could be regional trust funds – Regional Infrastructure Financing Funds (RIFFs). These could successfully embody and/or exploit the overseas development strategies of respective contributors. Regional centres are likely to have a more 'hands-on' approach, better grasp of specific issues and concentrate on assistance that is more specialized. Such an initiative has the added advantage of providing a significant boost to intra-regional trade as well, effectively aligning contributor-recipient incentives. Regional arrangements could also be more cost-effective as the concessional lending would be more than offset by lowered transactions' costs of intra-regional trade.[5] A caveat here, however, could be that the surplus-recycling nations could subtly link trade and/or foreign policy goals like neighbourhood trade, regional security and expansion and so on, through such a vehicle.

Policy Recommendations

Based on the above discussion, India could propose the setting up of an SPV – EMIFF, or Emerging Markets Infrastructure Financing Fund – at the G20. The Indian Prime Minster's suggestion of recycling capital surpluses towards infrastructure investments in emerging markets can be taken forward still. India can next utilize the sponsorship or support of the G20 forum and propose the establishment of a specially designated financing vehicle for infrastructure investments, suitably named as the EMIFF. While the G20 could discuss and evolve the size of the corpus, India could elaborate that the nature of contribution should embody low-cost, long-tenure financing to ensure the success and viability of the plan.

There are several advantages in choosing the SPV option. Primarily, such a facility would be under the G20 umbrella, and therefore, be part of an overall approach to global macroeconomic coordination and cooperation to boost and sustain global economic growth. Commitments from surplus countries would therefore, be easier to obtain; this is especially relevant for low-cost funding of projects with long duration. Second, and as highlighted in the previous section, a new institution designed for a specific purpose would be able to devise its own situation-specific rules, procedures and management. Three, it would be easier for the base MDB, for example the World Bank, to administer a specific programme assigned to it as part of the G20 coordination process.

Endnotes

1 Since the social rates of return on such investments exceeds that of private returns, the most attractive attribute of this proposal is that it would significantly boost global aggregate demand directly and through indirect channels. For example, building infrastructure would create a good investment climate, which is critical for attracting foreign direct investment (FDI) flows; currently, inadequate infrastructure acts as a perverse incentive for businesses in many emerging market economies (EMEs) where investment opportunities abound. Further, infrastructure investment projects will encourage domestic private investments in the recipient countries through their linkage and multiplier effects.

2 The Japanese Export-Import Bank played a major role in this process due to its ability to guarantee loans raised in the Japanese capital markets, which could be re-lent to the developing countries.

3 The agency to implement bilateral aid and loans under the jurisdiction of the Economic Planning Agency in Japan.

4 Most of the reserves are deployed in safe, low-yielding investments like short and long-term government securities, while some countries also invest a fraction through sovereign wealth funds (government-promoted investment vehicles) in a broader range of assets, such as US or European treasury bonds, agency and asset-backed securities, equities, commodities, real estate, and so on.

5 For instance, trade within the Asian region could benefit enormously by developing international highways that will link neighbouring countries for the transport of goods.

References

Bhattacharya, A., M. Romani and N. Stern. June, 2012. 'Infrastructure for Development: Meeting the Challenge', Policy paper prepared as collaborative effort between the Centre for Climate Change Economics and Policy, the Grantham Research Institute on Climate Change and the Environment and the Inter-Governmental Group of Twenty-Four, London School of Economics (LSE) and Intergovernmental Group of 24.

Eichengreen, Barry. 2004. 'The Dollar and the New Bretton Woods System', Henry Thornton Lecture, delivered at the Cass School of Business, London, 15 December.

Fay, M., M. Toman, D. Benitez and S. Csordas. 2011. 'Infrastructure and Sustainable Development', in *Post-crisis Growth and Development: A Development Agenda for the G-20*, edited by Shahrokh Fardoust, Yong beom Kim and Claudia Paz Sepúlveda, 329–82. Washington DC: World Bank.

Fischer, Stanley. 2001. 'Exchange Rate Regimes: Is the Bipolar View Correct?', Distinguished Lecture delivered at the Meetings of the American Economic Association, New Orleans, 6 January.

Forum on Debt and Development (FONDAD). 1995. *Multilateral Banks: An Assessment of their Financial Structure, Policies and Practices*. The Hague: FONDAD. Available at: www.fondad.org.

Foster V. and C. Briceño-Garmendia. 2010. *Africa's Infrastructure: A Time for Transformation*. World Bank, December 2009.

G20. June, 2011. 'Supporting Infrastructure Development in Low-Income Countries, Submission to the G20 by the MDB Working Group on Infrastructure, Interim Report. Available at: www.g20dwg.org/documents/pdf/view/13/.

IEA. 2010. *World Energy Outlook*. Paris, France: International Energy Agency.

IMF. 2011. 'Recent Experiences in Managing Capital Inflows – Cross-Cutting Themes and Possible Policy Framework', *Policy Paper February 2011*. Washington, DC: IMF.

McKinsey Global Institute. August 2011. 'Mapping Global Capital Markets'. McKinsey & Company.

Okuma, H. 1988. 'Japan in the World. The Capital Recycling Programme', *Trocaire Development Review* 69–83. Available at: www.trocaire.org/sites/trocaire/files/resources/policy/1988-japan-aid-programme.pdf.

Sengupta, A. 3 September 1988. 'Recycling the Japanese Surplus to the Developing Countries', *Economic and Political Weekly* 23(36): 1851–56.

WIDER. May 1987. 'Mobilizing International Surpluses for World Development: A WIDER Plan for a Japanese Initiative'. *WIDER Study Group Series No. 2*. Tokyo: World Institute for Development Economics Research.

4 G20: Impact of the Crisis with Special Reference to India and International Burden Sharing

D. K. Srivastava

Introduction

Starting as a crisis of sub-prime mortgages in the United States, the US financial crisis became intertwined with a global economic crisis during 2007–09. All major economies were adversely affected. While some countries went into deep recession, others escaped with limited erosion in their growth rates. But the crisis also accelerated the pace at which a new world economic order is emerging, the centerpiece of which is a group now referred to as the G20[1] group. Together the G20 economies comprise about 90 per cent of global gross national product, 80 per cent of world trade (including EU intra-trade) and two-thirds of the world population.[2] The epicentre of the world economic power, which had until recently been concentrated in the hands of the G-7[3] economies, is now more wide spread with considerable economic power slowly shifting to emerging economies like China and India.

In this paper, the author looks at the effects of the global crisis as it affected the G20 members with special reference to India. The global crisis also witnessed a weakening of the efforts regarding international burden sharing for a long-felt need for support for achieving both the MDG goals and international climate change related efforts. He also examines both conventional and innovative methods of financing the international effort for achieving the MDG objectives and the approach that India may develop in this context as part of the G20 group.

This chapter is divided into several sections. The following section looks at the position of the G20 economies as they emerge out of the global crisis. The next section examines the Indian economy as it faced and emerged out of the crisis. Next the author looks at the position of the G20 economies in the context of international burden sharing in the post-crisis world. The following section reviews the role of conventional and innovative methods of financing international economic goals. The final section provides the concluding observations. Appendix 1 looks at options and strategies that India can adopt in regard to international burden sharing.

The Global Economic Crisis and its Aftermath

The financial crisis

As is well known now, the 2008 financial crisis started with several of the financial institutions in the western world going bust as a result of defaults developing in the housing loan sector in the US and later spreading into other financial instruments. The trigger for the financial crisis was the collapse of the US sub-prime mortgage market and the reversal of the housing boom in other industrialized economies. The ripple effect spread into other financial sector activities, leading to failures of many well known financial institutions and banks. Later the effects spread into the wider economy engulfing almost all economies.

The sub-prime crisis is linked to the unbridled innovation in the evolution of financial instruments where, with securitization, banks and financial institutions pool various loans into salable assets. This enabled off-loading of risky loans onto others. Securitization was seen as the greatest financial innovation of the 20th century. With layers of securitization, one security was derived from another, and in each layer of the derivative, information of the primary risk became more distant and non-transparent.

Instruments like the collateralized debt obligations (CDOs), asset based securities (ABS); residential mortgage based securities (RMBS), and commercial mortgage based securities (CMBS) reflected such complex forms of securitization, which spread the risk but were very complicated and often hid the bad loans.

The surge in housing mortgages in the US to sub-prime borrowers was linked to the upsurge in the housing prices. Even when the borrowers were not assessed to be low risk on account of their income earning capacity, loans were extended on the basis of the mortgage where the price of the asset, viz., the residential property was expected to increase.

The interest rate in the US increased from 1 per cent to 5.35 per cent between 2004 and 2006. This lowered the demand for housing and also led to payment defaults on housing loans. Defaults occurred precisely when the asset prices also fell, triggering a slowdown in the US housing market. Sub-prime borrowers could only barely afford their mortgage payments when interest rates were low. With higher interest rates, defaults started on a large scale.

As defaults started primarily in the housing mortgages, problems became noticeable and confidence fell quickly. The crisis of confidence spread like a contagion. Investment banks that were sitting on the riskiest loans found a sudden drop in the demand for their assets. Assets started plummeting in value and existing lenders wanted to take their money back. But some investment banks had little in deposits and a major liquidity crisis developed. Banks and financial institutions started collapsing quickly and dramatically.[4]

From financial to economic crisis

Since the onset of the financial crisis, symbolically linked to the date of the fall of the Lehman Brothers on 15 September 2008, the shock spread from American housing to all economic sectors and from the US economy to other economies including both the developed and the developing world leading to a fall in output and employment in many countries.

Tables 4.1 and 4.2 show quarterly growth rates (year-on-year) for selected G20 economies, divided into two groups. In Group A, economies who suffered a negative growth for at least for four quarters are listed. Group B consists of economies that suffered a negative growth in less than four quarters or those that did not witness a negative growth in any quarter although they may have experienced an economic slowdown. The ten countries listed in Group A were the major world economies that suffered recession which lasted for four quarters or more.

The crisis hit all the major economies of the world. The Business Cycle Dating Committee of the National Bureau of Economic Research, which provides an informed judgment on the business cycles both on a monthly and quarterly basis, dated the onset of US recession in December 2007. June 2009 was dated as the trough after which the economy started recovering. The European Area Business Cycle Dating Committee of the centre for Economic Policy Research, which dates business cycles on a quarterly basis has dated the last peak for the European Area economies as the first quarter of 2008 signaling the start of the recession and the second quarter of 2009 as the trough signaling the start of the recovery.

In the G20 group, Australia, India, Indonesia, and China escaped with only an economic slowdown without experiencing an actual decline in income through a negative growth rate. For some of these economies, the profile of growth rates is given in Table 4.2. India's growth experience during the global crisis period is discussed in greater detail in a separate section.

Table 4.1: Quarterly growth rates in selected G20 countries suffering recession – from pre- to post-crisis period

(per cent)

	Canada	Germany	France	United Kingdom	Italy
2006Q1	3.88	2.55	2.11	3.16	1.84
2006Q2	3.24	3.50	2.86	2.71	1.83
2006Q3	2.31	3.68	2.33	2.59	2.00
2006Q4	1.90	4.51	2.37	2.70	2.74
2007Q1	1.45	4.01	2.57	2.59	2.26
2007Q2	2.17	2.76	1.99	2.88	1.74
2007Q3	2.63	2.64	2.58	2.91	1.51
2007Q4	2.54	1.76	2.15	2.36	0.00
2008Q1	1.71	2.68	1.83	1.88	0.27
2008Q2	0.87	1.65	0.68	1.04	-0.45
2008Q3	0.40	0.48	-0.18	-0.40	-1.76
2008Q4	-0.88	-1.97	-1.94	-2.75	-3.34
2009Q1	-2.51	-6.62	-3.86	-5.38	-6.52
2009Q2	-3.18	-5.53	-3.08	-5.90	-6.15
2009Q3	-3.05	-4.45	-2.67	-5.32	-4.70
2009Q4	-1.10	-2.00	-0.54	-2.84	-2.78
2010Q1	2.09	2.07	1.15	-0.32	0.51
2010Q2	3.41	3.92	1.58	1.64	1.25
2010Q3	3.44	3.93	1.72	2.66	1.10
	Japan	**Mexico**	**Turkey**	**United States**	**South Africa**
2006Q1	2.07	6.17	5.95	3.05	5.45
2006Q2	2.14	5.31	9.74	2.98	5.30
2006Q3	1.83	5.18	6.29	2.23	5.36
2006Q4	2.10	4.03	5.75	2.45	6.29
2007Q1	3.20	2.98	8.10	1.34	6.36

	Japan	Mexico	Turkey	United States	South Africa
2007Q2	2.42	2.89	3.81	1.79	5.45
2007Q3	1.84	3.47	3.18	2.33	5.26
2007Q4	1.80	3.69	4.19	2.32	5.23
2008Q1	1.17	2.35	7.01	1.91	4.33
2008Q2	-0.06	2.83	2.63	1.25	4.73
2008Q3	-1.09	1.69	0.86	-0.34	3.66
2008Q4	-4.67	-0.77	-6.97	-2.77	1.64
2009Q1	-10.09	-7.21	-14.57	-3.80	-0.60
2009Q2	-6.96	-9.57	-7.65	-4.11	-2.44
2009Q3	-6.15	-5.53	-2.66	-2.74	-2.43
2009Q4	-1.79	-2.03	6.01	0.20	-1.24
2010Q1	5.54	4.58	11.84	2.39	1.39
2010Q2	3.51	7.63	10.22	3.01	2.82
2010Q3	4.97	5.28	5.49	3.25	3.25

Source (Basic Data): World Bank Global Economic Monitor

Table 4.2: Quarterly growth rates (year-on-year) for selected G20 countries

(per cent)

	Argentina	Korea Republic	Australia	Indonesia	India
2006Q1	8.78	6.12	2.57	5.13	9.78
2006Q2	7.75	5.116	2.74	4.93	10.58
2006Q3	8.74	5.032	1.95	5.86	9.27
2006Q4	8.64	4.561	2.82	6.06	9.99
2007Q1	7.95	4.453	4.59	6.06	10.14
2007Q2	8.65	5.295	4.88	6.73	10.29
2007Q3	8.82	4.925	4.95	6.74	8.65
2007Q4	9.1	5.671	4.07	5.84	7.35
2008Q1	8.53	5.519	3.32	6.22	7.33
2008Q2	7.82	4.357	3.03	6.3	7.19
2008Q3	6.94	3.277	2.87	6.25	6.1

	Argentina	Korea Republic	Australia	Indonesia	India
2008Q4	4.05	-3.333	1.11	5.28	5.76
2009Q1	2.04	-4.298	1.03	4.6	6.33
2009Q2	-0.77	-2.183	0.81	4.16	8.68
2009Q3	-0.35	1.000	0.91	4.18	6.53
2009Q4	2.61	6.047	2.59	5.39	8.57
2010Q1	6.76	8.095	2.29	5.59	8.88
2010Q2	11.85	7.153	3.12	6.13	8.89
2010Q3	8.59	4.437	2.65	5.8	

Source (Basic Data): World Bank Global Economic Monitor

Structural roots of the crisis

Most analysts now consider that while the global economic crisis was visibly rooted in the financial crisis, it had deeper structural roots in persistent global economic imbalances. These imbalances set up a vicious and unsustainable cycle and unless corrected, the global economy will remain vulnerable to frequent shocks.

The key features of the global imbalances may be summarized as follows:

1. The US economy along with some other major western economies runs a large, persistent current account deficit reflecting deficient domestic savings.
2. These deficits are matched by surpluses emanating from three major channels:
   (a) Emerging markets, most importantly China has excess savings and correspondingly large current account surplus.
   (b) The oil exporting countries are flush with funds that they cannot domestically absorb. They also have current account surplus and excess savings.
   (c) To a lesser extent, metal exporting countries are in a similar situation.

The US current account, which measures the balance of investment and saving, has been in deficit since 1992. Until 1997, the annual saving shortfall was modest but it grew steadily thereafter, reaching a peak of nearly 6 per cent of GDP in 2006. The saving ratio in the US steadily fell over these years.

The dollar started to decline gradually from 2002 but the current account deficit only got bigger.

Figure 4.1: Current account imbalances – pre- and post-crisis

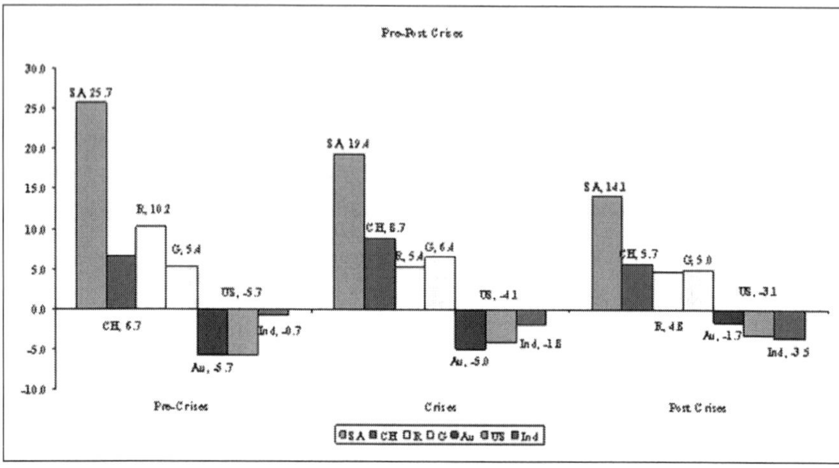

Source: International Monetary Fund, World Economic Outlook Database, April 2011
Key: SA: South Africa; CH: China; R: Russia; G: Germany; Au: Australia; Ind: India; US: United States

In 1996, the year before the Asian financial crisis began, economies designated by the IMF as emerging, developing and newly industrialized countries ran a collective current account deficit of $78 billion. Over the next decade this turned into a surplus of several hundred billion dollars, with China and oil exporters accounting for almost all of the increase in the past three or four years.

In 2006, the US's current account deficit peaked at 6 per cent of its GDP. Between 2000 and 2008 the country received over $5.7 trillion from abroad to invest, equivalent to over 40 per cent of its 2007 GDP. Over the same period the United Kingdom and Ireland absorbed around a fifth of their 2007 GDPs and Spain a vast 50 per cent. The financial system had the job of recycling the money to borrowers. Inevitably, credit became cheaper and savings declined. In the US, savings fell from around 10 per cent of disposable income in the 1970s to 1 per cent after 2005.

Figure 4.1 shows a comparison of selected countries in the pre-crisis period (average over 2004–06), crisis period (average over 2007–09) and post-crisis period (average over 2010–12) of current account balance relative to GDP. In the pre-crisis period, Saudi Arabia had a large current account surplus linked to the oil price surge. The US current account deficit fell as the world economy emerged out of the crisis. India's current account deficit appears to have increased during this period, but is still relatively smaller relative to India's GDP. Figure 4.2 shows the time profile of the current account balance relative to GDP for some of the important countries both on the surplus and deficit side.

Figure 4.2: Time path of current account imbalance of selected countries

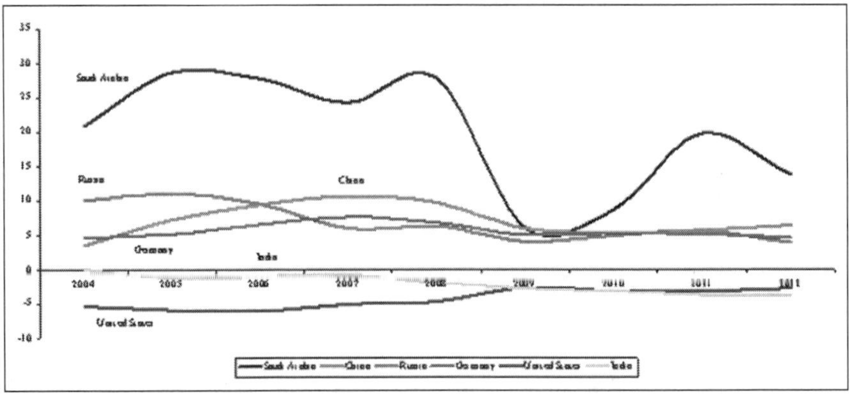

Source: International Monetary Fund, World Economic Outlook Database, April 2011

There is also a large accompanying demand for foreign exchange reserves. One reason for many of the Asian countries is that while they have excess savings today, they want to invest in foreign exchange reserves so that they do not have to face a sudden flight of capital as was experienced in the crisis of the 90s.

The excess saving emanating from China is partly the result of the Chinese exchange rate policy. Buying large amounts of dollars keeps domestic currencies weak encouraging exports and lowering domestic spending. The result is a high level of net national saving, much of which ends up in central banks' foreign exchange reserves. US, UK and other deficit countries showed a high appetite for cheap credit from abroad.

All countries whether producing manufactured goods like China, or oil or metals have excess savings that seek safe and liquid investment avenues abroad since domestic financial instruments are neither large nor adequately developed to absorb these large excess savings. Ricardo Caballero (2011),[5] and Caballero, Farhi and Gourinchas (2008) have argued that the emerging countries cannot create enough trustworthy saving vehicles to keep up with the pace of economic growth, because their financial markets are immature.

The US is still the favoured destination with a broad range of liquid markets for securities.

The need of the emerging markets for insurance has driven them to export capital to the US. The interaction between the two was fatal. After the dotcom bust, American firms turned cautious and investment spending became weak. This ruled out a natural home for foreign capital. Faced with strong external demand for AAA rated assets, the financial system got creative. Marginal home loans were packaged into supposedly safe securities. That supply of credit lifted house prices and spurred a boom in residential construction, which filled the gap in demand left by sluggish business investment.

These loans turned bad and losses mounted. At the same time banks had set aside too little capital to protect themselves against unexpected losses leaving the banks crippled when the rush for redemption of financial assets started.

The bait for capital inflows is that the US provides reliable and liquid assets, which cannot be found at home. Ideally its financial system might have provided an intermediary service – funneling emerging-market savings into emerging market projects. That would have lowered deficits in the US and surpluses abroad. Only a fraction of the capital that flows into America is absorbed by the current account deficit. Much of it finances capital outflows indicating the purchase of foreign assets by American residents.

This sets up a dynamic flow where the surpluses of one block of countries finance the deficits of the other. The problem is that persistent and large imbalances raise issues of sustainability and periodic breakdowns.

This profile of imbalance cannot be sustained for long. If current account surplus is maintained by keeping the exchange rate low, a strategy followed by China, then domestic inflation will eventually force correction. If the central banks flood the foreign-exchange market with their own money, domestic currency can be kept low against foreign currency, but inflation will be pushed up eventually eroding the gain in competitiveness from a cheap currency. China has postponed this outcome by 'sterilizing' its currency interventions by selling bonds to banks, companies and households. Since the financial system is tightly controlled savers do not have much choice.

Since structural forces behind the global saving glut are unlikely to abate quickly, there is a real risk that the dangerous imbalances will persist – with the US's public sector as the new consumer of last resort. Some see the

2007–09 disaster as a result of that Asian crash. Asian nations – especially China – have been determined to be part of global capital markets but not to run current account deficits, which would leave them vulnerable to sudden currency outflows. So they have been happy to see their money go abroad. In the words of Martin Wolf, an economic columnist at the *Financial Times*, they 'smoke but do not inhale'.

Obstfeld, Taylor, and Shambaugh (2009) view these 'excess' reserves as insurance for the domestic banking system. They argue that in economies with managed exchange rates and fast-growing bank deposits, there is increased risk of a 'double drain'. When crisis hits, fear of devaluation could spark a rush out of bank deposits into cash, and from cash into hard currency. Reserves are not only a prudent safeguard against a 'sudden stop' in foreign finance. They are also needed as insurance against the risk of 'sudden flight' by domestic savers. Financial depth, measured by the ratio of broad money to GDP, helps explain the size of reserves. In a more recent study they found that countries with insufficient reserves to insure their financial systems suffered bigger currency crashes during last year's turmoil. The currencies of countries with full war chests did not depreciate; some rose. If economies draw the lesson that their reserves were not big enough, global imbalances will be even harder to tackle.[6]

Taylor reckons the policy of accumulating reserves accounts for a significant and growing fraction of global surpluses – enough (in the early years of this decade) to finance as much as a third of the US's current account deficit. The self-insurance against financial fragility is part of a more general trend towards precautionary saving in the developing world. If it persists, as seems likely, it will throw the problem of deficient global demand back to the US.

Global oil and food prices

A key component of the new global order is going to be world oil and crude prices. In periods where world growth is robust, both sets of prices shoot up. Countries like India that are net importers of oil and more and more in need of food imports in periods of internal deficiencies will find themselves to be highly vulnerable to these global drivers. Crude prices are a key component of the global cycle of imbalances, as argued earlier. Figure 4.3 looks at the movement of crude oil prices (Brent; US$ per barrel) and index of world food prices (base 2001=100).

Figure 4.3: Crude oil and world food price indices – time profile

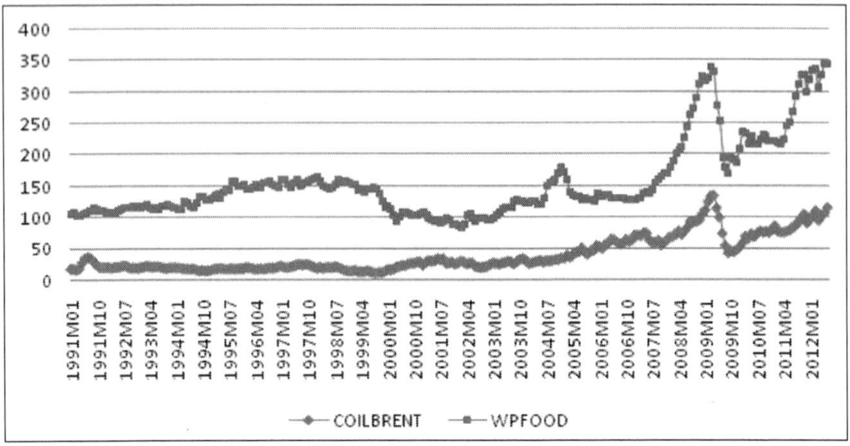

Source: International Monetary Fund, World Economic Outlook Database, April 2011

Hamilton (2009) notes that each of the five major oil crises since the early 70s has been linked to major economic crisis. He observes:

> Big increases in the price of oil that were associated with events such as the 1973–74 embargo by the Organization of Arab Petroleum Exporting Countries, the Iranian Revolution in 1978, the Iran-Iraq War in 1980, and the First Persian Gulf War in 1990 were each followed by global economic recessions. ...The price of oil doubled between June 2007 and June 2008, a bigger price increase than in any of those four earlier episodes. In my mind, there is no question that this latest surge in oil prices was an important factor that contributed to the economic recession that began in the U.S. in 2007:Q4.

Figure 4.4 shows that the two prices in terms of growth (inflation) rates' move together.

Figure 4.4: Crude oil and world food price index – co-movement in growth rates

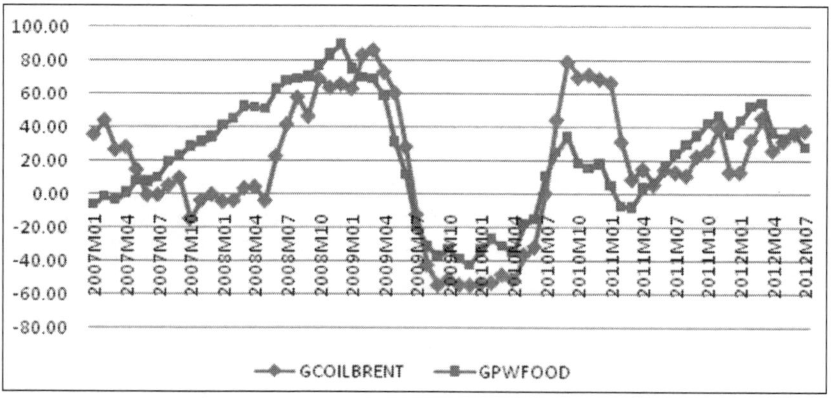

Source: International Monetary Fund, World Economic Outlook Database, April 2011

The source of oil demand is expected to shift more towards China and India. In a 2011 Report of the Economic Intelligence Unit on the Gulf Cooperation Council[7] Trade and Investment Flows (EIU, 2011), it is observed that rising from a 16 per cent share of global GDP in 1987, the emerging economies will be accounting for about 41 per cent share of global GDP by 2015. The report also says that in the coming years, oil demand will be an important factor in the shift of trade to emerging markets. The Indian economy is particularly vulnerable to movement of oil prices given its growth linked energy needs and world food prices given the growing size of its population.

The new fracking technology that resulted in an enormous boost in gas and oil output has had a stabilizing influence on the global crude oil prices. In the US, gas output has increased by one-third since its most recent trough in 2005, and oil production has risen by 30 per cent since its recent low in 2008. After falling sharply from \$97 to \$62 from 2008 to 2009, the average (average of Brent, Dubai and WTI) crude oil price per barrel rose but remained stable at around \$104–105 per bbl during 2011 to 2013.

Crisis and global adverse impact

There are however certain disturbing adverse impacts of the crisis that became noticeable. Two notable trends in the collective G20 experience, in the post-crisis world are proliferation of protectionist measures, and rise in unemployment.

Protectionist measures

A proliferation of protectionist measures by the G20 members has been prominently noted by several observers. Simon Evenett (University of St. Gallen) who has launched the Global Trade Alert (GTA) has noted that as of September 2009, the G20 members were responsible for 172 of the initiatives with protectionist overtones since the start of the crisis. The Peterson Institute for International Economics (PIIE) report estimates that G20 countries accounted for around 35 per cent of protectionist measures implemented or considered worldwide (Appendix Table 4.7).

The GTA classifies as 'most certainly' discriminatory and already implemented protectionist measures and calls these as 'final' measures. In contrast, the pipeline protectionist measures are termed 'ambiguous' by the GTA since in these cases: (1) the initiative has yet to be implemented, but if put in force will almost certainly discriminate against foreign commercial interests; and (2) when the initiative has already been implemented and is 'likely' to be discriminatory (but not 'most certainly' discriminatory); or (3) when the initiative contains a mix of policies and some are discriminatory and some that are not. The report calls all these cases 'pipeline' protection. Countries are then ranked using three metrics – number of protectionist measures implemented or in the 'pipeline', number of tariff lines affected, and number of trading partners affected.

All three metrics for gauging final protectionist measures exhibit two waves. They all spiked upwards at the end of 2008, and the number of protectionist measures and trading partners affected all peaked in the first quarter of 2009. The metrics displayed a second and lower peak in the middle of 2009. According to the GTA, the top five most protectionist countries are Russia, United States, India, Argentina and Brazil. The least protectionist countries across the metrics are Mexico, Turkey, Australia, Republic of Korea, South Africa, and Saudi Arabia. As emphasized earlier, these composite rankings do not gauge the economic impact of the measures implemented or considered.

Unemployment

The second disturbing trend is that while output growth has started picking up, unemployment rates are slow to show recovery. The IMF has also estimated that unemployment takes five quarters to reach its worst level after output starts to recover.

The crisis has particularly hit the industrial sector and the labour market. The United States experienced a 3.4 percentage point peak-to-trough decline in output (GDP), which resulted in a 3.9 percentage point peak-to-trough increase in unemployment. Germany experienced a larger 7.0 percentage point decline in output but the German unemployment rate only decreased by 0.3 percentage points. Among the G20 low and middle income members, China, India, and Brazil did better in terms of unemployment, while Turkey and Russia suffered increases in unemployment rates by margins in the range of 2.5–3.0 percentage points. It may be mentioned that the unemployment situation was not necessarily a deliberate policy outcome.

G20 Coordination: Stimulus and Exit

G20 governments responded to the crisis in terms of stimuli and also attempted a coordination of their exit strategies. They allowed automatic stabilizers from existing social safety nets to operate fully, implementing huge fiscal programs alongside monetary expansion to stimulate aggregate demand, and provided additional and targeted support to identified sectors that were severely impacted by the crisis. Some of the major initiatives are highlighted below:

London Summit, 2 April 2009

The leaders resolved to restore confidence, growth and jobs; repair the financial system to restore lending; strengthen financial regulation to rebuild trust; fund and reform the international financial institutions; promote global trade and investment and reject protectionism; and build an inclusive and sustainable recovery. As a result, the 'Global Plan for Recovery and Reform' was brought about. It was agreed that resources available to the IMF will be raised to $750 billion (for new SDR allocation of $250 billion, $100 billion of additional lending by the MDBs, and $250 billion support for trade finance) and to use the additional resources from agreed IMF gold sales for concessional finance for the poorest countries and to constitute an additional $1.1 trillion programme of support to restore credit, growth and jobs in the world economy.

Pittsburgh Summit, 24–25 September 2009

It was agreed that at least 5 per cent shift in the IMF quota to underrepresented countries would take place. A new framework for global macro-balances, where members agree on shared policy objectives, set out medium-term policy frameworks and work together to assess the collective implications of national policies for global growth, identifying potential risks to financial stability and agree on actions to meet common goals.

St. Andrews Meeting, 2 November 2009

In this G20 meeting, the 'Framework for Strong, Sustainable and Balanced Growth' was launched which adopted a detailed timetable and initiated a new consultative mutual assessment process to evaluate whether policies will collectively deliver the agreed objectives. The first challenge in using the framework is the transition from crisis response to stronger, more sustainable and balanced growth, consistent with the goals of sustainable public finances; price stability; stable, efficient and resilient financial systems; employment creation; and poverty reduction.

Toronto Summit, 26–27 June 2010

The 2010 G20 Toronto summit was the fourth meeting of the G20 heads of government. This meeting discussed the global financial system and the world economy. 21 representatives of the major economies in G20 came together in Toronto. In addition, leaders of six invited nations and eight intergovernmental organizations participated in the summit.

The summit provided an opportunity for the leaders to discuss plans to ameliorate the impact of the ongoing world recession. The summit's priorities included evaluating the progress of financial reform measures, developing sustainable stimulus strategies, debating projected global bank tax proposals, and promoting open markets.

Recognizing the scale of the crisis, the G20 countries coordinated the stimulus packages in a closely coordinated manner. In terms of timing, the stimulus packages were introduced in the last quarter of 2008 although in some cases like Japan and Spain stimulus packages were introduced earlier in the second quarter of 2008. In India, the stimulus efforts started in the last quarter of 2008, which was followed by a larger stimulus in February 2008 by a fiscal deficit financed increase in government expenditure and reduction in tax rates.

Given the fiscal slippage and inflationary pressures, most countries wanted an exit as soon signs of recovery in the respective economies became visible. As Giavazzi (2010), Minegeshi and Cournede (2010) and IMF (2010) argue many of the advanced G20 countries have delayed stimulus withdrawal since the recovery is still weak and uncertain. They point out that the advanced countries are worried that there are still significant asset losses in the pipeline; further the central banks require more time to gradually unload the assets acquired in the peak crisis period to shore up the financial market; and also the consideration that monetary tightening and a sharp increase in interest rates could adversely affect the yield curves of banks that may be borrowing short and lending long.

However, fiscal pressures indicate that fiscal consolidation cannot be delayed for long. Analyses undertaken at IMF suggest that the advanced countries should aim at a stable public debt to GDP ratio of 60 per cent. This may call for a reduction in the structural primary deficit of about 8 per cent on average (IMF, 2010). India also requires to pursue fiscal consolidation so as to move on to its potential growth path as discussed in the next section.

India: Impact of the global crisis and recovery

India also suffered from the global crisis but escaped with limited damage. Table 4.3 looks at the quarterly growth rates (year-on-year) of GDP at factor cost and its components in terms of eight sectors. Looking at the overall GDP at factor cost, it is from the fourth quarter of 2007–08 (January–March 2008) that the slowdown appears to have set in. It lasted for four quarters reaching a minimum of 5.6 per cent growth rate in 2008–09 Q3 (October–December, 2008) before recovery started. The growth rate remained low for another two quarters before it crossed 8 per cent again. Thus, the maximum adverse impact lasted for about six quarters.

Table 4.3: Quarterly growth rates (year-on-year) of GDP at factor cost and its components
(Years refer to financial year, thus, 2006 refers to 2005–06)

(per cent)

	Agriculture and allied sectors	Mining and quarrying	Manufac-turing	Electricity, gas, and water supply	Construction
	YAR	YMQR	YMANR	YEGWSR	YCRR
2006Q1	3.19	4.14	11.16	8.66	10.71
2006Q2	3.88	-2.06	8.55	3.98	9.61

	Agriculture and allied sectors	Mining and quarrying	Manufac-turing	Electricity, gas, and water supply	Construction
	YAR	YMQR	YMANR	YEGWSR	YCRR
2006Q3	7.78	0.03	8.69	6.3	14.69
2006Q4	5.19	3.04	9.91	7.46	14.27
2007Q1	3.08	6.36	14.68	8.3	11.62
2007Q2	2.95	7.65	15.12	10.63	10.57
2007Q3	3.76	9.82	14.18	11.63	9.38
2007Q4	4.66	10.69	15.75	9.46	10.74
2008Q1	3.14	1.08	12.07	10.17	10.68
2008Q2	3.85	4.65	10.32	9.14	13.1
2008Q3	8.65	4.45	10.71	7.05	9.64
2008Q4	2.13	5.08	8.32	7.84	7.05
2009Q1	4.75	0.98	6.41	5.14	9.74
2009Q2	2.6	0.02	6.26	6.18	7.19
2009Q3	-1.25	1.2	1.92	5.91	1.07
2009Q4	3.26	-0.3	0.55	4.09	5.66
2010Q1	1.79	6.86	1.95	6.21	5.41
2010Q2	1.19	6.63	6.08	7.52	5.09
2010Q3	-1.6	5.19	11.4	4.49	8.25
2010Q4	0.69	13.96	16.28	7.1	8.69
2011Q1	2.53	8.45	12.99	6.25	10.32
2011Q2	4.39	7.85	9.82	3.39	8.7
2011Q3	8.95	5.97	5.64	6.4	7.97

Source (Basic Data): National Income Accounts, CSO.

In terms of timing and extent of adverse impact, the maximum effect was on manufacturing, followed by mining and quarrying, electricity, gas and water supply and construction sectors. Figure 4.5 provides a profile of these sectors in terms of quarterly growth rates of GDP at factor cost at 2004–05 prices.

Figure 4.5: Indian manufacturing sector – quarterly growth rates (year-on-year)

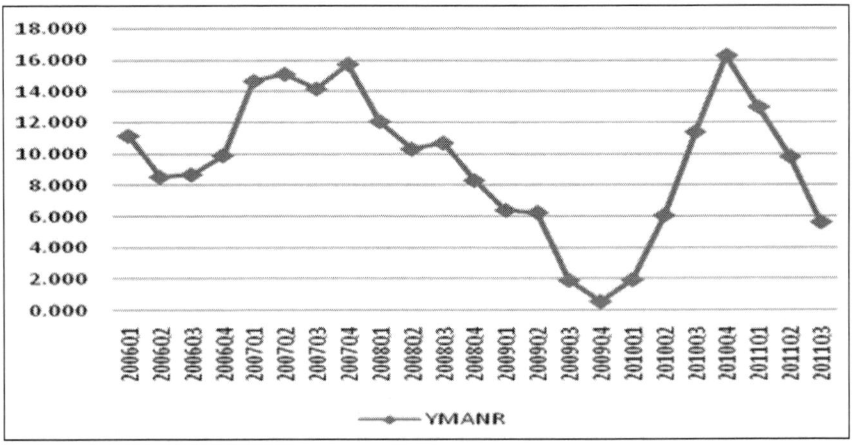

Source: National Income Accounts, Ministry of Planning and Statistics, Government of India

It is notable that as soon as the impact of the global crisis appeared to be ending by the fourth quarter of 2008–09, India went through another crisis emanating internally from the agricultural sector where the growth rate was extremely low or negative throughout the four quarters in 2009–10.

Table 4.4: Quarterly growth rates (year-on-year) of GDP at factor cost and its components
(Years refer to financial year, thus, 2006 refers to 2005–06)

(per cent)

	Trade, hotels, transport, storage and communications	Financial, real estate and business services	Community, social and personal services	GDP at factor cost
	YTHTCR	YFIEBR	YCSPSR	YR
2006Q1	12.9	11.5	7.12	9.25
2006Q2	11.93	13.12	7.72	8.91
2006Q3	11.44	11.73	8.25	9.69
2006Q4	12.07	14.74	7.38	9.99
2007Q1	11.02	14.14	5.99	9.81
2007Q2	12.65	14.48	2.95	10.13

	Trade, hotels, transport, storage and communications	Financial, real estate and business services	Community, social and personal services	GDP at factor cost
	YTHTCR	YFIEBR	YCSPSR	YR
2007Q3	11.97	15.22	1.31	9.38
2007Q4	11.06	14.18	0.9	9.59
2008Q1	11.87	13.97	4.16	9.35
2008Q2	9.55	13.78	7.01	9.39
2008Q3	10.69	13.34	5.32	9.73
2008Q4	10.85	11.88	9.8	8.49
2009Q1	10.09	10.07	8.29	8.04
2009Q2	10.43	9.79	9.36	7.81
2009Q3	4.3	10.76	22.58	5.59
2009Q4	5.7	12.26	8.78	5.76
2010Q1	5.51	11.48	13.04	6.32
2010Q2	8.21	10.92	19.41	8.64
2010Q3	10.85	8.52	7.61	7.33
2010Q4	12.35	7.9	1.6	8.57
2011Q1	11.03	7.88	7.76	8.85
2011Q2	12.09	8.25	7.37	8.87
2011Q3	9.4	11.24	4.77	8.19

Source (Basic Data): National Income Accounts, CSO.
Note: YTHTCR: GDP at from trade, hotels, transport, storage and communications; **YFIEBER:** GDP from financial and business services; YCSPSR: GDP from community, social, and public services; YR: GDP at factor cost at 2004–05 prices

In coping with the crisis, two types of imbalances have emerged in India. First, while a stimulus package was needed to counter the global recession, it had to be financed through a higher fiscal deficit. This meant that the targets of the Fiscal Responsibility and Budget Management Act, 2003 for the central government had to be postponed. The state governments also witnessed some slippage in respect of their respective fiscal responsibility legislations but the slippage was limited in most cases.

Figure 4.6: Indian construction sector – quarterly growth rates (year-on-year)

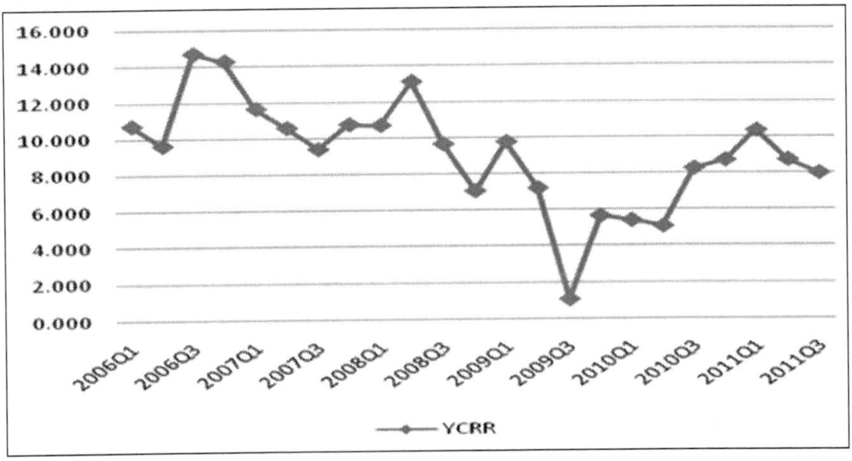

Source: National Income Accounts, Ministry of Planning and Statistics, Government of India

As discussed earlier, as soon as the world economy started recovering, the crude oil prices shot up. Since India depends heavily on imported crude for its energy requirements, this had a direct impact on the current account deficit as the deficit on the balance of trade ballooned. Alongside crude oil prices, the world food prices have also firmed up. This makes India very vulnerable particularly in years where agricultural output is going through a trough.

Figure 4.7: Indian electricity, gas, and water supply sector – quarterly growth rates (year-on-year)

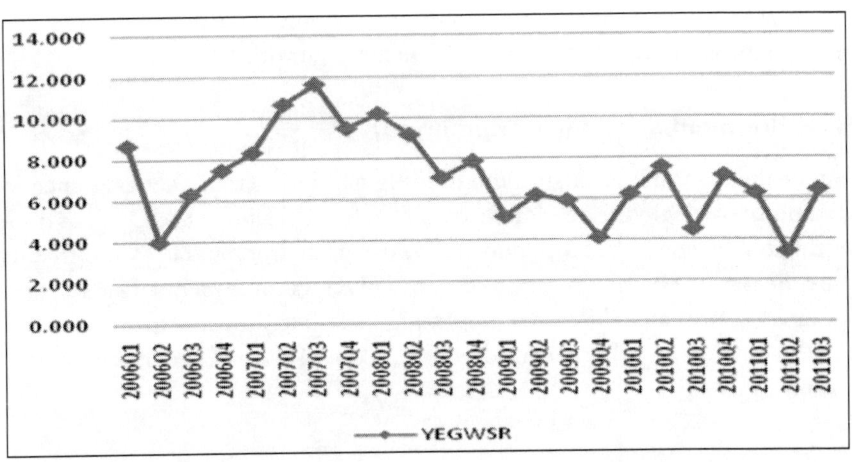

Source: National Income Accounts, Ministry of Planning and Statistics, Government of India

Table 4.5 shows that following the crisis both fiscal imbalance as represented by the fiscal deficit on the combined account of the central and state governments and the current account deficit in India widened considerably.

Table 4.5: Fiscal and current account deficits in India relative to GDP – recent years

(per cent to GDP at market prices)

	2004–05	2005–06	2006–07	2007–08	2008–09	2009–10
Revenue deficit	3.5	2.7	1.3	0.2	4.2	5.2
Fiscal deficit	7.2	6.5	5.4	4	8.5	9.7
Current account deficit	–0.4	–1.2	–1	–1.3	–2.4	–2.2
Trade balance	–4.7	–6.2	–6.5	–7.4	–9.7	–9.8

Source: National Income Accounts (various Issues) and Economic Survey, Government of India, 2010

International Burden Sharing

The term international burden sharing is increasingly being used to refer to the question of sharing costs for the provision of collective goods or global initiatives between countries. More recently, the debate on international burden sharing is widening to cover issues of achieving the MDG goals, climate change, peace keeping, inter-country migration, etc. These are all areas where national policies are often not enough and global externalities need to be accounted for in a global policy framework.

Development assistance: Funding gap

According to some estimates, the funding gap in international assistance to finance activities in the developing countries for achieving the MDGs has been estimated at about $156 billion per year for environmental commitments and about $180 billion per year for MDG commitments (Table 4.6). Although estimates differ but funding gap is likely to be in the range of $ 300–400 billion per year considering both the MDG and the environmental commitments.

Table 4.6: Funding gap estimates

Funding gap for environmental commitments (per year) [1]	$156.000.000.000
Funding gap for official development aid (per year) [2]	$180.000.000.000
Funding gap to meet international developments and environmental commitments (per year) [3]	$336.000.000.000

Source: Innovative financing for the MDGs: A Precondition for Success, The ITUC and the Ubuntu Forum, September 10, 2010

1 http://www.leadinggroup.org/IMG/pdf_Financement_innovants_web_def.pdf

2 http://www.leadinggroup.org/IMG/pdf_Financement_innovants_web_def.pdf

3 http://www.leadinggroup.org/IMG/pdf_Financement_innovants_web_def.pdf; per year between 2012–17

Christian Masset, French Secretary-General for G20 has also highlighted large funding gaps. He mentioned that for climate change the Copenhagen Agreement agreed to raise US$ 100 billion per year by 2020; MDG needs were estimated at US$ 200 billion per year while ODA figures were only US$120 billion per year.

Crisis and impact on ODA

The ODA flows suffered an erosion in the immediate aftermath of the global economic crisis. The ODA has started recovering since but remains well below the commitment of 1 per cent of GDP of donor countries. In 2009, total net ODA from members of the OECD's Development Assistance Committee (DAC) rose slightly in real terms (+0.7 per cent) to $119.6 billion, representing 0.31 per cent of DAC members' combined gross national income. Debt relief, which had been especially high in 2005 and 2006 due to exceptional Paris Club packages for Iraq and Nigeria, fell sharply. The combined net ODA of the 15 members of the DAC that are EU members fell slightly (-0.2 per cent) to $ 67.1 billion, representing 0.44 per cent of their combined GNI. DAC-EU ODA represented 56 per cent of total DAC ODA.

In 2009, net bilateral ODA to Africa was $ 27 billion, representing an increase of 3 per cent in real terms over 2008. $ 24 billion of this aid went to sub-Saharan Africa, an increase of 5.1 per cent over 2008. The largest donors by volume were the United States, France, Germany, the United Kingdom and Japan. Five countries exceeded the United Nations ODA target of 0.7 per cent of GNI – Denmark, Luxembourg, the Netherlands, Norway and Sweden.

In 2009, Japan's net ODA fell by 10.7 per cent in real terms to $9.5 billion, representing 0.18 per cent of its GNI. The fall was mainly due to the fact that debt relief, notably for Iraq, fell compared to 2008. However, contributions to international financial institutions increased significantly in 2009.

On 17 February 2010, the OECD released its first estimate of the 2010 ODA outcome, based on a special review of donors' budget plans for 2010. This estimate has now been updated in light of the DAC donors' 2009 performance and some further adjustments to the 2010 targets. In general, GNI reported by DAC donors for 2009 was slightly higher than previously estimated and the GNI prospects for 2010 are also slightly improved.

The OECD now estimates that the recent economic contraction has, by cutting nominal GNI, reduced the dollar value of the commitments made for 2010 to around $126 billion (in constant 2004 dollars), or $46 billion over the 2004 level, compared with the original estimate of $50 billion.

While most countries have maintained their commitments for 2010, others, including some large donors, have reduced or postponed the pledges they made for 2010. On the basis of current 2010 budget proposals and latest GNI figures the overall expected ODA level for 2010 is estimated at $108 billion expressed in 2004 dollars, an increase of $28 billion over the 2004 baseline, with the ODA/GNI ratio rising over the same period from 0.26 per cent to an estimated 0.32 per cent.

Some will surpass that goal. Sweden, with the world's highest ODA as a percentage of its GNI at 1.01 per cent, is followed by Luxembourg (1 per cent), Denmark (0.83 per cent), the Netherlands (0.8 per cent), Belgium (0.7 per cent), the United Kingdom (now estimated at 0.60 per cent), Finland (0.56 per cent), Ireland (0.52 per cent) and Spain (0.51 per cent). But others are unlikely to reach the target, although some have made significant progress since 2004: France (estimated at between 0.44 and 0.48 per cent, 0.46 per cent is used in the attached projections), Germany (0.40 per cent), Austria (0.37 per cent), Portugal (0.34 per cent), Greece (0.21 per cent), and Italy (0.20 per cent).

Despite various shortfalls against commitments, ODA increased by nearly 30 per cent in real terms between 2004 and 2009, and is expected to rise by about 36 per cent in real terms between 2004 and 2010. ODA as a percentage of GNI rose from 0.26 per cent in 2004 to 0.31 per cent in 2009 and is expected to rise to 0.32 per cent in 2010.

Traditional vs. innovative methods of international assistance

A distinction is being made between traditional methods of international assistance by budgetary allocation vis-à-vis innovative methods, which comprise a range of measures including a Financial Transactions Tax. Some of the other measures include: (1) a guaranteed scheme to raise money on the markets and advance market financing; (2) micro contributions based on global air ticket levy; (3) micro tax on tobacco; (4) market mechanisms like auction of credit of carbon dioxide (CO_2) emissions; (5) cancellation of debt; and (6) voluntary contributions from business or citizens.

The relevant issues relate to: (1) the relative roles of traditional methods of funding international assistance *vis-à-vis* innovative methods; and (2) the scope of further developing the innovative methods.

Financing development assistance: Traditional methods

The traditional methods are required for funding international assistance and should continue to be the main vehicle for funding international assistance. There was a period during the international financial crisis when traditional funding fell because of the global economic slowdown. But as most economies emerge from out of the slowdown and internal fiscal pressures ease, more and more reliance can be placed on the traditional methods.

The shortfall in traditional funding has been due to the fact that most donor countries have failed to meet the Monterrey Consensus commitment to allocate 0.7 per cent of their Gross National Income (GNI) to ODA. Furthermore, in most developing countries the budget allocated for the social, and especially the health sector, has been insufficient as it fails to meet the 15 per cent Gross National Product (GNP) requirement dedicated to the health sector stated in the Abuja declaration of African leaders in 2001.

However, ODA funds continue to be deficient relative to needs or relative to commitments and these are also highly volatile. The Landau Report lists several reasons for such volatility. It observes:

> This volatility stems from several causes: the budgetary procedures in donor countries; changes in their priorities; administrative delays in making or implementing decisions; and implementation of conditionality

> when the beneficiary's performance deteriorates. The poorer the country, the greater is the volatility. Generally, it is impossible to ascribe this volatility to objective and identifiable causes. It is therefore impossible to anticipate. Aid is not only volatile; it is also, and above all, unpredictable.

In situations such as a global recession, the ODA funds fall from all sources rather than from individual countries.

There are other difficulties with this traditional mechanism. The ODA system works through a network of bilateral and multilateral relations between recipient and donor countries requiring coordinating mechanisms between countries whose objectives may or may not converge. Donors exercise discretionary powers over their contributions using a variety of means including conditionalities. The efficiency of such a system depends on how well designed the programmes are and how well these are implemented. These difficulties notwithstanding, suitable alternative funding mechanisms have not yet become important enough from the viewpoint of volume of resources. The traditional methods of funding international assistance will therefore continue to be the main vehicle for assistance to achieve the MDG goals.

There are good reasons for continued reliance on the traditional methods. In the longer run, as the MDGs are achieved, and per capita income of the poorer countries increase, their markets will provide growing markets for the products of the developed countries. Achieving the MDGs will not only provide a more stable economic order but it will also lead to a relatively faster growth of demand for services as people become more educated and healthier. Such a demand structure would be more consistent with the changing structure of output of international economy, which is becoming more and more service sector oriented. These changes will lead to an increased share of world trade in world output and greater integration of the world economy. Clearly, there is a case for supporting the traditional methods of financing development assistance, which has been linked with the size of the GDP of the economy. There may be case for establishing a link between the volume of assistance and the share of a country's exports in world exports. The larger the share of exports, the greater is the expected benefit to individual countries from the growth of the world economy. The share of each developed country can be earmarked according to the size of the economy, which is indicative of fiscal capacity and the size of exports, which is directly linked to the benefit of individual countries from a stable growth with a suitable weighting scheme.

Financing development assistance: Innovative methods

Innovative financing mechanisms can serve as a complementary mechanism for international funding for achieving the MDGs. Apart from the financial transactions tax and revenues from emissions trading, other methods at present seem to have a limited resource potential relative to needs. For assessing the role of innovative financing mechanisms, generally the following five principles may be considered as relevant:

Scaling-up: Innovative financing mechanisms should significantly increase funding in order to bridge the financing gap necessary to achieve the MDGs. Under this principle, among the various mechanisms being considered only the financial transactions tax (FTT) seems to qualify.

Additionality: The innovative mechanisms are being created to fill the funding gap after traditional funding methods are taken into account. These cannot replace Official Development Assistance and should not be taken as a substitute of ODA.

Sustainability: In order to have a significant and sustainable impact on the MDG's, innovative financing mechanisms should have the ability to finance long-term programmes in a sustainable and reliable way.

Multilateralism: The innovative funding mechanisms should work on the basis of participation of several countries together rather than being applied by individual countries.

Some of successful innovative funding mechanisms currently being used in the field of health are UNITAID, an international facility for the purchase of drugs against HIV/AIDS (Human Immunodeficiency Virus/Acquired Immunodeficiency Syndrome), malaria and tuberculosis, is supported by the 'air ticket solidarity levy,' which is a tax on airline tickets. By 2009, 13 countries had started applying this domestic tax on the airline tickets.

Another innovative method is issuance of bonds in the capital markets with guarantees by the donor countries. So far, around €2 billion has been collected for The Global Alliance for Vaccines and Immunisation (the GAVI Alliance). Available information indicates that International Finance Facility for Immunization (IFFIm) can finance up to 20 year grants by issuing bonds in the capital markets backed by donor countries. Advance market commitments (AMC) are mechanisms supporting the GAVI Alliance aimed at providing incentives for Research & Development (R&D) for new vaccines through the guarantee of a viable market to the new product. In this method, the critical condition that needs to be satisfied is viability and sustainability. Since the money is raised from the market, the debt needs to be serviced and eventually returned. In case of R&D on vaccines, returns can flow from patents and sale of vaccines. The success depends on beneficiary governments or organizations committing themselves to buy or subsidize the purchase of the vaccines at agreed prices. This mechanism has been implemented for pneumococcal vaccines to demonstrate both the feasibility of the AMC mechanism and its impact on accelerating the introduction and mass production of these vaccines.

In another innovative mechanism, called Product Redmark (RED), which supports the Global Fund for Aids, Tuberculosis and Malaria (*The Global Fund*), global companies contribute a share of their profits on goods from sales branded with the RED trademark. Similarly, Debt2Health is a mechanism that supports *the Global Fund*. Under this mechanism, debt negotiation between creditor and debtor countries is facilitated by *The Global Fund* whereby the creditors agree to forego part of the repayment of the money due to them against the commitment of the debtor to invest an agreed amount on Global Fund approved programmes. By the end of 2009, € 200 million were pledged under this mechanism.

Another innovative mechanism is voluntary contributions on travel and tourism products. These funds are collected by the Millennium Foundation through a donation to Massive Good, which lets travellers make an optional $2, £2 or €2 'micro–contribution' every time they purchase a travel service. These funds go to UNITAID in its fight against HIV/AIDS, tuberculosis and malaria. These funds can also go towards improving maternal and child health in the developing world.

A potentially important innovative mechanism is the so called 'de-tax', which is a 'proposal to earmark a share of VAT Taxes generated by participating businesses for health systems development'. De-tax is currently being discussed by the G20 countries.

Financial transactions tax/currency transactions tax

Potentially the most important innovative mechanism from the viewpoint of generating resources to make a significant dent in the funding gap is the Financial Transactions Tax (FTT) and/or the Currency Transaction Levy (CTL). This is a potential mechanism that would let governments apply a tax on foreign exchange transactions. The tax can be managed through computerized payments made in connection with the settlement of every trade. With a low rate like the 0.005 per cent rate that is currently being discussed, a reasonable amount of funding can be generated. Mr. Christian Masset (CM) estimates that a tax rate of 0.005 per cent could raise between $30 to 40 billion a year.

Since the FTT has been proposed in different forms (e.g. Cash Transactions Tax, Bank Transaction Tax, Spahn Tax, Transfer Tax, Robinhood Tax), initially, it may be levied on a voluntary basis by countries with some degrees of freedom in determining the tax rate as also the specific form. More uniform structures can be considered over a longer period of time. The FTT and its variants have been advocated not only as a revenue raising device but also a means of stabilizing the financial markets and curbing excessive speculative activities.

It may be useful to determine country-wise targets for assistance and the countries can then be given freedom to determined how far they want to rely on the traditional methods and how far they want to rely on innovative methods.

The FTT revenues may be earmarked for meeting the MDG funding gap and the revenues from the GHG emission permits for the climate change related funding gap.

Market for greenhouse gas (GHG) emission permits

Auctioning of permits to emit greenhouse gases could be an important innovative financing mechanism earmarked for environmental purposes. Germany announced that it would allocate €225 million from the 2009 proceeds of these auctions to fund development activities. Carbon emissions trading have been steadily increasing in recent years. The emissions trading methods or the cap and trade methods also have a double advantage in the sense that they minimize the overall cost of achieving a given reduction in the carbon emissions.

The World Bank has facilitated the establishment of a number of carbon funds like 'prototype' carbon fund, bio-carbon fund, community development carbon fund, and umbrella carbon facilities, and several country specific funds. The size of these funds taken together has grown from $145 million in 2000 to nearly $2.3 billion in 2011.

More recently the European carbon trading market has seen a near-collapse. In 2008, Europe's carbon price was €20 a tonne. By mid-2013, it had fallen to €2.6 or $3.34 a tonne. This is the result of the prolonged European economic crisis. The collapse of the carbon trading system has seriously jeopardized the flow of international finance to the developing world.

Given India's high growth potential and large size of the economy, India is in the unique position of being a participant in extending international assistance to a number of developing countries. At the same time, given the relatively large gaps in a number of MDGs, it is also a deserving recipient of international assistance provided such assistance is of high quality and a well directed towards deserving sectors and areas. In the Appendix, some of the key considerations for developing India's approach to international assistance both as a recipient and as a contributor is developed.

Conclusion

This chapter reviews the experience of G20 economies as they faced the 2007–09 economic crisis and surfaced out of the crisis. The paper notes that post-crisis, the centre of gravity of the world economy has widened from G7 to G20, in which economies like India and China will progressively have a major role to play. Although the immediate causes of the crisis are found in the financial crisis starting with the collapse of the sub-prime lending in the US linked to the housing mortgage market, there are deeper roots to the crisis. These can be traced back to deep seated structural imbalances in the world economy.

There are some important economies like China and Saudi Arabia that maintain large current account surplus, while other major economies like the US and the UK that maintain large current account deficits. This sets up a dynamics that sees capital from the surplus economies where by and large the financial markets are underdeveloped move to the deficit economies where the financial markets are deep and innovative. The large demand for financial assets relative to supply induces dilution of safety of the assets increasing their risk content. Unless these global imbalances are managed better, the global economy will remain vulnerable to economic shocks.

The main source of the current account surplus is the movement of crude oil prices and prices of primary inputs like metals and high domestic saving ratio like that in China. The main source of deficit is the low saving ratio in economy like the US. Crude oil prices and the global food prices represent sources of vulnerability to the Indian economy.

Although Indian economy emerged out of the 2008 financial crisis with limited damage in the immediate aftermath of the crisis, its growth has suffered in more recent years falling well below its potential growth, usually estimated in the range of 8 to 8.5 per cent.

In the immediate aftermath of the crisis, the global efforts towards international burden sharing for financing expenditure especially for achieving worldwide MDG goals and international climate change related efforts. Given India's potential economic strength, the country will be increasingly called to contribute to the international effort. In spite of the economic strength, India presents a paradoxical picture because of unflattering achievement levels in regard to poverty indicators, and education and health indicators. India will be better off both contributing to international aid effort and receiving such aid. It may be possible to establish a link between the two especially in the field of health.

In international funding for assistance towards achieving the MDGs and environmental objectives, the funding gap is large. Suggestions are being made to fill up this gap by a set of innovative mechanisms of financing. So far, these mechanisms have been utilized in a limited way for assistance directed towards the health sector. The two innovative mechanisms with relatively larger revenue potential are the FTT or any of its variants and the revenues from the emissions trading. But in practice theses methods are yet to be developed at a scale that can fill up the funding gaps. The innovative methods of financing assistance should be seen as playing a complementary role to the traditional methods.

Appendix: International Burden Sharing – Developing India's Approach

India has the potential for growing at 8 per cent plus on a sustainable basis, given its demographic dividend. But to make this possible, policy effort needs to be directed to productively absorb the growing number of people who are joining the working force. They need to be educated, skilled and provided adequate health facilities. While India has performed satisfactorily in meeting some of the MDGs, there are considerable deficiencies in others. G20 can be a major partner in extending technical and financial assistance to India to provide support to achieve its growth potential. In turn, as India's growth story unfolds, it can itself become an effective contributor to the international burden sharing in extending assistance to other deserving developing countries.

Introduction

India's economy presents a paradoxical view. On the one hand, India is one of the top growth performers having achieved a 9 per cent plus growth rate before the onset of the global recession. Although at present India's GDP growth rate has fallen to below 5 per cent, it has the potential to sustain an 8 per cent plus average growth rate at least for another two and a half decades, given its demographic dividend. At the same time, India is still plagued by large and persistent poverty, severe undernourishment, unflattering health and other social indicators, and acute regional imbalances. With its growing economic prosperity, India should be contributing to the global efforts for achieving a large number of social and economic goals in a number of developing countries. Yet, it requires considerable support from international initiatives.

In order to formulate a suitable strategy, two features of the Indian economy stand out: (1) the demographic dividend; and (2) the increasing globalization of the Indian economy.

Appendix Figure 4.8 shows the projected share of working age population (in the age group of 15 years to 60 years) to total population in India based on UN country-wise population projections. The minimum of this ratio at about 54 per cent was in 1970 and the highest of the ratio at about 64 per cent is projected to occur around 2033. There is noticeable acceleration of this ratio soon after 2000. Although it continues to rise, there is deceleration after 2007. The window from now to up to 2035 is the critical growth window for India with the growing availability of labour force and a falling dependency ratio. It benefits growth from the output side both by a larger size of the working population and by increasing the saving rate and therefore the supply of investible resources.

Figure 4.8: Share of working population to total population in India

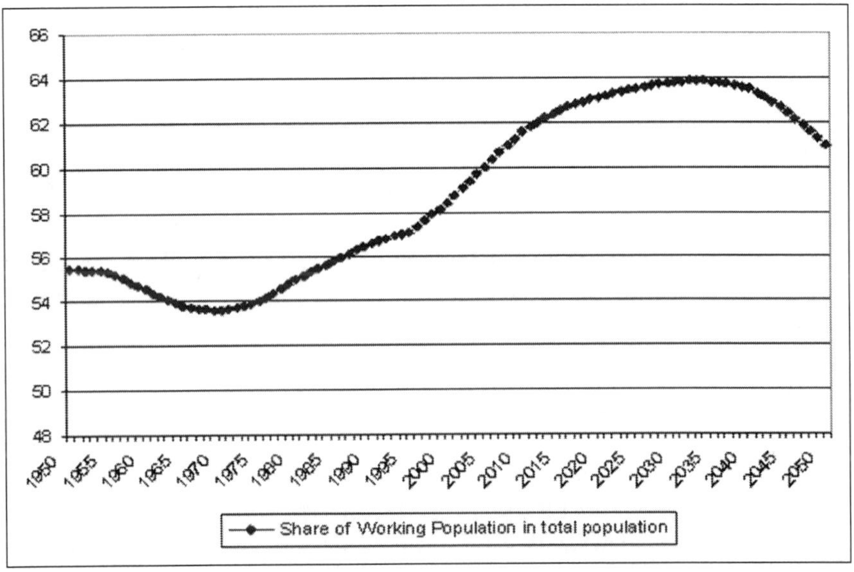

Source: Population Division, Department of Economic and Social Affairs, United Nations

MDGs: India's Achievements and Distance to Traverse

In terms of India's own needs, it is useful to review the progress that India has made in respect of a number of social and economic indicators including poverty reduction and the considerable ground that is still to be covered. In doing so, it is useful to draw a perspective with reference to the UN Millennium Development Goals (MDGs). The first three of the eight fundamental goals relate to eradication of poverty and hunger, education, and gender equality. Goals four to six relate to health focusing on reducing child mortality, improving maternal health, and combating HIV/AIDS, malaria and other diseases. Goals seven and eight are related to environmental sustainability and partnership for global development.

Poverty in India

Income poverty

There is an extensive debate as to the extent of poverty in India. The estimates are sensitive to the definition of poverty and poverty line. The officially defined poverty lines are close to the purchasing power parity (PPP) $1 per day benchmark for rural areas and somewhat higher for urban areas. As per official data, during 1973–74 to 2004–05, the reduction in the all-India rural poverty head count ratio (HCR) was more than 27 percentage points from 56.4 to 27.5 per cent. Thus, the extent of poverty nearly halved with rural poverty head count ratio falling more than the urban poverty head count ratio.

The changing poverty profile in India has two notable features. One, poverty has become less but spatially more concentrated. Rural poverty is concentrated in a few poor states. Urban poverty is also spatially concentrated but this list includes some of the middle to higher income states also. Secondly, poverty has become more urbanized in the sense that the number of urban poor in total poor has increased in almost all states. The increasing urbanization and spatial concentration of poverty call for a qualitative change in policies aimed at poverty reduction, making these state-specific and targeted.

Chen and Ravallion (2008) have argued that revisions in the poverty lines based on Purchasing Power Parity (PPP) measures resulting from the 2005 International Comparison Program (ICP) price data indicates that that the incidence of poverty in the world including India is higher than past estimates have suggested. The main reason is that in the past PPPs had implicitly underestimated the cost of living in most developing countries. Their correction for the bias in past PPPs has added 400 million people to the global count for 2005, when judged against an international poverty line that is representative of the national poverty lines found in the poorest countries. They assess that the developing world outside China will not attain the MDGs without a higher rate of poverty reduction than has been seen over 1981–2005. For the MDG goal of eradicating extreme poverty and hunger, India must reduce by 2015 the proportion of people below poverty line from nearly 37.5 per cent in 1990 to about 18.75 per cent. Clearly there is much distance to travel. Since income-poverty is increasingly being recognized as too narrowly defined, the author also looks at some other dimensions of poverty.

Nutritional poverty

Researchers are increasingly noticing an extremely disturbing aspect of poverty relating to nutritional deficiency. For example, Meenakshi and Vishwanathan (2003) observe that nutritional poverty in India is high. The head count ratios based on calorie thresholds have increased between 1983 and 1999–2000 for rural households in most states.

Malnourishment

Women's malnourishment increases the risk to maternal mortality apart from being essential for a person's wellbeing and human development. Based on national family health survey data (NFHS 3, 2005–06), Jose and Navaneetham (2008) provide an interstate perspective on women's malnutrition. They look at body mass index (BMI), chronic energy deficiency (CED) and incidence of anemia (iron deficiency) and find that malnutrition is high in most Indian states.

Other millennium development goals

In respect of some of the other MDGs also, while some ground has been covered, there is still considerable ground that has to be covered. For universal primary education, India should increase the primary school enrolment rate to 100 per cent and wipe out the drop-outs by 2015 against 41.96 per cent in 1991–92. The drop-out rate for primary education is still high. The gross enrolment ratio in primary education has tended to remain near 100 per cent for boys and recorded an impressive increase for girls.

1. To ensure gender parity in education levels in Goal-3, female participation at all levels has to reach a female male proportion of equal level by 2015. The female male proportion in respect of primary education was 71:100 in 1990–91.

2. For Goal 4, the under five mortality rate (U5MR) from 125 deaths per thousand live births in 1988–92 to 42 in 2015. The U5MR has decreased during the period 1998–2002 to 98 per thousand live births. The infant mortality rate (IMR) has also come down from 80 per thousand live births in 1990

3. For Goal-5, India should reduce maternal mortality rate (MMR) from 437 deaths per 100,000 live births in 1991 to 109 by 2015.

4. For Goal-6, the prevalence rate of HIV has increased from 0.74 per thousand pregnant women in 2002 to 0.86 in 2003. This increasing trend needs to be reversed. The prevalence and death rates associated with malaria and tuberculosis (TB) are consistently coming down.

5. Goal-7 aims at ensuring environmental sustainability. The proportion of population without sustainable access to safe drinking water and sanitation is to be halved by 2015.

6. Goal-8 is regarding the developing global partnership for development. Measured on the basis of access to internet this has been increasing significantly but beyond a point further progress will be linked to progress and spread of education.

Appendix Table 4.7 summarizes the position in respect of these goals as per latest available data.

Table 4.7: Selected MDG indicators – current status in India

Goal 2	Net enrolment in primary education (% both sexes)	94.2
Goal 3	Gender equality and women empowerment	
	Gender parity index in primary level enrolment	1
	Literacy rates of 15–24 years old (% both sexes)	82.1
	Seats held by women in National Parliament	8.3
Goal 4	Reduction of child mortality	
	Mortality rate of children under 5 years old (per thousand live births)	76
	1 year old children immunized against measles (%)	59
Goal 5	Improve maternal health	
	Maternal mortality ratio (per 100 thousand births)	450
Goal 6	Combat HIV/Aids, Malaria and other diseases	
	People living with HIV, 15–49 years old (%)	0.3
	Prevalence of tuberculosis (per 100,000 people)	299
Goal 7	Ensure environment sustainability	
	land area covered by forests (%)	
	Carbon dioxide emissions per capita (metric tonnes)	1.20203
	Access to improved drinking water sources (% of total population)	89
Goal 8	Develop global partnership for development	
	internet users per 100 people	10.7

Source: United Nations Millennium Development Goals (UNMDG) Monitor

While improvement is tangible in most fields, there is a lot of ground that is yet to be covered. AIDS is the main issue where the prevalence rates may go up if adequate remedial measures are not taken.

India's Growth and Growth Potential

While India's needs are large and compulsive, given the size of its population and the spread of inequality and poverty across regions and income groups, its growing economic strength is also undeniable. India and China along with Brazil, Russia, and South Africa together named as BRICS are large and fast growing economies. Analysts increasingly recognize the potential of the growing economic size of these economies and correspondingly the changing nature of the contribution that they can make in tackling some of the most pernicious problems affecting mankind. The prospects of the Indian economy have been analysed in a number of forecasting exercises. One of the first one in this context was Goldman Sachs' BRIC paper in 2003, which has been periodically updated.

A 2007 update entitled BRICS and Beyond (Goldman Sachs, 2007), before the onset of the global economic crisis, noted that India can sustain a 8 per cent plus growth rate up to 2020 revising its earlier 2003 projection of an average 5.7 per cent growth. The main condition on which India's future will depend is taking advantage of the bulge in the working age population in the window in which the demographic dividend will remain operative by educating and imparting skills to them and ensuring that they remain healthy so that they can productively participate and contribute to enhancement of productivity.

Appendix Figure 4.9 shows India's growth performance as measured by growth of GDP at factor cost at 2004–05 prices. The author shows both actual growth rate and trend growth rate, which has been estimated using the Hodrick-Prescott filter. In 2007–08 the trend growth rate peaked at just below 8 per cent. That year the actual growth was 9.3 per cent. In 2013–14, advanced estimates show that growth rate has fallen to 4.9 per cent while trend growth rate is close to 6 per cent. There was temporary spurt in the growth rate in 2010–11 when the actual growth had again touched 9 per cent. A suitable revival strategy can restore growth to 8 per cent plus on a sustainable basis. This would require non-inflationary fiscal and monetary stimuli in the short run and structural changes aimed at improving the efficiency in resource-use and productive absorption of the available working age population in the long run.

Figure 4.9: India's recent growth experience: actual and trend

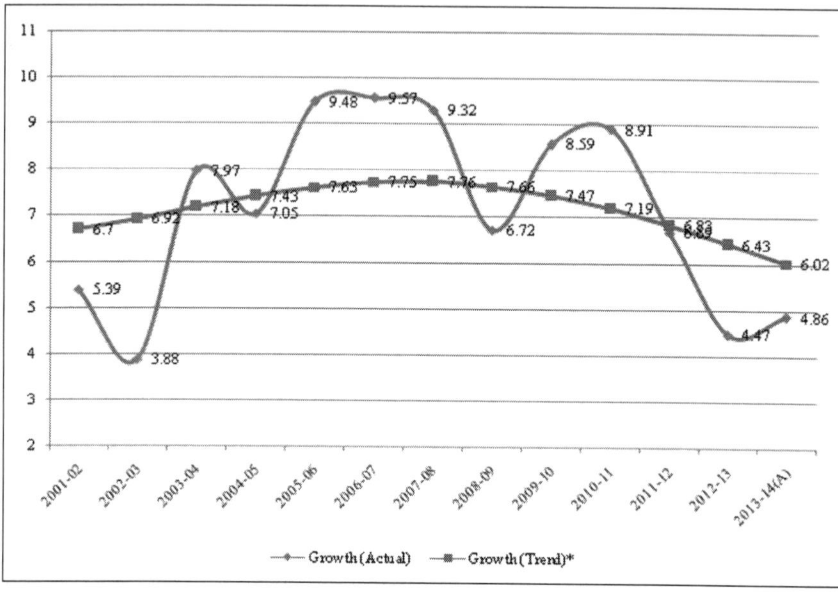

Source: National Income Accounts, Ministry of Statistcis and Plan implementation, Government of India

Case for India's Participation in Financing Global Initiatives

Given India's need to pay attention to its health and education sectors, not only its budgetary allocations for these sectors have to increase but also it can leverage the available funds from the Global Initiatives on a cost sharing basis to increase both the quality and volume of funds directed towards these sectors, particularly the health sector.

The volume of resources, given the needs have to flow both from national budgetary resources and from international sources. Since in any case budgetary allocation has to be increased and India's model shows increasing fiscal space getting created as the overall, tax GDP ratio rises to close to 22 per cent of GDP from the present 18 per cent and the burden of interest payments falls with the debt-GDP ratio falling as result of pursuit of fiscal responsibility legislations at the central and state governments, the additional fiscal space for increasing primary expenditures will increase by about 7 to 9 percentage points of GDP. A good part of this should be devoted to education and health in the social sectors and physical infrastructure in the economic sector. Using some of these additional resources for cost sharing, additional funds can be accessed from cost sharing.

1. As a rapidly expanding economy with high stable growth, India will need to play a more significant role in contributing to global human welfare.

2. Support to India's role in world affairs by other countries, particularly developing countries will increase as India extends a helping hand in addressing some of the worst diseases in poorer countries.

3. There are considerable negative externalities in the spread of diseases like aids emanating from neighbouring countries like Bangladesh, Nepal, Sri Lanka, Thailand and other nearby countries. Any reduction of the incidence of the disease in the neighbourhood would also help reduce the incidence in India.

4. Health and economic development have a clear linkage. The sustainability of projected high growth depends critically on taking advantage of the demographic dividend.

5. Access to the fund allocation from the international aid programme would follow a policy of prioritizing allocation for high impact interventions. Quality of intervention would improve both in the selection of the project but also as a result of follow up monitoring and inputs from international subject specialists.

6. As a contributor, India will have better representation in the decision making bodies for allocation of funds in different geographical locations. India can look forward to higher allocation for its own needs as also in its neighbouring countries or countries where it may have closer relations or where it sources natural resources from and where it is obliged to contribute to the welfare of the citizens of those countries.

India's economy shows high growth potential combined with the need to improve its social and economic indicators. Growth releases the necessary fiscal resources, which can be directed towards achieving better health and education outcomes, which in turn are necessary to sustain the potentially achievable high growth performance. Increasing globalization casts additional responsibilities on India.

Although Indian economy emerged out of the 2008 financial crisis with limited damage in the immediate aftermath of the crisis, its growth has suffered in more recent years falling well below its potential growth, usually estimated to be close to 8 per cent. In the immediate aftermath of the crisis, the global efforts towards international burden sharing for financing expenditure especially for achieving worldwide MDGs and international climate change relate efforts. Given India's potential economic strength, India will be increasingly called to contribute to the international effort. In spite of the economic strength, India presents a paradoxical picture because of unflattering achievement levels in regard to poverty indicators, and education and health indicators. India will be better off both contributing to international aid effort and receiving such aid. It may be possible to establish a link between the two especially in the field of health.

Endnote

1 G20: G7+ Argentina, Australia, Brazil, China, India, Indonesia, Mexico, Russia, Saudi Arabia, South Africa, Republic of Korea, Turkey+ European Union

2 http://www.g20.org/about_what_is_g20.aspx, last accessed 25 May 2011.

3 G7: France, Germany, Italy, Japan, United Kingdom, United States and Canada

4 Financial crises at a smaller scale have been taking place since the early seventies. But the scale of the 2007 financial crisis was quite unprecedented. Eichengreen (University of California at Berkeley) and Bordo (Rutgers University) identify 139 financial crises between 1973 and 1997 (of which 44 took place in high-income countries), compared with a total of only 38 between 1945 and 1971. Crises are twice as common as they were before 1914, the authors conclude.

5 Caballero (2011) builds a stylized model of the workings of a global economy where one of its key driving factors is economic agents continuous struggle to find assets in which to park financial resources. This struggle naturally comes with euphoria and disappointments, as many of the 'parking lots' are built too quickly or are not of the desired size. There are also global asymmetries, as some countries are endowed with more empty land than others and their growth potential may also differ. Caballero uses this caricature of the world economy to describe several of the main driving forces behind recent global macroeconomic events and to discuss 'quantitative' easing policies.

6 In a Peabody Award winning programme, NPR correspondents argued that a 'Giant Pool of Money' (represented by $70 trillion in worldwide fixed income investments) sought higher yields than those offered by US Treasury bonds early in the decade. This pool of money had roughly doubled in size from 2000 to 2007, yet the supply of relatively safe, income generating investments had not grown as fast. Investment banks on Wall Street answered this demand with the MBSs and CDOs, which were assigned safe ratings by the credit rating agencies. In effect, Wall Street connected this pool of money to the mortgage market in the US, with enormous fees accruing to those throughout the mortgage supply chain, from the mortgage broker selling the loans, to small banks that funded the

brokers, to the giant investment banks behind them. By approximately 2003, the supply of mortgages originated at traditional lending standards had been exhausted. However, continued strong demand for MBSs and CDOs began to drive down lending standards, as long as mortgages could still be sold along the supply chain. Eventually, this speculative bubble proved unsustainable.

7 GCC: Bahrain, Kuwait, Oman, Saudi Arabia, Qatar, and United Arab Emirates (UAE)

References

Berkmen, P., G. Gelos, R. Rennhack and J. P. Walsh. December, 2009. 'The Global Financial Crisis: Explaining Cross-Country Differences in the Output Impact', *IMF Working Paper.*

Caballero, Ricardo. 2010. 'A Caricature (Model) of the World Economy', prepared for the Ninth Macroeconomic Policy Research Workshop 'Understanding Financial Frictions', Magyar Nemzeti Bank, Budapest.

Caballero, R. J. and A. Krishnamurthy. 2009. 'Global Imbalances and Financial Fragility, National Bureau of Economic Research', *NBER Working Papers 14688.*

Caballero, R. J., E. Farhi and P. Gourinchas. 2008. 'Financial Crash, Commodity Prices and Global Imbalances, National Bureau of Economic Research', *NBER Working Papers 14521.*

Chen, S. and Martin Ravallion. 2008. 'The Developing World Is Poorer Than We Thought, but No Less Successful in the Fight Against Poverty', *Policy Research Working Paper 4703.* Washington, DC: World Bank.

Corsetti, G., A. Meier and G. J. Muller. 2009. 'Fiscal Stimulus with Spending Reversals', *IMF Working Paper* and *CEPR Discussion Paper 7302.*

Economic Intelligence Unit (EIU), GCC. 2011. 'Trade and Investment Flows: The Emerging Market Surge', *The Economist*, London.

Giavazzi, F. February, 2008. *Union Budget.* New Delhi: Ministry of Finance, Government of India.

_______. 9 September 2009. *Issues in the Design of a Fiscal Exit Strategy.* Bocconi University and MIT.

_______. April 2010. 'Fiscal and Monetary Policies in the Crisis: The Exit Stage', *Inter-American Development Bank Discussion Paper No. IDB-DP-100.*

Hamilton, James D. 2009. 'Oil Prices and the Economic Downturn', Testimony before the Joint Economic Committee of the United States Congress, 20 May.

International Monetary Fund (IMF). 4 February 2010a. 'Exiting from Crisis Intervention Policies', Prepared by the Fiscal Affairs, Monetary and Capital Markets, and Research Departments, approved by O. J. Blanchard, C. Cottarelli and J. Viñals.

_______. 2010b. 'Strategies for Fiscal Consolidation in the Post-Crisis World'. Fiscal Affairs Department, approved by Carlo Cottarelli.

_______. April 2010c. *Global Financial Stability Report.*

_______. 14 May 2010d. 'Navigating the Fiscal Challenges Ahead', *Fiscal Monitor.*

_______. July 2010e. *International Financial Statistics.*

Jose, Sunny and K. Navaneetam. 2008. 'A Factsheet on Women's Malnutrition in India', *Economic and Political Weekly*, 16(August): 61–67.

Meenakshi, J. V. and Brinda Vishwanathan. 2003. 'Calorie Deprivation in Rural India, 1983-1999/2000', *Economic and Political Weekly* 38(4): 369–75.

Minegeshi M. and B. Cournede. 2010. 'Monetary Policy Responses to the Crisis and Exit Strategies', *Working Papers No. 753, ECO/WKP(2010)9*. France: OECD Economics Department.

Ostry J. D., A. R. Ghosh, J. I. Kim and M. S. Qureshi. 1 September 2010. 'Fiscal Space'. *IMF Staff Position Note.*

Obstfeld, M. 2009. 'International Finance and Growth in Developing Countries: What Have We Learned?', *NBER Working Papers No. 14691*. National Bureau of Economic Research.

_______. 2009. 'Lenders of Last Resort in a Globalized World', *IMES Discussion Paper Series 09-E-18*. Japan: Institute for Monetary and Economic Studies, Bank of Japan.

Obstfeld, M. and K. Rogoff. 2009. 'Global Imbalances and the Financial Crisis: Products of Common Causes', *CEPR Discussion Paper 7606.*

Obstfeld, M., J. C. Shambaugh and A. M. Taylor. May 2009. 'Financial Instability, Reserves, and Central Bank Swap Lines in the Panic of 2008', *American Economic Review* 99(2): 480–86. American Economic Association.

Zhang Z. and W. Zhang. 10 December 2009. 'The Road to Recovery: Fiscal Stimulus, Financial Sector Rehabilitation, and Potential Risks Ahead', *Working Paper 18/2009.* Hong Kong: Hong Kong Monetary Authority, Bank of International Settlement.

5 India's Growth Prospect: Structural Impediments

Kirit S. Parikh

Accelerating Growth

India was one of the richest countries in the world when Robert Clive landed here. When the British left in 1947, it had become one of the poorest. As Prime Minister Manmohan Singh observed at Oxford University:

> As the painstaking statistical work of the Cambridge historian Angus Madison has shown, India's share of world income collapsed from 22.6% in 1700, almost equal to Europe's share of 23.3% at that time, to as low as 3.8% in 1952. Indeed, at the beginning of the 20th Century, 'the brightest jewel in the British Crown' was the poorest country in the world in terms of per capita income.

However, the Indian economy has grown steadily since independence. Not only is the economy growing, economic growth has also been accelerating. Table 5.1 shows decadal growth rates of GDP, which are estimated simultaneously to have no discontinuities in the estimated GDP. The acceleration from less than 3.5 per cent growth rate in the 1960s and 1970s to 7.2 per cent in the 20-noughties has been steady. However, the growth rate has fallen to around 4.5 per cent for 2011–12 and 2012–13. The growth rate in 2013–14 is expected to be similar. As a consequence the target of growth rate of 9 per cent suggested in the Twelfth Plan approach document has been reduced to 8 per cent in the Twelfth Plan document (Planning Commission, 2013). The election of 2014 with Narendra Modi as Prime Minister has however regenerated hope to have 10 per cent growth rate or more in the Thirteenth Plan and beyond.

Table 5.1: Decadal growth rate of GDP at factor cost (2004–05 prices)

Period	Per year
1951–59	3.9

Period	Per year
1960–69	3.4
1970–79	3.3
1980–89	4.8
1990–99	5.5
2000–09	7.2

Source: Estimate by author based on time series from Handbook of Statistics, (Table 2, 15 September 2010), Reserve Bank of India (RBI)

Can India attain double–digit growth and maintain it for two or three decades? That is what the country needs to meet the human development goals and fulfill its 'tryst with destiny' (Nehru, 1947) as despite progress in poverty reduction India still has many poor people, see Table 5.2.

Table 5.2: Poverty across NSS rounds – head count percentage

	Year	1973–74	1983–84	1993–94	1999–00	2004–05 (mixed recall)*	2004–05 (uniform recall)**	Tendulkar poverty line 2011–12*
Rural	Poverty line (₹/ person/month)	49.63	89.5	205.84	327.56	356.3	356.3	816
	HCR (%)	56.44	45.65	37.27	27.09	21.8	28.3	25.7
	Gini Coefficient	0.28	0.3	0.28	0.26	0.25	0.3	
	Poverty line (₹/ person/month)	56.64	115.65	281.35	454.11	538.6	538.6	1000
Urban	HCR (%)	49	40.8	32.4	23.6	21.7	25.7	13.7
	Gini Coefficient	0.3	0.33	0.34	0.34	0.35	0.37	
	As per Tendulkar Committee Report:							
	Year			1993–94		2004–05		2011–12*
Rural	HCR (%)			50.1		41.8		25.7
Urban	HCR (%)			31.8		25.7		13.7

Note:* http://www.planningcommission.nic.in/news/pre_pov2307.pdf
*comparable with 1993–94 estimates, ** comparable with 1999–2000 estimates

Source: http://planningcommission.nic.in/data/datatable/1705/final_38.pdf, http://planningcommission.nic.in/data/datatable/1705/final_42.pdf, Handbook of Statistics on Indian Economy, (Table 162, 15 September 2010) RBI.

The author thinks that India can if it follows the right policies and takes care of a number of impediments that plague it today and may in future.

Economists have looked at sources of growth. Adam Smith (1776) looked at it. What is contributed by factor accumulation and what is due to productivity growth have been examined for many countries. Solow's classical paper (1957) has generated a whole industry to measure TFPG. In India also many estimates of TFPG have been made (see Ahluwalia, 1991; Goldar, 2000, 2002; Goldar and Mitra, 2002; Virmani, 2004; Das, 2010)

The endogenous growth literature has developed these ideas further. Romer (1986) and Lucas (1988) and the literature that followed them have emphasized human capital formation for growth. TFPG is also an indication of technical progress and innovation. Joseph Schumpeter (1942) was one of the most well known proponents of their importance for economic growth.

A more technological explanation of TFPG, or Solow residual, is advanced by Ayres and Warr (2006, 2010). They show that energy use efficiency explains almost all of TFPG in the US.

What this shows is that sustained growth requires capital accumulation, increasing human capital and technological progress. Technical progress becomes even more important in the context of growing scarcity of natural resources of land, water and conventional energy resources and the constraint imposed by environmental limitation, such as imposed by climate change on the use of certain resources such as coal.

Inequality and poverty are also perceived as constraints to rapid growth. In the absence of access to credit the poor may not be able to acquire education and skills that can give them better income. This slows down human capital formation and in turn economic growth (Galor and Zeira, 1993). Inequality can also impede growth if it generates pressures for redistributive policies, which can adversely affect investment (Alesian and Rodrik, 1994). This may be particularly relevant for democratic and federal India where state and central governments of all parties seem to provide freebies to win votes. This seriously limits government's ability to provide public goods and services. Infrastructure development, education and health suffer. Also this raises fiscal deficit, which can also adversely affect growth. Apart from inequality, pressures for redistributive measures can also be generated when a country becomes a middle-income country. The country then slides into the middle-income trap (ADB, 2011). Thus, the structural impediments that India faces are the following:

1. development of infrastructure of power and transport;
2. education and skills development for human capital accumulation;
3. land and water scarcity that threatens food security;

4. access to energy at prices that maintain competitive edge;
5. the danger of the middle–income trap; and
6. governance.

The chapter will deal with the various impediments in turn. That these are important can be seen in the regression below estimated using the Cochrane-Orcutt procedure using data from 1951–52 to 2008–09:

log GDP= 0.74 log (road length) t–2 + 0.86 log (MW inst) t–1 + 0.21 log (secondary pass) t–2

t statistic (13.43) (6.26) (2.62)

Adj. R square: 0.99

Durbin Watson Statistics: 1.86

Where

GDP = gross domestic product at factor cost (base year 2004–05) in ₹ Crores.

Source: The data was taken from Handbook of Statistics, (Table 2. 15 September 2010), RBI.

Road length is in kilometers. (Source: Basic Road Statistics, Ministry of Road Transport and Highways, Table 1.7, 2010)

Megawatt or MW inst=installed power plant capacity (thousand mw). The data was taken from Economic Survey 2010–11(1.24A)

Secondary pass has been estimated as being equal to enrolment rates times (1-drop-out rate).

The gross enrolment ratio is the ratio of total enrolment, regardless of age, to the population of the age group that officially corresponds to the level of education shown (secondary).

Source: World Development Indicators or WDI, United Nations Educational, Scientific, and Cultural Organization (UNESCO) Institute for Statistics (1971 to 2008).

Infrastructure

Power

Vladimir Lenin's observation that 'Communism is Soviet power plus the electrification of the whole country' underlines the importance of electricity. Indian planners have put great emphasis on it. At the time India embarked on planned growth in 1950, its installed capacity was 1713 MW and generated 5.1 billion units (BU) of electricity. The country has come a long way since. By the end of March 2014 the installed capacity had increased to 243029

MW and the generation in 2013–14 was 966.4 BUs. Yet power shortages have been endemic. Despite the various measures undertaken, progress has been relatively little. Table 5.3 shows that, if anything, energy shortage increased till 2009 and peak shortage remained above 10 per cent. Since 2010–11 they have come down a bit and in March 2014 peak and energy shortages were 3.95 and 3.6 per cent respectively. However, the reduction in 2013–14 is largely due to the slowdown of the economy and particularly industrial output. If the economy is to pick up, power shortages may pick up too, unless action is taken to improve supply. The problem of increasing supply is compounded by the shortage of coal that many power plants face today. Domestic production of coal, despite having adequate reserves, has been falling short of requirement and India has been importing more than 100 metric tonnes (MT) of coal in recent years.

Table 5.3: All India electricity shortages

	2002–03	2003–04	2004–05	2005–06	2006–07	2007–08	2008–09	2009–10	2010–11	2011–12
Peak (MW)	-9945	-9508	-10254	-11463	-13897	-18073	-13024	-15157	-12031	-13815
Peak deficit (%)	-12.2	-11.2	-11.7	-12.3	-13.8	-16.6	-11.9	-12.7	-9.8	-10.6
Energy deficit (MU)	-48093	-39866	-43258	-52735	-66092	-73336	-86001	-83950	-73236	-79313
Energy deficit (%)	-8.8	-7.1	-7.3	-8.4	-9.6	-9.9	-11.1	-10.1	-8.5	-8.5

Source: http://www.cea.nic.in/reports/planning/power_scenario.pdf.

The shortages have persisted at state level too. Table 5.4 shows the average shortages over 2002–03 to 2009–10 and the growth rate of state domestic products over the same period.

Table 5.4: Average electricity shortage 2002–03 to 2009–10

States	**Average peak deficit (%)**	**Average energy deficit (%)**	**Average growth of state domestic product or SDP (%)**
Chandigarh	0.8	0.6	10.5
Delhi	3.4	1.2	10.0
Haryana	8.0	7.5	8.7
Himachal Pradesh	1.4	2.0	7.4

States	Average peak deficit (%)	Average energy deficit (%)	Average growth of state domestic product or SDP (%)
Jammu and Kashmir	19.4	19.0	5.5
Punjab	17.1	8.6	5.5
Rajasthan	6.6	2.3	6.3
Uttar Pradesh	19.3	18.6	6.0
Gujarat	22.4	10.9	10.0
Madhya Pradesh	18.4	15.4	5.9
Maharashtra	22.5	16.4	8.0
Andhra Pradesh	10.2	4.2	7.5
Karnataka	10.9	5.9	7.3
Kerala	6.9	3.9	8.4
Tamil Nadu	6.9	3.4	6.8
West Bengal	3.8	2.4	6.4
Arunachal Pradesh	12.5	11.2	5.9
Assam	10.2	7.0	5.5

Source: http://www.cea.nic.in/reports/planning/power_scenario.pdf and Central Statistical Organization

When growth rates are regressed across states against peak shortages and energy shortages over 2002–03 to 2009–10 one gets an elasticity of -0.1.

Regression results:

Log (average growth SDP) = 2.18 – 0.103 log (average peak deficit)

t statistics (18.52) (–2.01)

R square = 0.20

Log (average growth SDP) = 2.15 – 0.111 log (average energy deficit)

t statistics (23.84) (–2.40)

R square = 0.26

Thus, while it may seem that India has become used to dealing with power shortages, the reality is it has not been able to eliminate shortages. The reason for this is the poor financial performance of distribution companies (DISCOMs). Power theft and leakages along with high transmission and distribution (T&D) losses have strained the finances of DISCOMs. Table

5.5 shows AT&C (aggregate technical and commercial) losses. Large private distribution companies show reduction in AT&C losses. Some state controlled DISCOMs have also reduced their AT&C losses. However many DISCOMs show large losses. When the Bihar State Electricity Board cannot account for 50 per cent of electricity, its finances are bound to be stressed. It would not be able to expand electricity supply to rural areas nor would it be able to attract private investors to set up power plants in the state. For financial year (FY) 2011, the total losses of state electricity boards (SEBs) are estimated to be ₹ 68000 crore.

Table 5.5: AT&C loss (per cent)

Sl. No.	State	Utility	2003–04	2004–05	2005–06	2006–07	2007–08	2008–09
1.	Bihar	Bihar State Electricity Board	50.33	48.17	55.49	41.99	47.71	DNF
2.	Jharkhand	Jharkhand State Electricity Board	64.12	64.84	63.85	58.44	34.38	53.19
		Jamshedpur Utilities and Services	DNF	DNF	DNF	DNF	0.45	3.23
		Damodar Valley Corporation	10.94	7.41	7.47	12.56	13.45	9.11
3.	Orissa	Central Electricity Supply Utility (CESU)	50.57	51.12	49.18	47.58	45.93	45.23
		North Eastern Electricity Supply Company of Odisha (NESCO)	51.85	42.09	43.24	40.74	35.88	38.60
		Southern Electricity Supply Company of Odisha (SOUTHCO)	49.27	40.22	43.86	46.61	48.73	50.97
		Western Electricity Supply Company of Odisha (WESCO)	46.36	41.66	41.75	39.99	40.65	36.51
4.	Sikkim	Sikkim Power Department (Sikkim PD)	DNF	DNF	DNF	DNF	DNF	DNF
5.	West Bengal	West Bengal State Electricity Distribution Company	41.64	37.36	36.20	30.75	24.07	26.38

Sl. No.	State	Utility	2003–04	2004–05	2005–06	2006–07	2007–08	2008–09
		Calcutta Electricity Supply Corporation (CESC)	17.89	16.81	15.80	15.06	14.16	13.51
		DPSC	6.89	6.10	5.21	5.00	4.87	4.47
		Durgapur Projects Ltd	10.74	10.26	9.95	9.77	9.90	9.50
6.	Arunachal Pradesh	Arunachal PD	DNF	DNF	DNF	DNF	DNF	DNF
7.	Assam	Central Assam Electricity Distribution Company Limited (CAEDCL)	DNF	DNF	DNF	DNF	DNF	DNF
		Lower Assam Electricity Distribution Company Limited (LAEDCL)	DNF	DNF	DNF	DNF	DNF	DNF
		Upper Assam Electricity Distribution Company Limited (UAECDL)	DNF	DNF	DNF	DNF	DNF	DNF
8.	Manipur	Manipur PD	75.00	54.79	58.53	68.19	63.06	82.92
9.	Meghalaya	Meghalaya State Electricity Board (MeSEB)	DNF	33.89	44.69	32.94	31.62	31.63
10.	Mizoram	Mizoram PD	60.39	49.09	44.27	58.27	43.10	58.84
11.	Nagaland	Nagaland PD	DNF	DNF	DNF	DNF	DNF	DNF
12.	Tripura	Tripura PD	NA	NA	40.38	36.69	36.08	34.94
13.	Delhi	North Delhi Power Limited	44.86	33.81	26.52	23.74	21.63	18.96
		BSES Rajdhani	45.05	40.64	35.53	29.91	27.18	20.94
		BSES Yamuna	54.29	50.13	43.87	39.03	29.82	24.39

Sl. No.	State	Utility	2003–04	2004–05	2005–06	2006–07	2007–08	2008–09
		New Delhi Municipal Council (NDMC)	DNF	DNF	DNF	DNF	DNF	DNF
14.	Haryana	Dakshin Haryana Bijli Vitran Nigam (DHBVN)	36.99	36.86	34.24	32.38	25.94	26.72
		Uttar Haryana Bijli Vitran Nigam (UHBVN)	40.49	42.80	42.35	35.53	33.68	DNF
15.	Himachal Pradesh	Himachal Pradesh (HP) State Electricity Board SEB	38.64	35.89	29.99	26.16	25.85	23.13
16.	Jammu and Kashmir	J&K PD	70.79	66.78	66.64	67.56	73.43	72.93
17.	Punjab	Punjab State Electricity Board (PSEB)	DNF	DNF	24.67	24.08	22.69	19.90
18.	Rajasthan	Ajmer Vidyut Vitran Nigam (AVVN)	45.40	43.71	44.44	36.86	35.22	29.55
		Jodhpur Vidyut Vitran Nigam (Jodhpur VNN)	44.79	47.27	46.17	36.05	35.39	29.54
		Jaipur VNN	35.08	37.89	37.78	34.00	30.85	27.61
19.	Uttar Pradesh (UP)	Dakshinanchal Vidyut Vitran Nigam (DVVN)	53.73	52.76	51.03	44.35	45.51	34.92
		Madhyanchal Vidyut Vitran Nigam (MVVN)	NA	41.76	41.52	37.81	36.21	31.63
		Paschimanchal Vidyut Vitran Nigam (VVN)	DNF	DNF	DNF	DNF	DNF	DNF
		Poorvanchal VVN	DNF	DNF	DNF	DNF	DNF	DNF
		Kanpur Electricity Supply Company (KESCO)	NA	NA	NA	NA	NA	42.94

Sl. No.	State	Utility	2003–04	2004–05	2005–06	2006–07	2007–08	2008–09
		Noida Power Company	11.97	11.67	10.33	10.77	9.26	8.50
20.	Uttarakhand	Uttarakhand Power Corporation Limited (UPCL)	52.98	37.31	34.78	38.20	37.12	33.26
21.	Andhra Pradesh	Central Power Distribution Company (CPDC)	29.31	12.51	20.12	17.89	17.90	17.43
		Eastern Power Distribution Company (EPDC)	14.73	13.55	13.95	12.90	9.01	9.16
		Northern Power Distribution Company (NPDC)	27.55	22.66	20.46	19.18	14.58	15.45
		Southern Power Distribution Company (SPDC)	17.21	20.39	16.50	17.07	15.33	14.44
22.	Karnataka	Bangalore Electricity Supply Company (BESC)	27.00	29.60	34.26	26.63	26.12	18.18
		Chamundeshwari Electricity Supply Corporation (CESC) Ltd	DNF	DNF	42.85	35.97	35.70	26.08
		GESC	37.52	45.88	53.28	45.12	40.68	42.00
		Hubli Electricity Supply Corporation (HESC)	28.45	41.89	39.68	37.15	37.75	33.33
		THRECS	49.65	56.65	40.59	1.72	48.95	38.50
		Mangalore Electricity Supply Company (MESC)	DNF	DNF	DNF	DNF	DNF	DNF
23.	Kerala	Kerala Electricity Supply Board (KESC)	28.46	26.22	24.59	23.43	21.63	DNF
		Rubber ParkLimited (RPL)	56.45	38.01	6.38	3.83	1.87	2.79
		Techno Park Limited	22.60	20.20	16.19	14.45	16.30	13.83

Sl. No.	State	Utility	2003 –04	2004 –05	2005 –06	2006 –07	2007 –08	2008 –09
24.	Pondicherry	Pondicherry PD	DNF	DNF	DNF	DNF	DNF	DNF
25.	Tamil Nadu	Tamil Nadu Electricity Board	20.71	19.34	20.37	19.65	18.92	18.95
26.	Chhattisgarh	Chhattisgarh State Electricity Board (CSEB)	36.67	37.16	35.36	34.45	31.89	37.77
27.	Goa	Goa PD	DNF	DNF	DNF	DNF	DNF	DNF
28.	Gujarat	Dakshin Gujarat Vij Company (DGVC)	DNF	DNF	18.00	16.44	15.23	DNF
		Madhya Gujarat Vij Company (MGVC)	21.02	21.56	17.21	12.31	12.95	11.78
		Paschim Gujarat Vij Company (PGVC)	DNF	45.47	41.34	33.77	35.40	30.07
		Uttar Gujarat Vij Company (UGVC)	DNF	DNF	23.86	17.38	20.04	11.46
		Torrent Power Limted (Ahmedabad)	DNF	DNF	11.52	10.04	13.94	14.30
		Torrent Power Limited (Surat)	DNF	DNF	9.50	8.12	6.71	9.76
29.	Madhya Pradesh	MP (Madhya Kshetra Vidyut Vitaran Company) MKVVC	DNF	DNF	48.08	48.80	47.31	39.71
		MP Paschim Kshetra Vidyut Vitaran Company (PKVVC)	DNF	DNF	37.08	34.59	37.78	35.34
		MP Poorv Kshetra Vidyut Vitaran Company (KVVC)	DNF	DNF	41.33	42.82	42.06	40.88

Sl. No.	State	Utility	2003–04	2004–05	2005–06	2006–07	2007–08	2008–09
30.	Maharashtra	Maharashtra State Electricity Distribution Company (MSEDC)	DNF	DNF	DNF	33.98	26.08	24.14
		Tata	DNF	DNF	DNF	DNF	5.66	–0.32
		Bombay Electricity Supply and Tramways Company (BEST)	12.92	12.43	14.80	13.63	10.93	14.16
		Reliance	9.27	11.32	12.90	10.97	12.79	15.58
		Mula	53.53	44.41	45.09	51.70	39.37	43.17

DNF= data not furnished, N.A = not available

Source: http://www.forumofregulators.gov.in/Data/policy_Imp/AT%20&%20C%20LOSS%20DATA%20-%20STATE%20&%20UTILITES%20WISE.pdf

The high AT&C losses were interpreted as inefficiency of public sector state electricity boards. Power is a state subject and till 1980s, there were hardly any private power suppliers. With the reforms of 1991, private investors were encouraged, partly to provide competition and partly to increase pace of investment in the sector. By March 2014, 28 per cent of generating capacity was with central sector, 38 per cent with state sector and 34 per cent with private sector plants. To improve competition the Electricity Act 2003 was enacted, which facilitated open access to overcome the inability of state DISCOMs to provide uninterrupted electricity at stable voltages on demand. By permitting consumers to buy electricity from any supplier it was expected to attract private producers and also to put competitive pressure on state DISCOMs. Open access has not worked well as the incumbent DISCOMs have put various obstacles in the path of new suppliers. See Table 5.6.

Table 5.6: Progress of open access

State	As on	Applications received		Cases approved		Cases implemented		Cases rejected		Cases pending	
		No.	MW	No.	MW	No.	MW	No.	MW	No.	MW
Andhra Pradesh	3.6.09	11	1056	4	51	4	51	4	3	3	999
Jammu and Kashmir	nil	Nil	Nil	Nil	Nil	Nil	Nil	Nil	Nil	Nil	Nil
Assam	nil	Nil	Nil	Nil	Nil	Nil	Nil	Nil	Nil	Nil	Nil
Bihar	nil	Nil	Nil	Nil	Nil	Nil	Nil	Nil	Nil	Nil	Nil

State	As on	Applications received		Cases approved		Cases implemented		Cases rejected		Cases pending	
Delhi	nil	Nil	Nil	Nil	Nil	Nil	Nil	Nil	Nil	Nil	Nil
		No.	MW	No.	MW	No.	MW	No.	MW	No.	MW
Chhattisgarh	30.11.09	16	404	6	66	5	53	10	338	0	0
Gujarat	30.4.09	44	5534	40	5523	40	5523	4	10.8	0	0
Haryana	30.11.07	2	573	0	0	0	0	1	10.8	1	563
Himachal Pradesh	21.8.07	3	32	0	0	0	0	0	0	3	32
Jharkhand	27.11.07	1	40	0	0	0	0	0	0	0	0
Karnataka	31.03.09	11	332	7	290	4	256	2	13.45	2	29
Kerala	Jan. 2004	1	30	1	30	0	0	0	0	0	0
Madhya Pradesh	15.12.09	33	61	33	61	33	61	0	0	0	0
Maharashtra	31.08.09	64	14452	57	14311	7	163	3	3	8	142
Meghalaya	DNF	D.N.F	D.N.F	D.N.F	D.N.F	D.N.F	D.N.F	D.N.F	D.N.F	D.N.F	D.N.F
Orissa	31.5.09	1	50	1	50	1	50	1	50	1	50
Punjab	31.7.09	4	79	4	79	4	79	0	0	0	0
Rajasthan	1.12.09	33	294	31	280	31	280	0	0	2	8
Tamil Nadu	31.10.09	17	1959	0	0	0	0	0	0	17	1959
Tripura	nil	Nil	Nil	Nil	Nil	Nil	Nil	Nil	Nil	Nil	Nil
Uttar Pradesh	30.9.09	29	973	29	973	29	973	0	0	0	0
Uttarakhand	nil	Nil	Nil	Nil	Nil	Nil	Nil	Nil	Nil	Nil	Nil
West Bengal	15.5.08	4	86	3	36	0	0	1	50	0	0

Source: http://www.forumofregulators.gov.in/state_wise_OA.aspx (Forum of Regulators)

Many of the DISCOMs with low AT&C losses are urban DISCOMs that have very few, if any, farmer customers.

Initially the large AT&C losses arose because state supplied electricity to farmers without metering it at a fixed charge. With zero marginal cost farmers have little incentive to save on electricity use. The unmetered supply to farmers provided a shield to others to steal electricity with the cooperation of the staff of DISCOMs. For years the agricultural consumption was estimated as a residual, assuming T&D loss to be 20 per cent. Only when state electricity regulators were established some 15 years ago and when some of them insisted on measuring consumption by farmers on a sampling basis that suddenly the growth rate of agricultural consumption came down and AT&C losses went up.

Also many regulators do not act independently and follow the explicit or implicit directives of the state government. As a result, tariffs have not been revised even when cost of production has gone up. Moreover they do not insist on universal supply obligation as a result of which many state DISCOMs do not buy electricity even when it is available at reasonable cost and instead impose power cuts as they do not have the money to pay for it. Thus wind power plants did not find buyers for their electricity in Tamil Nadu. The high AT&C losses and the low tariff that regulators impose make DISCOMs financially stressed.

Many states provide highly subsidized electricity to farmers. The law requires states to compensate DISCOMs for the subsidy to farmers. However, since electricity to farmers is not metered there is a dispute about how much electricity is actually provided to farmers. The DISCOMs often do not get fully compensated.

Gujarat now supplies electricity to farmers through separate feeders so that how much electricity goes to farmers can be measured at the distribution transformer level and can be controlled. Since farmers are provided electricity at fixed time and at stable voltages, they also find it convenient and by and large support it.

If India wants double-digit growth, it must make the power sector healthy.

To deal with power shortages to provide stable 24/7 power the following needs to be done:

- Make state electricity regulatory commissions (SERCs) truly independent and free of political interference, so that electricity tariff can be fixed on sound economic principles.
- Separate feeders for all agricultural consumers so that power consumed by them can be metered at the transformer level and proper compensation can be provided to DISCOMs.
- Ensure that the restructured accelerated power development and reforms programme (RAPDRP) reduces AT&C losses by March 2016.
- Denationalize coal and permit private investors, national and international, in coal mining.

One bright light is that 90 per cent of the villages i.e., 536,860 villages were electrified as on February 2011. This would help rural development provided uninterrupted power at stable villages is supplied.

Roads

Roads are a critical infrastructure. Poor roads mean more time to travel from one city to another or one place to another even within a city. This wastes fuel as well as time of persons, increases cost of travel and transport and makes the economy that much less efficient. 10 years back a World Bank study had assessed the cost to the Indian economy to be ₹ 60000 crore a year of poor road infrastructure.

The National Democratic Alliance (NDA) government (1999–2004) had launched a major highways programme to build the corridors of divided lane highways consisting of a golden quadrilateral (GQ) connecting Delhi-Mumbai-Chennai-Kolkata-Delhi and a North-South Corridor and an East-West Corridor. Subsequently the United Progresive Alliance (UPA) government launched more schemes under the National Highways Development Programme (NHDP). Unfortunately the rate of progress in this has been less than desirable.

Table 5.7 gives the progress in various NHDP schemes. In many schemes the targets have not been reached, at least not on time.

Table 5.7: Status of different phases of NHDP (as on 30 April 2012)

Phase	Total length in km	Length completed in Km	Length under Imp.	Awarded work not started	To be awarded
I. GQ	5846	5840	6		0
II. EW - NS corridors port connectivity and others	7142	6018	691	12	421
III. Upgradation, 4-6 laning	12109	3798	2802	3669	1840
IV. 2-laning with paved shoulders	14799		3318	1866	9615
V. 6- laning of GQ and High density corridors	6500	940	1181		4379

Phase	Total length in km	Length completed in Km	Length under Imp.	Awarded work not started	To be awarded
VI. expressways	1000	nil	nil		nil
VII. Ring roads, bypasses and flyovers and others	700 km of ring roads by pass - flyovers etc	14	27		659

Source: Mid Term Appraisal for Eleventh five year plan, Annexure Table No.16.2, (http://planning commission.nic.in/plans/mta/11th_mta/chapterwise/chap16_transpost.pdf) and Planning Commission (2013a).

The slow development of roads during the last few years is partly due to the emphasis on Public Private Partnership (PPP) as the major method of road construction and the lack of agreement on how to go about it between the Planning Commission on the one hand and the Ministry of Road Transport on the other.

Recently, however, following the adoption of Chaturvedi Committee report (2009), situation seems to have improved in 2009–10, see Table 5.8.

Table 5.8: Contracts awarded under build-operate-transfer (BOT) (toll/annuity) during the Eleventh Plan

Year		BOT (toll)			BOT (annuity)	
	Number of contracts	Length (km)	*TPC (₹ crore)	No. of contracts	Length (km)	TPC (₹ crore)
2007–08	8	1108.8	8057	1	36.2	209
2008–09	7	638.7	8151			
2009–10 (upto March)	38	3188.2	31638	3	171.8	1775

*TPC – Total Project Cost

Source: Eleventh Plan Mid Term appraisal,
http://planningcommission.nic.in/plans/mta/11th_mta/MTA.html

The target of limited access expressways of 1000 km by December 2015 is pitifully small when compared to China, which has 74000 km of expressways by the end of 2010 (KPMG, 2013).

In this connection, India's emphasis on six laning of highways is misplaced. India should instead go for development of restricted access expressways. Open access highways lead to ribbon development and encroachment that reduce the carrying capacity of the highway.

Despite the poor quality and congestion of Indian roads, traffic is moving from railways to roads and today roads carry 45 per cent of passenger traffic and 65 per cent of freight.

Improving roads network with expressways can significantly reduce logistic costs in India, which is 14 per cent of total value of goods compared to 10 per cent for China and 6 per cent to 8 per cent for developing countries. The cost of rail and road transport in India was estimated to be 7 US cents/km compared to 3.7 cents in Japan and 2.0 cents in Canada. (Vaidyanathan, 2007)

Apart from expressways, rural road connectivity is important for all around inclusive economic growth. The PMGSY (Pradhan Mantri's Gram Sadak Yojana) has made good progress but yet much remains to be done. As per the Mid-Term Appraisal (MTA) of the Eleventh Plan, by March 2009, only 62,484 habitations were provided all weather road compared with the target of 1,67,000 habitations.

To speed up the development of roads, the processes of awarding projects to private sector under the PPP mode needs to be streamlined. Elaborate contracts that take thousand stitches in time to save nine delay projects and do not save on litigation.

Railways

As they are fuel efficient, railways are important for movement of goods and people. In fact a tonne km of goods transport by trucks uses six to eight times as much diesel as movement by railways does. A tonne kilometer (tkm) of goods moved by rail emits 29.9 grams of CO_2 compared with 160 gms moved by road. Similarly one passenger kilometre (pkm) by rail emits 75 gms of CO_2 compared with 175 gms by road and 229 gms by air, (Twelfth Plan).

For containing CO_2 emissions and also to reduce diesel consumption it is imperative that India develops railways into an efficient, attractive and preferred mode of transport. Indian Railways have the fourth largest network in the world with 64,460 km of routes and 113,994 km of lines on March 2011. The progress of railways has been poor. Only 11,864 km of lines have been added since independence and the hilly states are poorly connected with skeletal lines. Less than 50 per cent of the modest targets of capacity addition of the Eleventh Plan were realized, (Twelfth Plan).

The low rate of capacity creation is due to poor resource generation and efficiency of Indian Railways. Net return on capital at charge has been less than 4.5 per cent in recent years except from 2006 to 2008 when it was around 20 per cent. Loss in passenger service in 2010–11 was nearly ₹ 20000 crores, which was nearly three times the net revenue of ₹ 7,144 crores. Employee productivity in freight movement is one third that of China in NTKM (net tonne kilometre)/employee terms. It was higher in passenger movement as India's trains are highly over crowded.

Railways have been losing their share in goods movement as the tariff structure involves huge cross subsidy from freight traffic to passenger traffic. Freight yield in purchasing power parity terms is 72 per cent higher in China and 100 per cent higher in USA. For passenger traffic it is one third that of China and one ninth that of Japan. Apart from high tariff, loss of freight traffic is also due to low speed and uncertain delivery. Speed of goods trains averages 25 km per hour compared to 50 km per hour in USA. Railways can win back the share of freight traffic by increasing speed, ensuring on-time delivery, lowering tariff and containerization to increase safety and door-to-door delivery. For these dedicated freight train corridors (DFTC) are being planned between Delhi and Mumbai and Delhi and Kolkata.

Unfortunately very little progress has been made on the construction of these, even through budgetary outlays were made as far back as 2006. Only in late 2011, various wrinkles seem to have been ironed out and tender bids are being invited. Though the target for completion is 2016–17, given the difficulties of land acquisition it is likely to be delayed. Efficient, timely and low cost freight movement is vital for economic growth. Lack of this is a major impediment. With the permission of private players in container movements some progress has been made. More services need to be out sourced and overstaffing needs to be reduced (every minister adds to staff and initiates a new line to his constituency, which spreads railways meager resources thinly delaying completion of projects) to improve efficiency. Cross subsidy also needs to be eliminated.

Railways are losing passengers not only to roads but also to airlines. Air traffic has been growing at a rapid rate. India's air traffic was 100 million passengers in 2007 and is projected to be 581 million passengers in 2027 making India third in the world following USA and China (CAPA 2009, quoted in Yenneti and Joshi, 2010).

While private airlines provide competition to Air India and the demand for air travel is now met without the hassle of old days when one needed influence and had to beg and plead to Indian Airlines staff if a sudden need to travel arose. One can thus expect that air travel need would be met. However, given the constraints of containing greenhouse gas (GHG) emissions that will become ever more stringent with time, one should plan for the alternative of super fast trains between cities. China is building this network at a rapid rate and plans to build a network of 6000 km of super fast trains. In December 2009, its Harmony Express reached a maximum speed of 394.2 km per hour, faster than any train in the world.

Ports

Rapid growth would require greater integration in the world economy and much larger trade. For this, development of ports is critical. Today India has 12 major ports and 187 non-major ports. The ports are congested and the turnaround time at most ports is high and increasing. The average turnaround time was 3.41 days in 2004–05 and 4.38 days in 2009–10.

Table 5.9: Port-wise performance indicators of major ports

	Average pre-berthing detention (days)		**Average turn round time (days)**		**Average output per shipping berth-day (tonnes)**	
	2008–09	2009–10	2008–09	2009–10	2008–09	2009–10
Kolkata	0.62	0.22	4.6	5.38	3481	2331
Haldia	3.38	1.36	4.21	4.98	7643	6084
Paradip	2.32	0.05	4.78	9.04	12635	13853
Visakhapatnam	1.28	0.79	3.93	4.78	11171	10470
Ennore	0.18	0.02	2.35	2.35	28429	21565
Chennai	1.39	0.04	4.16	4.04	10970	11706
Tuticorin	1.1	0.4	3.66	3.97	5574	6505
Cochin	0.7	0.1	2.14	2.08	10599	10829

	Average pre-berthing detention (days)		Average turn round time (days)		Average output per shipping berth-day (tonnes)	
	2008–09	2009–10	2008–09	2009–10	2008–09	2009–10
N. Mangalore	0.65	0.03	3	3.06	13644	13876
Mormugoa	1.9	0.83	3.61	5.63	20797	18618
J. L. Nehru	0.97	0.27	1.97	2.02	22472	25627
Mumbai	1.31	0.3	4.76	4.2	6156	7015
Kandla	2.61	0.95	5.2	5.03	12998	13372
All ports	1.63	0.49	3.86	4.38	12033	1247

Source: http://shipping.nic.in/showfile.php?lid=125 (Ministry of Shipping)

Port capacities must be augmented and efficiency improved if it is not to stifle growth by making exports more expensive and non-competitive

Education and Skill Development

The Sarva Shiksha Abhiyan has made significant progress in primary school enrollment and in most states the rate exceeds 100 per cent. While dropout rate from elementary education (class one to seven) has come down from 54.60 per cent in 2001–02 to 43.06 per cent in 2007–08 and Table 5.10 shows this, it remains disturbingly high reflecting on the quality of schools. Only 16 per cent of the children entering primary school in 2006–07 will graduate from secondary school if the dropout rates remain at the level of 2006–07.

Table 5.10: Dropout rates at primary/elementary and secondary schools in India (1960–61, 1965–66, 1970–71 and 1975–76 to 2006–07)

Year	Primary			Elementary			Secondary		
	(I–V) classes			(I–VIII) classes			(I–X) classes		
	Boys	Girls	Total	Boys	Girls	Total	Boys	Girls	Total
1960–61	61.7	70.9	64.9	75	85	78.3	NA	NA	NA
1965–66	63.17	70.49	66.83	NA	NA	–	NA	NA	–
1970–71	64.5	70.9	67.7	74.6	83.4	77.9	NA	NA	NA
1975–76	60.21	66.18	63.195	74.3	82.8	–	NA	NA	–
1976–77	61.8	67.8	64.2	74	82.2	77.1	82.5	89.4	85.2

Year	Primary			Elementary			Secondary		
	(I–V) classes			(I–VIII) classes			(I–X) classes		
	Boys	Girls	Total	Boys	Girls	Total	Boys	Girls	Total
1977–78	56.9	66.7	62.7	73.9	81.7	76.9	82.1	88.7	84.7
1978–79	58.7	65.5	62.6	74	81.2	76.8	82.5	88.6	84.9
1979–80	57.3	63.7	59.8	73.5	81.5	76.6	81.2	87.8	83.7
1980–81	56.2	62.5	58.7	68	79.4	72.7	79.8	86.6	82.5
1981–82	51.1	57.3	53.5	68.5	77.7	72.1	79.4	86.8	82.3
1982–83	49.4	56.3	52.1	66	74.9	69.6	78.2	86.2	81.4
1983–84	47.8	53.9	50.3	66.1	75.3	69.8	76.4	84.8	79.7
1984–85	45.6	51.4	47.9	61.8	70.9	65.4	74.7	83.3	78.1
1985–86	45.8	50.3	47.6	60.7	70	64.4	73.9	83.1	77.6
1986–87	46.8	51.2	48.6	61.4	70.1	64.9	73.3	81.3	76.4
1987–88	43.3	49.4	46.9	58.8	67.5	62.3	72.1	80	75.3
1988–89	46.7	49.7	47.9	59.4	68.3	65.4	72.7	79.5	75.4
1989–90	46.5	50.3	48.1	61	68.7	64.1	71	77.7	73.7
1990–91	40.1	46	42.6	59.1	65.1	60.9	67.5	76.9	71.3
1991–92	40.3	44.3	42	56.1	62.4	58.7	69.6	76.3	72.3
1992–93	43.8	46.7	45	58.2	65.2	61.1	70	77.3	72.9
1993–94	36.1	38.6	37.2	58.4	63.4	60.5	69.7	75.4	72
1994–95	40.7	42.5	41.4	56.5	62.2	58.9	69.7	75.5	72.1
1995–96	41.4	43	42.1	56.6	61.7	58.8	66.7	73.7	69.6
1996–97	39.7	40.9	40.2	54.3	59.5	56.5	67.3	73.7	70
1997–98	37.5	41.5	39.2	53.8	59.3	56.1	66.6	73	69.3
1998–99	40.9	42.3	41.5	54.2	59.2	56.3	64.5	69.8	66.7
1999–00	38.8	41	40.3	53.3	57.7	55.1	64.9	69.9	67
2000–01	39.7	41.9	40.7	50.3	57.7	53.7	66.4	71.5	68.6
2001–02	38.4	39.9	39	52.9	56.9	54.6	64.2	68.6	66
2002–03	35.85	33.72	34.89	52.28	53.45	52.79	60.72	64.97	62.58
2003–04	33.74	28.57	31.47	51.85	52.92	52.32	60.98	64.92	62.69
2004–05	31.81	25.42	29	50.49	51.28	50.84	60.41	63.88	61.92
2005–06	28.71	21.77	25.67	48.67	48.98	48.8	60.1	63.56	61.62
2006–07	24.57	26.75	25.6	46.44	45.22	45.9	58.61	61.5	59.88

Source: http://education.nic.in/stats/Timeseries0506.pdf (MHRD)

As seen earlier secondary pass affects growth with lag of two years, which means primary education affects growth after a decade or so. Thus it is important to reduce dropout rates. For sustained growth over long term, India needs to act now.

Completing elementary education is a requirement for admission into Industrial Training Institutes (ITIs) or Industrial Training Centres (ITCs). There were 8039 ITIs/ITCs as on April 1, 2010 with a seating capacity of 11.35 lakh. This is an increase of 2925 ITIs/ITCs in three years, which is 57 per cent of ITIs/ITCs set up in 60 years after independence (MTA, P.211). India can set up ITIs/ITCs as needed but the major impediment to skill formation would be dropout rate at elementary level.

Land and Water Security

If Indian economy grows rapidly, the demand for agricultural products would increase. Also with higher incomes, the product mix demanded would change. With growing population this will require structural transformation of the agricultural sector. This transformation will have to take place when net cultivable area is decreasing slowly and when use of available water is seriously constrained by environmental concerns. Also the Planning Commission in its MTA has questioned the estimates of available water and lowered it significantly.

Analysis with a multi-sectoral inter-temporal optimizing model has shown that even though by 2040 the share of agricultural GDP may come down to around 5 per cent, agricultural output may seriously constrain growth given the limited availability of land and water and assuming that significant import of food grains would not be politically acceptable. Table 5.11 shows scenarios of the model with different Total Factor Productivity Growth (TFPG).

Table 5.11: Macroeconomic aggregates of scenarios of TFPG

	Rate of growth 2007–039				
Assumptions and dependent variables	**Base run (B)**	**Faster non-agricultural productivity growth (2011)**	**Faster agricultural productivity growth (2011)**	**Faster productivity growth in both sectors (2011)**	**'Chinese' productivity growth (2019)**
TFPG in agriculture	1.5	1.5	2.0*	2.0*	3.0**
TFPG in non-agriculture	1.5	2.5*	1.5	2.5*	3.0**
Consumption per capita	6.76	7.14	8.07	8.19	10.04

Rate of growth 2007–039					
Assumptions and dependent variables	**Base run (B)**	**Faster non-agricultural productivity growth (2011)**	**Faster agricultural productivity growth (2011)**	**Faster productivity growth in both sectors (2011)**	**'Chinese' productivity growth (2019)**
GDP	7.63	7.70	8.70	8.61	10.19
GDP agriculture	4.09	4.12	4.73	4.76	5.92
Food expenditures per capita	1.11	1.14	1.20	1.21	1.37
Rural food expenditures per capita	1.29	1.32	1.38	1.39	1.51
Urban food expenditures per capita	0.89	0.93	1.02	1.04	1.28

* Achieved over recent past

** Chinese Rates over last two decades

Source: Parikh *et al.* (2014)

It may be noted that the foodgrains imports in the base run exceed 40 Mt by 2020 and 60 Mt by 2040. Such level of imports may not be politically acceptable, even when the world market is able to supply them. One concludes that at least 2 per cent growth rate of TFPG in agriculture is needed for an 8 per cent aggregate GDP growth rate, and for a 10 per cent aggregate growth, TFPG of agriculture would have to be 3 per cent. Such TFPG can give the required agricultural growth of a bit over 4 per cent and over 5 per cent respectively. These are important constraints for achieving more than 8 per cent or more than 10 per cent of economic growth over the next 30 years.

The TFPG in agriculture has been around 1.5 per cent in the last 10 years and raising it to 2 per cent or even 3 per cent poses important challenges. If not improved, TFPG in agriculture can be an impediment to economic growth of the country.

In these scenarios the author had assumed that net cultivable land will remain constant at 140 Mha. However with growing urbanization with a projected urban population exceeding 550 million by 2040, cultivable land will go down and so higher TFPG will be required.

Land scarcity has affected and slowed down both development of infrastructures and industries. The Land Acquisition Act of 2013 is a recipe for interminable delays in starting any project. The act provides for Social Impact Assessment (SIA) for every piece of land acquired, however, small. Land acquisition can only begin after SIA is reviewed by an expert committee. This can be delayed further if it is challenged in a court. The act should be amended forth with to restrict SIA to acquisitions above a certain limit and to streamline the process. Also certain provisions of compulsory R&R (resettlement and rehabilitation) need to be modified.

A strategy for urbanization that provides for organic growth of cities and maintains or improves the quality of urban life is required. Without it rapid economic growth will be harder to realize.

Access to Energy

Energy scarcity and high-energy prices have been the bugbears of Indian economy. The oil shocks in 1973 and 1979 and the Kuwait war in 1991, all had adverse impact on India's growth. The high oil price in 2008 and since, has affected India's economic growth, inflation, financial health of oil firms and fiscal deficit.

India is short of oil and gas. Nearly 75 per cent of its consumption of petroleum product, which was around 150 Mt in 2011–12, is based on imported crude products. Domestic production of crude oil has remained at around 33mt since 1992, while crude imports in 2009–10 were 153 Mt as per Economic Survey, 2011. Natural gas production has gone up recently but optimistic forecasts do not expect it to provide more that 15 per cent of its commercial energy needs.

Coal remains India's major energy resource but even that will not last forever. The known extractable reserves of coal will run out in 40 years if consumption of it keeps growing as it has been. Table 5.12 shows the projection of commercial energy needs for 2031–32 from the expert group report on integrated energy policy (Planning Commission, 2006) the ranges are based on scenarios developed with a programming model (Parikh et al, 2009).

Table 5.12: Ranges of commercial energy requirement, domestic production and imports for 8 per cent growth for 2031–32

Fuel	Range of requirement in scenarios	Assumed domestic production	Range of imports*	Import Per cent
	(R)	(P)	(I)	(I/R)
Oil (Mt)	350–486	35	315–451	90–93
Natural gas (Mtoe) including coal bed methane (CBM)	100–197	100	0–97	0–49
Coal (Mtoe)	632–1022	560	72–462	11–45
TCPES**	1351–1702	—	387–1010	29–59
* Range of imports is calculated across all scenarios as follows:				
Lower bound = minimum requirement – maximum domestic production				
Upper bound = maximum requirement – minimum domestic production				
** Total commercial primary energy supply				

Source: Integrated Energy Policy, Expert Committee, Planning Commission of India

The table shows that India's import dependence for commercial energy could be as much as 29 to 59 per cent. The lower number is the result of policies to push energy efficiency in energy use and production and development of renewable sources of energy.

The requirement of coal would be at least 632 Mt, which in terms of Indian coal comes to 1580 Mt. Domestic production of coal in 2009–10 was 566 Mt. Expanding coal production thus poses a huge challenge in itself. The growing concern for environmental problems of coal mining and the go no-go classification of forests by Ministry of Environment and Forests (MOEF), make it even more of a challenge.

Though coal was India's major resource in 2011, it has not been able to produce the coal it needs and almost 20 per cent of its coal needs may have to be met by imports. Even if it is able to produce all the coal it needs in future, the constraints imposed by climate change and the requirement to restrict CO_2 emissions may make it difficult to use it all.

Thus meeting energy needs of a fast growing economy will require developing other options. Among these are nuclear, wind and solar energy. Nuclear power takes its own time to develop and is not likely to make any significant contribution in the next couple of decades. Wind can be mobilized quickly but its total energy potential is limited. The estimates of potential vary from 45000 MW by Ministry of New and Renewable Energy (MNRE),

150000 MW by some wind industry entrepreneurs to 350000 MW by some US scientists (Phadke *et al.*, 2011). Since wind power plants have a load factor of less than 20 per cent in India even the most optimistic assessment of India's wind power potential of 350000 MW, in terms of energy generated it will be equivalent to a 100000 MW of coal power plants. Solar has high potential, can be mobilized quickly but it costs a lot today.

Energy availability can thus constrain India's economic growth unless it develops economically viable new sources of energy. It is equally, if not more, important to make the energy sector efficient.

For this it is imperative that the sector is made competitive and that energy prices reflect their true opportunity costs. India is far from this situation. The government still sets prices of major oil products and coal. India already sees the shortage of domestic coal as coal India has not been able to meet demand and the sector has not been opened to private sector. The present policy of subsidizing diesel is unviable and can lead the government into a fiscal mess that can disrupt economic growth.

Middle Income Trap

A recent ADB (2011) study has raised the issue of middle income trap. Countries after reaching the middle income status, can find themselves stagnating when they are unable to compete with low income low wage economies in manufacturing export and are unable to compete with advanced economies in sectors requiring high skill and innovations. What are the dangers that India can get caught in this trap?

In India, a democratic country with high incidence of poverty, political parties compete in initiating welfare programmes for the poor. As the country's economy grows, more resources would be available with the government and the tendency of initiating new programmes can get a boost at the same time old programmes are never wound up. With substantial income coming from public welfare programmes, wages would rise. India then would not be able to compete in low wage manufacturing exports. The dangers of fiscal profligacy are also not insubstantial.

The growing uncertainty and currency problems in the Eurozone, coupled with persistent, almost double digit, inflation and resulting high interest rate do raise concerns about the country's ability to stay on high growth path. While India has diversified it exports to different countries, the industrialized countries still constitute an important part of India's exports. See Table 5.13.

Table 5.13: Percentage share of exports measured in ₹ by regions

Region	2007–08	2010–11
EU Countries (27)	21.17	18.65
Other west European (WE) countries	1.62	1.47
East Europe	0.07	0.06
Southern Africa	2.21	2.28
West Africa	2.13	1.81
Central Africa	0.16	0.19
East Africa	2.58	2.21
North America	13.49	10.73
Latin America	3.47	4.08
East Asia	0.87	0.78
Association of Southeast Asian Nations (ASEAN)	10.05	10.86
West Asia and North Africa (WANA)	18.64	22.59
Northeast Asia	16.23	16.74
South Asia	5.90	5.12
Central African Republic (CARs) countries	0.14	0.12
Other Commonwealth of Independent States (CIS) countries	0.92	1.02
Unspecified	0.34	1.28

Source: Website of Ministry of Commerce, http://commerce.nic.in/eidb/ergnq.asp

On the other hand, the pool of highly skilled people is sizeable and growing with the recent emphasis on expansion of higher, technical and professional education. Thus India should be a source of innovation. To be able to compete in the world for products and services based on innovations requires skilled workers. Arresting dropout rates at the elementary education level and expanding ITIs and ITCs become critical for creating a skilled workforce. Also India's own domestic markets are large and international or export competitiveness can be less critical. Of course an open economy needs to be internationally competitive irrespective of the size of its trade. However, countries do mange to provide some measure of protection through various means. Though one would not argue for such protection, when the chips are down countries resort to such measures and a democratic country is more likely to succumb to pressures from stakeholders.

Thus, if India maintains some measure of fiscal discipline, the danger of getting bogged down in the middle income trap can be avoided.

Governance

The spate of scandals that have come out in the open in recent months has created a sense of despair that the country is full of corruption and the effectiveness of governance is slipping.

However, there are a number of signs that the situation will improve and that lack of good governance would not keep the economy from growing. Yet corruption can affect inclusiveness of growth and deprive the poor and powerless from getting their legitimate share of prosperity. Among the hopeful signs are the following:

1. Ministers and industrial and business barons are in jail.
2. Right to Information (RTI) Act is increasing accountability.
3. An open society and a vigilant and intensely competitive media keep people on their toes.
4. Internet has empowered people in previously unimagined ways.

All these have lead to the election in May 2014 of a new Government, which promised growth and governance. Better governance is possible if those guilty of corruption are punished in time. This is one area where there is little progress. One hopes that the Modi government would deal with this problem on a priority basis. Judicial reform to deliver quick justice is vital to good governance.

Conclusion

There are a number of impediments in the path of the Indian economy that can prevent it from growing rapidly. Among the dangers are poor infrastructure, endemic power shortages, land and water availability, growing scarcity of energy, increasing dependence on imported energy, pending energy reforms and high dropout rates at primary and elementary school levels.

Most of these can be overcome with appropriate policies and measures taken in time.

In acknowledgement the author thanks Alwin D'souza for his help in preparing this chapter.

References

Ahluwalia, I. J. 1991. *Productivity and Growth in Indian Manufacturing.* Delhi: Oxford University Press.

Alesina, A. and D. Rodrik. 1994. 'Distributive Politics and Economic Growth', *Quarterly Journal of Economics* 109(2): 65–90.

ADB. 2011. *Asia 2050: Realizing the Asian Century.*

Ayres, R. U. and B. Warr. 2006. *Economic Growth, Technological Progress and Energy Use in the U.S. Over the Last Century: Identifying Common Trends and Structural Change in Macroeconomic Time Series.* Fontainebleau, France: INSEAD.

_______. 2009. *The Economic Growth Engine: How Energy and Work Drive Material Prosperity.* Cheltenham, UK and Northampton, Massachusetts: Edward Elgar Publishing. Retrieved 22 November 2010.

CAPA. 2009. 'China and India Domestic Traffic Soars. India: Centre for Asia Pacific Aviation', quoted in Yenneti, K. and Joshi, G. 2010. 'CO_2 Emission Reduction Potential from Civil Aviation Sector in India through Improvements in Operational Procedures: A Case of Delhi Mumbai Air-route', *India Infrastructure Report 2010, 3i Networks*, Chapter 18, 287–309. Oxford University Press. Available at: http://www.idfc.com/pdf/report/Chapter-18.pdf.

Central Electricity Authority. 2012. *Power Scenario at a Glance.* New Delhi. Available at: http://www.cea.nic.in/reports/planning/power_scenario.pdf.

Das, D. 2010. *Essays on Productivity and Efficiency in Indian Manufacturing.* PhD thesis. Mumbai: Indira Gandhi Institute of Development Research (IGIDR).

Estupiñán, N., A. Gómez-Lobo, R. Muñoz-Raskin and T. Serebrisky. 2007. 'Affordability and Subsidies in Public Urban Transport: What Do We Mean, What Can Be Done?', *World Bank Policy Research Working Paper #4440.*

Forum of Regulators. Available at: *http://www.forumofregulators.gov.in/Data/policy_Imp/AT%20&%20C%20LOSS%20DATA%20-%20STATE%20&%20UTILITES%20WISE.pdf.*

Galor, O. and J. Zeira. 1993. 'Income Distribution and Macroeconomics', *Review of Economic Studies* 60(1): 35–52.

Goldar, B. and S. C. Aggarwal. 2004. 'Trade Liberalization and Price-Cost Margin in Indian Industries', *Working Paper no. 130.* New Delhi: Indian Council for Research on International Economic Relations.

Goldar, B. 20–22 December 2000. 'Productivity Growth in Indian Manufacturing in the 1980s and 1990s', Paper presented at a conference to honour Prof. K. L. Krishna, organized by the Centre for Development Economics, Delhi School of Economics, on the theme 'Industrialization in a Reforming Economy: A Quantitative Assessment,' New Delhi.

_______. 2002. 'TFP Growth in the Indian Manufacturing in the 1980s', *Economic and Political Weekly* 37(49): 4966–68.

Goldar, B. and A. Kumari. December, 2003. 'Import Liberalization and Productivity Growth in Indian Manufacturing Industries in the 1990s', *Developing Economies* 41(4): 436–60.

Goldar, B. and A. Mitra. 2002. 'Total Factor Productivity Growth in Indian Industry: A Review of Studies', in *National Income Accounts and Data Systems,* edited by B. S. Minhas. Delhi: Oxford University Press.

Report of Expert Committee, Planning Commission of India. 2006. *Integrated Energy Policy.* New Delhi.

KPMG. 2013. *Infrastructure in China - Sustaining quality growth, KPMG, China.* Available at: http://www.kpmg.com/CN/en/IssuesAndInsights/ArticlesPublications/documents/Infrastructure-in-China-201302.pdf. Accessed on 27 August 2014.

Lucas, R. 1988. 'On the Mechanics of Economic Development', *Journal of Monetary Economics* 22(1): 3–42. Doi:10.1016/0304-3932(88)90168-7.

Ministry of Finance. 2012. *Economic Survey, 2011-12.* New Delhi: GOI.

Ministry of Human Resource Development (MHRD). Available at: http://education.nic.in/stats/Timeseries0506.pdf. Accessed on 15 February 2013.

Ministry of Shipping. Available at: http://shipping.nic.in/. Accessed on December 2011.

Nehru, Jawaharlal. 1958. *Jawaharlal Nehru's Speeches,* Vol 1, second edition. New Delhi: Publications Division, Ministry of Information and Broadcasting, Government of India.

________. 2010. 'Speech on the Granting of Indian Independence, 14 August 1947', *Modern History Sourcebook.* Internet History Sourcebook Project.

Parikh K. S., V. Karandikar, A. Rana and P. Dani. August 2009. 'Projecting India's Energy Requirements for Policy Formulation', *Energy – The International Journal* 34(8): 928–41.

Parikh, K. S., P. Ghosh and Hans P. Binswanger-Mkhize. 2014. 'Rapid Economic Growth in India: Technical Change in Agriculture, Irrigation and Food Security', *Integrated Research and Action for Development (IRADe) discussion paper.* New Delhi.

Patricia, C. A. 2010. 'Financing Indian Cities: Opportunities and Constraints in an Nth Best World', *World Bank Policy Research Working Paper 5474.*

Persson, T. and G. Tabellini. 1994. 'Is Inequality Harmful for Growth?', *American Economic Review* 84(3): 600–21.

Phadke A., R. Bharvikar, J. Khangura and J. Sathaye. 2011. 'Reassessing Wind Potential Estimate in India: Prelimainary Results and implications', *LBNL Discussion paper.*

Planning Commission of India. Availabel at: http://planningcommission.nic.in/data/datatable/1705/final_38.pdf, http://planningcommission.nic.in/data/datatable/1705/final_42.pdf,

________. 2010. *Mid Term Appraisal for Eleventh Five Year Plan,* (Annexure Table No.16.2).

________. 2013. *Twelfth Five Year Plan: 2012–2017: Faster, More Inclusive and Sustainable Growth,* Vol.1: 35. New Delhi.

______. 2013a. *Twelfth Five Year Plan: 2012–2017: Faster, More Inclusive and Sustainable Growth,* Vol. II: (Table 15–20). New Delhi.

Reserve Bank of India. 15 September 2010. *Handbook of Statistics,* (Table 2).

Romer, P. 1986. 'Increasing Returns and Long Run Growth', *Journal of Political Economy* 94(5): 1002–37.

_______. 1990. 'Endogenous Technological Change', *Journal of Political Economy* 98(5): 71–102.

Schumpeter, J. 1935. 'The Analysis of Economic Change'. *REStat* 17(May): 2–10.

_______. 1942. *Capitalism, Socialism and Democracy*. New York, London: Harper & Brothers.

_______. 1947. 'The Creative Response in Economic History', *JEH* 7(2): 149–57.

Smith, A. 1776. *An Inquiry into the Nature and Causes of The Wealth of Nation*. Random House Inc. London: W. Strahan & T. Cadell.

Solow, R. 1956. 'A Contribution to the Theory of Economic Growth', *Quarterly Journal of Economics* 70(1): 65–94. Doi:10.2307/1884513. The MIT Press.

_______. 1957. 'Technical Change and The Aggregate Production Function', *Review of Economics and Statistics* 39(3): 312–20.

The Electricity Act. 2003. Available at: www.powermin.nic.in.

The Wall Street Journal. 18 January 2011. *Road-Building Rage To Leave U.S. In Dust.*

Vaidyanathan, G. 2007. 'Current Status of Logistics in India', *PIANC Magazine No. 126,* February 2007, février 14.

Virmani, A. May 2004. 'Sources of India's Economic Growth: Trends in Total Factor Productivity', ICRIER *Working Paper No. 131.*

Section 3

Energy Security and Environmental Sustainability

6 The Co-benefit Principle and the Durban Platform: Towards an Inclusive Framework for Negotiating Climate Finance

A. Damodaran

Introduction

The benchmark of an efficient and just system of financing global public goods has centered on the maxim of 'new and additional resources that are predictable, adequate and equitable'. Despite the importance accorded by the global community for financing activities that address climate change issues, nothing much has been achieved in tangible terms. The concept of 'adequacy' of climate financing can be judged by the supply of funds relative to needs. Alternatively it can be taken to mean flow of funds that are sufficient to cover relevant costs (Muller, 2008). However, the flow of funds for development and global environmental causes has not been encouraging even in years when the global economy was booming. In 2007, ODA flows through bilateral and multilateral channels were only of the order of $103.7 billion (UNFCCC, 2008, p. 91). This represented on an average 0.23 per cent of the GDP of developed countries as against the Monterry ODA Target of 0.7 per cent of Gross National Income (Ibid, 2008).

While funds that are available for adaptation and mitigation are inadequate, the case of 'adaptation' is in particular fragile, since private funds do not have a propensity to invest in adaptation projects as compared to mitigation projects. The balanced emphasis on both mitigation and adaptation in the 'Durban Platform on Enhanced Action' adopted by the Parties to the Convention in 2011 and the incorporation of the 'loss and damage' window for poor countries by the Conference of Parties to the UNFCCC at its nineteenth session in Warsaw (UNFCCC, 2013), throws up in sharper relief the 'resource inadequacy' problem for climate change.

Nearly 60 per cent of total global investment in environmental projects has been mobilized from domestic sources (ibid, p. 90). Annual availability of adaptation funds has been less than $500 million/year (ibid, p. 92). By comparison, funds annual available for mitigation is pegged close to $1 billion/year. These figures pale into insignificance when reckoned against the figures of revenue generation from Clean Development Mechanism (CDM) and joint Implementation (JI) projects ($9 billion) in 2007 (Ibid, p. 92).

Estimates vary about the scale of funding required for adaptation. While the World Bank guesstimates current needs to be of the order of $9 to 41 billion, United Nations Development Programme (UNDP) estimates are higher at $86 billion. The UNFCCC places adaptation funding requirements to be in the range of $28–67 billion (Muller, 2008). The World Bank's estimates are based on anticipated flows from ODA, FDI and domestic investment towards adaptation activities. It is reckoned by the Bank that 10 to 20 per cent of the ODA and concessional flows amounting to $4 billion to $8 billion will flow for adaptation activities. The Bank likewise estimates that 10 to 20 per cent of FDI flows amounting to $2–$4 billion will find its way to funding adaptation activities. Gross domestic investment is expected to contribute $3 billion to $30 billion which works out to be 2–10 per cent share of aggregate domestic investment (Muller, 2008).

The terms 'new' and 'additional' that are part of the maxims of climate financing have complex implications. By the term 'additional' is meant 'over and above ODA' (Muller, op.cit). In a deeper sense, from a developing country perspective, the term 'new' could mean a new source of financing that is different from existing ones.

Allocation, Delivery and Governance of Financial Resources: Case of Global Environmental Facility (GEF) and UNFCCC's Adaptation Funds

Article 11 of the UNFCCC provides for a financial mechanism that functions under the aegis of the Conference of Parties (COP) of the Convention. This proviso forms the basic principle underlying a financial mechanism that is set up to fund climate relevant activities as envisaged by the Convention. Delivery of financial resources for climate relevant activities will depend upon a combination of factors. The first factor involves the adoption of resource allocation criteria that is based on a mix of efficiency and equity principles. The second factor refers to the ease by which needy countries can access the financial mechanism.

It is noteworthy that the GEF has been the primary financial mechanism for the UNFCCC ever since its inception. It assists both mitigation and adaptation activities.

Sagasti *et al.* (2005) argue that the efficiency of a financial mechanism refers to both the total amount of development financing available and to the match between financial instruments and the needs of developing countries. Presently in the GEF scheme of things, allocation follows the principle of geographical and sectoral balances (UNFCCC, 2008). The system seeks to follow the precepts of transparency and cost effectiveness, based on a combination of global environmental benefits and country performance (GEF EO, 2008 as cited in UNFCCC, 2008). However the resource allocation framework of the GEF is considered to be complex (ibid). There are issues relating to effectiveness and efficiency, predictability (in project selection) and the length of the GEF project cycle (ibid, p. 90).

There are a few dedicated adaptation funds in existence. Currently adaptation financing focuses on global and national environmental benefits. The Strategic Priority on Adaptation (SPA) funds under the Global Environmental Facility (GEF) Trust Fund requires generation of global environmental benefits. LDCF (Least Developed Countries Fund) and SCCF (Special Climate Change Fund) under GEF apply only when climate change affects core sectors of development such as agriculture, water, health or infrastructure. It does not carry the requirement of generating global environmental benefits (UNFCCC, 2008). GEF considers costs of adaptation as costs imposed on vulnerable countries to meet their immediate adaptation needs, which, in turn, are understood to be the additional costs imposed by climate change to render development climate-resilient (ibid). Since *ex ante* calculation of additional costs of adaptation is complex, the GEF has developed a sliding scale for LDCF and SCCF funding, which serves as a proxy for estimating additional costs. In terms of the sliding scale, smaller projects receive proportionately more GEF funding than bigger ones, since they are assumed to have a higher adaptation component (GEF, 2006). The scale provides an indication of the possible maximum amount of GEF funding that can be made available for a given project of a specific size (UNFCCC, 2008).

The allocation criterion described above has evolved over a period of time. However it is necessary to take into account certain other factors when planning for climate financing in the light of the new changes in climate governance regime brought in by the Durban Platform. In the case of adaptation, given the intrinsic difficulties of estimating additional costs, or separating global environmental benefits from domestic benefits, a financing criterion that focuses on 'incremental cost allocation and cost effectiveness' (based on the truism that Incremental Costs on Investment (IC) ought to be less than International Benefits (IB) (King, 1993) may not be enough. The ideal allocation criteria should be based on outcomes and incremental finance should focus on poorer or disadvantaged sections of human communities. This can complement existing approaches that are based on a 'sliding scale' to fund adaptation projects.

The GEF, is an operational entity set up by the COP of the Convention to carry out all business functions. The recently established 'Green Climate Fund' (GCF) is also structured as an operational entity (Laltanzio, 2013 and Muller 2014a and 2014b). In case of the GEF the operational entity 'pools' the received financial resources and disburses grants, concessional loans and risk guarantees etc through a fiduciary arrangement based on a Trust Fund approach. The Trust Fund is administered by a 'fund managing Trustee' such as the World Bank, which also provides for a mechanism for monitoring and evaluating utilization of all financial resources. (Reed *et al.*, 2009, 8–11). The operating system routes its resources through an intermediary or an implementing agency (World Bank, UNDP, ADB etc) which, in turn, provides technical advice to catalyse project preparation, design, execution and implementation. Delays in project cycles and disbursement of funds, currently noted as affecting the efficiency of financial mechanisms such as the GEF Trust Fund, are largely attributed to the intermediation processes.

The Adaptation Fund Board seeks to address this inadequacy by providing direct access to financial resources by the operating entity than seek its routing through an intermediary institution. China and G77 had in the past proposed a like framework for future adaptation financing mechanisms (UNFCCC, 2008, p. 45).

The needs of developing countries as relevant to adaptation funding include both the ability to access funds and ability to use these funds, in line with the country's adaptation requirements. Thus, flow of funds that are consistent with national action plans not only makes equity sense but also 'efficiency' sense. The proposal to give up on intermediation is welcome insofar as it cuts down on delays in the project cycle. But given the fact that most of the intermediaries (or implementation agencies) carry out country programmes in countries of action, it will be advisable to involve these agencies with project monitoring and evaluation in the post project approval phase. Countries that are short of capabilities in project design may find the role of intermediary institutions useful in the project cycle. (Reed *et al.* 2009).

Coming to the issue of management of these funds, it is clear that adaptation being a nationally driven process, their governance of the Adaptation Fund needs to be sufficiently broad based. However the allocation criteria that meet the needs of recipient countries and donors, should lie at the foundation of the functioning of an adaptation finance mechanism. A system that improves predictability in project selection satisfies donor interest, while programme based approaches to financing adaptation activities, enhance the acceptability of adaptation projects to recipient countries.

Predictability of Climate Financing

The issue of predictability of fund flows for adaptation activities is complex since it is guided by many factors[1]. Leave alone 'predictability' in flow of additional resources, there is great uncertainty even about maintaining existing levels of flows. Economic cycles and uncertainties associated with annual budgetary priorities have created considerable uncertainty about the flow of public financial resources from developed countries. Financial mechanisms like the GEF also face uncertainties in their periodic replenishment exercises. (UNFCCC, 2008) Private funds are even more unpredictable as they are vulnerable to changes in the economic environment as signaled by the capital markets. Beyond 'best endeavor' statements, there has been no firm and targeted commitments by developed countries when it comes to financing mitigation and adaptation activities in developing countries. The world economic crisis of 2008 had cast a big question mark on the adequacy and predictability of environmental financing. The $100 billion/year, GCF salted from 2020, will also be constrained by the 'absence of predictability'. Indeed there is considerable uncertainty about the sources that will fill the coffers of the GCF and the systems by which resources need to be allocated by the Fund (Laltanzio, 2013; Muller, 2014a and 2014b).

The Dimensions of Equity Articulated in Classical Climate Financing Negotiations

There are four dimensions of 'equity' that have been conventionally articulated in the climate financing negotiations by developing countries. The first dimension is the adherence to the principle of common but differentiated responsibility specified in Article 3.1 of the UNFCCC. The second dimension relates to honouring the needs of the economically less advantaged members of the United Nations Framework Convention on Climate Change (FCCC). Where the principle of equity underlies financing systems, the notion of returns on investment is not the most significant consideration in resource allocation and deployment. In the context of environmental financing of global public goods, equity connotes allocation of funds to nation states or local communities that require them most. Nation states and poor local communities, which are not in a position to bear the costs of conservation ought to be the focus of an equity driven environmental financing system rather than nation states or communities that are able to conserve resources at the least cost. Typically private capital tends to flow to projects that afford the highest risk adjusted returns, while international and national public finances like ODA and related budget grants, would gravitate towards projects that are high in social returns.[2]

The third dimension of equity arises from climate financing being independent and supplementary to other forms of financing. The equity dimension of climate financing is not captured, if environmental financing is done at the cost of essential financial resources that a community requires for its developmental needs. Here the concept of equity comes closer to the notion of additionality. Indeed environmental financing could be at the expense of ODA flows. As mentioned, the Monterry target on ODA remains to be realized. Therefore, environmental financing of global public goods projects should not be at the expense of potential ODA flows. This will weaken the development process in least developed countries that have been dependent on ODA. New revenue raising instruments like auctioning of emission trading permits or new carbon taxes contribute to the mobilization of resources that are new and additional. As far as climate change is concerned, financing of adaptation measures, from new and additional sources that are 'over and above the Monterry target on ODA, would form the equity foundations of the post 2012 global environmental financing architecture.

The fourth dimension of equity relates to 'appropriateness' of financial flows. This is of special relevance to the adaptation issue. Following Muller (2008, p. 22–23), appropriateness refers to a financial measure, which considers adaptation to be a historical debt of developed countries towards developing countries (ibid, p. 22). In terms of this paradigm that views historical debt as an equity issue, since the costs of adaptation have been imposed by developed countries on developing countries over time, any effort to have an adaptation financing system as a loan or even a conditional grant is perverse and inappropriate. Thus loans and grants for adaptation are not appropriate even if they are concessional. Only unconditional transfer payments are appropriate. The full incremental costs of adaptation must be met by these transfer payments (Sethi, 2008).[3] The concept of historical debt is thus philosophical and fundamentally linked to 'equity' though this point is getting to be sidetracked. Friman and Linner (2008) explain how the takeover of the 'historical obligation debate' by the 'technology school' (the Scientific and Technical Advisory Panel (STAP) in the UNFCCC has undermined the equity notion of the concept.

Relevance of Classical Climate Finance Maxims in the Post Durban Platform Phase

The adoption of the Durban Platform for Enhanced Action in December 2011 by the COP of the UNFCCC in its seventeenth session in Durban, marks a major shift in the paradigm of Convention related obligations. The Durban Platform envisages both mitigation and adaptation obligations for all the parties to the convention, unlike in the pre-Durban phase when only developed countries had the obligation to carry out mitigation measures (Bodansky, 2012). Though the GCF has been established to take care of the requirements of developing and least developed countries to implement both mitigation and adaptation programmes, the progress with resource mobilization for the fund is tardy. The fund does not look like being able to meet the scale of assistance required by least developed countries to implement the twin obligations. Thus the norm of adequacy will not stand test under the new circumstances. For the same reason the notion of additionality also stands on weaker foundation in light of post Durban realities. It appears that the option of 'new' instruments would have to be explored more intensely to facilitate resource mobilization. This will be in shape of market based instruments, private sector investments and other non public funds – both national and international. Such 'new sources' of funding will be sensitive to the issues of transfer of technologies, intellectual property rights regimes, risk management and finally 'risk adjusted return on investments'.

Co-benefits Approach to Climate Financing and Equity

An unexplored dimension of equity in both the current and classical negotiations on climate financing is that of the relationship between adaptation activities and mitigation commitments. The Third Assessment

Report of the Inter-Governmental Panel on Climate Change (IPCC) states, that until 2050 AD, the global mitigation efforts that are designed to cap GHGs (Green House Gases) at 550 parts per million (ppm) would benefit developing countries significantly, particularly when combined with enhanced adaptation action (IPCC, 2007). From the equity perspective it is important that the co-benefits of adaptation and mitigation are premised on common and differentiated responsibilities (Damodaran, 2012). Fund flows for adaptation programmes are primarily driven by national resources and grants. Required as they are to quantitatively reduce CO_2 emissions below the 1990 baseline, it is important for developed countries to take up firm commitments to carry out mitigation activities in the larger interests of reducing the financial burden on developing countries on adaptation activities.

In the absence of mitigation measures, adaptation is a costly necessity to prevent the livelihood driven sectors of developing countries from collapsing (Stern, 2006). However, with active mitigation measures, adaptation processes are less costly. India spends 2 per cent of its GDP on adaptation and is expected to spend more as the worst impacts of climate change intensify (Saran, 2009). Agricultural systems in the developing world are already threatened by climate variability which increases their vulnerability to food insecurity (Bates Bryson *et al.*, 2008). The hydrological systems in the developing countries of Asia and Africa are threatened by climate change, resulting in serious imbalances in water budgets. Coastal areas in developing countries are also threatened by sea level rise.

Low levels of mitigation efforts would only serve to increase adaptation costs for developing countries further (Lewellyn and Chaix, 2007).

Table 6.1 brings out this fact in relation to the situation of coastal, semi-arid agriculture, degraded forests and the water resources sectors with reference to Karnataka in India. Based on modal values of costs and benefits accruing to the various sectors in current prices , elicited through field surveys conducted in 2008, the relative loss of benefits and relative incremental costs have been estimated in columns five and six of Table 6.1. Amortized value of capital and operational costs have been taken to estimate the relative costs of various mitigation options, while as far as benefits are concerned, the same has been estimated in terms of damages avoided. It is evident that the softest adaptation measures are way below the most rigorous adaptation measures in terms of incremental costs or lost benefits. The higher the degree of abatement achieved through mitigation, the lower the adaptation costs (Damodaran, 2009 and 2012).

Table 6.1: Relative benefits or costs from adaptation projects for different mitigation scenarios

Sl. No.	Sector 2	Adaptation activity 3	Mitigation level 4	Modal values at current prices in ₹	
				Benefit[2] 5	Cost[3] 6
1	Agriculture	Drought resistant plant variety	Low	0.30	–
		Just in time sustainable irrigation	Medium	0.60	–
		Business-as-usual[1]	High status quo (irrigated crops)	1.00	–
2	Coastal zone	Sea walls	Low	–	1.00
		Bio-shields (mangrove plantations)	Medium	–	0.17
		Business–as–usual[1] (Routine protection measures)	High	–	0.003
3	Degraded land	Low transpiration	Low	–	1.00
		Medium transpiration	Medium	–	0.38
		Business-as-usual (high transpiration)	High	–	0.25
4	Water (groundwater)	Artificial recharge	Low	–	1.00
		Natural recharge	Medium	–	0.09
		Business-as-usual[1]	High	–	0.01

Notes: Business-as-usual – current level of utilization of the natural resource without any adaptation activity being undertaken.

Optimal yield of finger millets in Karnataka (probability) in dry land and irrigated conditions

Cost of undertaking the adaptation activity

Source: Damodaran (2009) with modifications

The Economic Rationale of Mandatory CO_2 Mitigation

Flexible mechanisms like clean development mechanisms (CDM) and joint implementation (JI) though CO_2 mitigating in nature, are not substitutes for graduated and definitive tangible emission reductions by developed countries in their own soil. Being of small scale their impacts in reversing GHG emissions are weak. Besides they can weaken the foundations of efficient price discovery by carbon markets. This will be evident from Figure 6.1 where MC_{m1} is the marginal curve of mitigation while MC_a is the marginal cost of adaptation. It is evident from Figure 6.1 that the lower the abatement level, the higher the marginal cost of abatement and vice versa. At the point where MC_a intersects MC_{m1} curve, the carbon price is 'P', which corresponds` to an abatement level Q. Let it be assumed that Q is equivalent to the 'Quantitative Emission Reduction or Limitation Objectives' (QERLO) targets to be met by Annexure 1 countries under the Kyoto Protocol. Beyond Q, if abatement is sought to be achieved through 'low cost or low quality and discounted CDM and JI projects credits, the effect will be the creation of a kink in the $MC_{m.}$ curve. The new MC_{m2} curve which commences from Q along the MC_a curve represents a low cost abatement trajectory for increased abatement beyond the QERLO. As abatement increases to Q_2 the price of carbon falls to 'P_1' from 'P'. Ideally the carbon price should have risen if Annexure 1 countries had contributed to the increase in abatement level to Q_2 and this would have happened if allowances to emit were distinguished from voluntary mitigation units like certified emission reduction units (CERs). At the carbon price of 'P1' the gap between MCm and MCa is the maximum, with supply of mitigation action being OQ_1 as compared to the demand for adaptation action which is OQ_2. This is clearly a non equilibrium situation that potentially creates a deadweight loss represented by the arc 'Q_1YQ_2'. Besides, low carbon prices pulls down CER prices arising from CDM projects which acts as a disincentive to non-Annexure 1 countries. (Damodaran, 2010)

Mandatory CO_2 reductions enable the social cost of carbon to be better reflected by carbon markets, thus enabling the realization of a carbon market structure that recognizes the principle of 'equitable burden sharing'. Any national effort on the part of developing countries to achieve mitigation can only be a supplement to the efforts on the part of developed countries.

Thus apart from reasons of fulfilling the Kyoto obligations, developed countries need to undertake mitigation measures in the interests of developing countries that will have to bear the brunt of climate change. As a carbon product, a CER from a CDM project in a developing country needs to realize an average revenue equal to MC_{m1}. Over a period as MC_{m1} shifts parallely due to cost–effective technological solutions, mandatory mitigation costs lower, resulting in lower carbon prices that are achieved without market distortion.

Figure 6.1: Efficient carbon price discovery – the rationale of mandatory mitigation

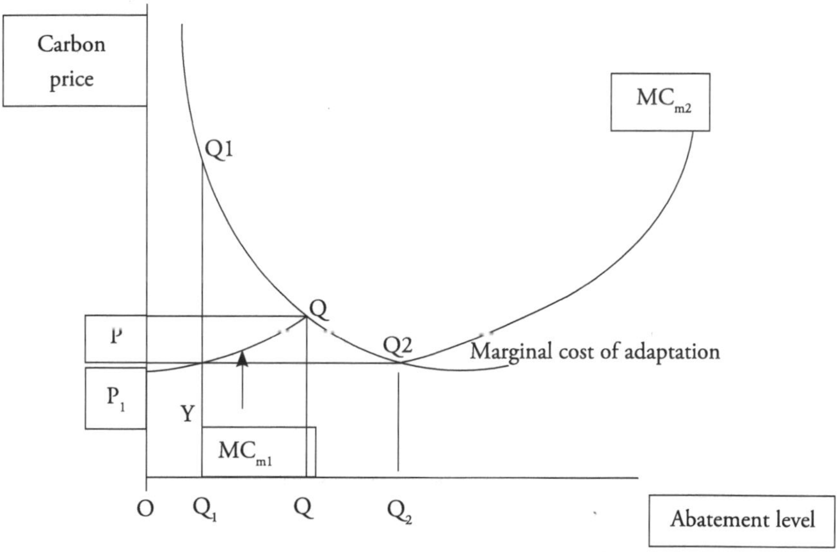

Source: Damodaran (2009)

Carbon Markets: Resource Mobilization Source Versus Technological Transformation Tool of C

Carbon markets are a good source of climate financing if designed well (Stavins, 2007). Developing countries (including emerging economies) can source their financial resources from carbon markets for carrying out their adaptation and mitigation obligations arising from the Durban Platform. Carbon markets that are designed in the manner described are more equitable and helpful to developing countries. Indeed the present system of sourcing adaptation funds from the carbon allowance markets is based on a sound conceptual basis.

Developing countries, and notably India, have maintained that financial flows from market mechanisms such as 'Cap and Trade' can only be supplemental to and not a substitute for multilateral financing mechanisms that have been envisaged for adaptation and mitigation (Saran, 2009). Much of the concerns about carbon markets arises from their non-transparency and deviation from the fundamental philosophical character of FCCC obligations. In case these deficiencies are addressed, carbon markets can be rendered more efficient and equitable. But this is only part of the problem.

However the more important constraint with carbon markets has been their limited 'transformational ability' to bring about pervasive technological change that can backstop global warming and the other externalities of climate change in a cost-effective manner.

Carbon markets should be based on strong mitigation action if they have to acquire a greater transformational ability in terms of pervasive technological change. A carbon market should enable enhanced mitigation action through periodic tightening of emission standards, if it has to be 'transformational' in the technological sense of the term. However, since standards cannot be revised frequently and need to follow a cycle of three to five years to there are limits to which carbon markets can be expected to deliver transformation.

Carbon Markets: Resource Mobilization Source Versus Technological Transformation Tool

[illegible]daptation and mitigation are viewed in their mutual interdependence, [illegible] be helpful in altering the livelihoods of poor people in developing cou[illegible] Adaptation has an organic linkage to national action programmes on clim[illegible]e change in developing countries and hence enjoys greater national commitment. However, mitigation activities encourage development of transformational and backstopping technologies (such as renewable energy) unlike adaptation activities which are confined to conventional technologies that are not back stopping in nature. Though there are opportunities for private sector to contribute to adaptation funding, these may not be in the direction of back stopping technologies as much as they are on 'calamity management'. Further adaptation projects suffer from what Grubb (2008) refers to as the 'risk of maladaptation' arising from uncertainty in regional climate predictions, masking of natural climate variability and adoption of failure prone capital intensive projects. Indeed maladjustment may cause even routine technologically shallow adaptation projects to have a high risk factor.

Coastal zone projects, water sources and agriculture R&D are three promising areas for adaptation action in the Indian situation. However, adaptation 'projects' associated with the coastal and water conservation have a high beta factor and risks of uncertainty about returns, when it comes to returns on investments. Breach of sea walls, non-realization of anticipated property values on shore lands that are protected by expensive sea walls, decline in groundwater quality from artificial recharge projects etc are potential risks on returns from such projects. (Damodaran, 2006 and 2009). This is more so when capital-intensive adaptation projects are taken up to provide for slow progress on the mitigation front. Indeed the higher the levels of mitigation, the lower the risks from adaptation projects and hence higher the risk adjusted return on adaptation projects. Private capital flows on adaptation projects will be higher if risks are less in relation to mean returns and this can happen only if mitigation measures are accelerated. Viewed in this manner there is a deeper logic to the emphasis of the Durban Platform on both adaptation and mitigation by all countries. The GCF's emphasis on supporting both adaptation and mitigation projects in developing and least developing countries also receives considerable support from the co-benefit approach. Indeed the co-benefit principle has gained considerable traction since COP 17 at Durban in December 2011.

Let 'Ω' be the optimal investment in mitigation projects and 'I' actual investments, given normal risks (σ), then

$$\sigma = \begin{cases} 0, & \text{if } I \geq \Omega \\ y, & \text{if } I \leq \Omega \\ x, & \text{if } 0 < I < \Omega \end{cases}$$

In Figure 6.2, the concave curve represents the efficient frontier of investment. As the curve shifts from P_1 to P_2 and investments on mitigation projects rises, the risks on adaptation projects decreases from OX to OY. This contributes to improved risk adjusted return from adaptation projects.

Figure 6.2: Benefits of mitigation on risk return patterns from adaptation projects

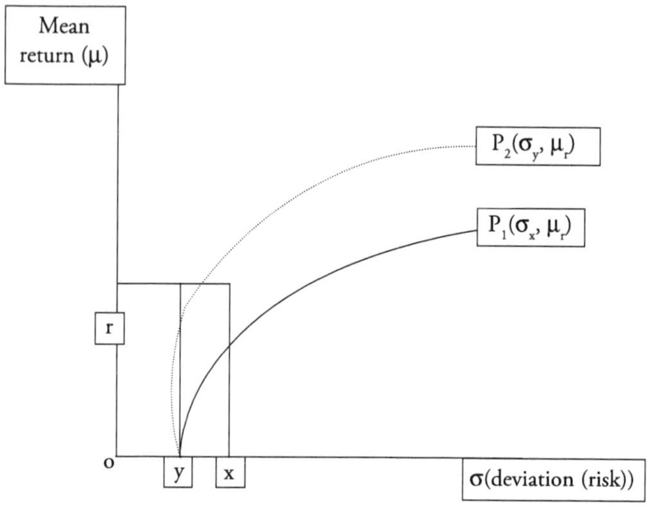

Source: Damodaran (2009)

Why the Co-benefit Principle is Currently Stymied? A Game-theoretic Explanation

Barrett (2012) classifies the game theory problematique in the climate/environmental arena into three: 'co–ordination games', 'Prisoners Dilemma' and 'catastrophic avoidance suboptimal'. Ray and Vohra (1997) have analytically demonstrated the relevance of equilibrium binding agreements, while Carraro (1998) has modeled the impact of coalitions in the Kyoto Negotiations through a two stage game theoretic framework.

In this chapter the author looks specifically at possibilities of Nash/stable equilibria, which is one of the three outcomes of a Prisoners Dilemma game situation. The author also sees possibilities for a 'focal point equilibrium' to emerge (Schelling, 1960) in case the co-benefit principle becomes the foundation principle for climate financing negotiations in the post Durban Platform phase.

Despite its intuitive and philosophical appeal, the co-benefit principle has not been entirely internalized in the past by donors of climate funds. This has been in spite of the emphasis of both the Durban Platform and the

GCF on mitigation and adaptation action by developing countries. This co-benefit principle also does not appear to be appreciated by recipients of climate funds. The current multilateral and bilateral assistance schemes in developed countries view adaptation financing as an alternative to mitigation financing rather than viewing the latter as obviating the magnitude of the former. Indeed this casts special challenges to operational entities like the GCF which is already burdened by procedural aspects of resource allocation (Muller, 2014a).

The resource allocation game involving developed country/major economy donors and developing/least developed country recipients is illustrated in Table 6.2. It describes a matrix of possibilities entailed by a two-fold ('high' and 'low') allocation regime of financial resources between mitigation and adaptation activities.

Table 6.2: Resource allocation options between mitigation and adaptation*

		Mitigation	
		H	**L**
Adaptation	**H**	HaHm	HaLm
	L	LaHm	LaLm

*(H–High Level of Financing, L–Low Level of Financing)
Source: Author's compilation

The current (or the pre-Durban Platform) scenario with regard to resource allocation for adaptation vis-a-vis mitigation can be contrasted from the incipient post Durban Platform phase in terms of changing equilibrium positions entailed by the changing climate change policy regimes in the two phases.

Thus the current scenario is 'La Lm' (which is undesirable) and the 'best endeavor' of negotiators from developing countries appears to be reach 'HaHm'

LaLm ⟶ HaHm

As an equity ideal, though the trajectory from the current depressing scenario is to be welcomed, there has been no progress towards the 'best endeavor' ideal since, developed countries feel that the 'HaHm' is infeasible given their resource constraints.

In terms of the game theory paradigm, the situation of a stable (Nash) equilibrium can be traced to HaLm or LaHm.

HaLm is a stable (Nash) state, since moving from LaHm to LaLm is morally infeasible for donor countries while moving to HaHm is burdensome. Thus donors (developed countries) prefer HaLm as the stable solution

For recipient/developing countries the stable/Nash solution is LaHm since movement to HaHm is infeasible while a shift to LaLm involves material loss to them.

Thus assuming the game to be 'Я' and 'Ng' to be no of countries involved in negotiations, 'S' to be the Strategy of the ith player and P to be the payoff from playing a game of strategy, one can represent the game as

Я = Ng {Si } iεNg {Pi} iεNg

where

LaLm $\longrightarrow$ HaHm

And where HaLm and LaHm are stable (Nash) equilibrium since

HaLm $\not\longrightarrow$ HaHm: HaLm $\not\longrightarrow$ LaLm: LaHm $\not\longrightarrow$ LaLm: LaHm $\not\longrightarrow$ HaHm

In terms of relative payoffs, the situation in Table 6.2 can be summarized as below:

Developed country donors

P_{11}(HaHm) < P_{12}(HaLm)> P_{21} (LaHm) < P_{22}(LaLm)

This is so due to higher unit costs and risks of mitigation projects as compared to low unit costs and the low technological content of adaptation projects.

Developing country recipients

P_{11}(HaHm) < P_{12}(HaLm) < P_{21} (LaHm) < P_{22}(LaLm)

Given the realities of the post Durban Platform phase and the assuming the acceptance of the co-benefit principle by all parties to the UNFCCC, it is possible that developing countries would prefer P_{21}(LaHm) as it could offer them maximum pay-off. Apart from expecting developed countries to spend more on securing mitigation of their CO_2/GHG emissions, developing countries would like developed countries to provide them more resources on promising mitigation projects that can reduce their CO_2 emissions while also meeting their development needs.

Incipient trend: Towards 'focal point equilibrium'?

The current (pre-Durban Platform) scenario as far as payoffs go is P_{22} (LaLm):

The best endeavour is to move to P_{22} (LaLm): $\rightarrow$ P(HaHm)

The feasible trajectory, which can be conceived as the twin Nash Equilibria are : P_{12}(HaLm) and P_{21} (La Hm)

It is likely that one of the two Nash Equilibria states, viz P_{21} (L_a H_m) will emerge as a 'focal point equilibrium' if the co-benefit principle emerges as the guiding principle of the Durban Platform and the GCF. The result can be that even in developing countries, in the wake of the Durban Platform, the focus will be on mitigation technologies that are backstopping in nature and are linked to development needs of these countries. The ideal candidates are renewable energy technologies that relieve energy shortages in developing countries, while at the same time mitigating CO_2 emissions through avoided emissions.

However, one casualty of this development is that the maxim of 'additionality' that was one of the key climate financing norms/maxims in the pre Durban Platform situation would get diluted in the process.

To sum up as per Table 6.2, the current dispensation favours a regime of high resource allocation for adaptation as compared to mitigation (H_aL_m). This is on account of the fact that adaptation projects, despite being capital intensive, entail less capital and unit costs as compared to mitigation projects. On the other hand, in order to achieve a cap in rise in temperature below 2^{0}C, the objective should be to attain the stable equilibrium of 'LaHm'. The 'LaHm' equilibrium position would be in the spirit of the Durban Platform and the decisions arrived at the Warsaw Summit of November, 2013.

'LaHm' can be achieved if climate financing can secure technological transformation by developing and commercializing backstopping technologies that are cost-effective in nature, rather than relying on adaptation projects that are 'calamity managing' than backstopping in nature (sea walls, large emergency water reservoirs etc). This aspect needs to be looked into by the negotiators in the forthcoming rounds of negotiations associated with climate financing.

Resource Mobilization Models – Negotiation Strategies and Outcome in the G20 Forum

The G20 has been addressing climate change and climate financing issues.

Indeed, commencing from the Pittsburgh and Toronto Summits, the G20 forum has been actively focused on climate finance in general and resource mobilization in particular (Damodaran, 2010 and World Bank, 2011). At the recent G20 Summit at St Petersburg held in September 2013, the Group signed an agreement to reduce the emissions of GHG and to support the a universal climate agreement by 2015 under the aegis of UNFCCC. In pursuance of this decision, the G20 is expected to focus on the fine print of resource mobilization.

The forthcoming negotiations on resource mobilization will involve two parties viz developed countries and the major (emerging) economies, which could include the BRICS bloc, that has been under pressure to not only take up mitigation obligations but also to contribute to financial resource mobilization to address climate change.

Table 6.3 illustrates the matrix of possibilities and options available to the developed and other major economies of the G20 to mobilize resources for climate change.

Table 6.3: Possible negotiating positions on resource mobilization options in G20*

		Emerging economies		
		P	**CM**	**PDI**
	P	P,P	P,CM	P,PDI
Developed countries	**CM**	CM,P	CM,CM	CM,PDI
	PDI	PDI,P	PDI,CM	PDI,PDI

*(P–public investment: CM– carbon market: PDI– private direct investment)
Source: Author's compilation

Table 6.3 illustrates the various possible negotiating positions in the G20 involving the developed countries and other major economies that include BRICS countries. As mentioned both in the UNFCCC and the G20 forums there has been considerable pressure on emerging economies like Brazil, India, China and South Africa to take more intense commitments by way of mitigation options. There is pressure on these countries to play a larger role than at present to provide resources for climate change. Given the struggle for resources to support climate financing systems, it is to be expected that negotiations will be intense, with players fighting for their 'core positions' and finally opting for 'fall back' positions that pave the way for consensus.

Table 6.3 demonstrates a 3x3 matrix of resource mobilization possibilities for developed countries and emerging economies. The three options are public financing (P) (national and international), private direct investment (PDI) and carbon markets (CMs). Historically emerging economies have forcefully argued for the primacy of public financing and have been extremely skeptical about carbon markets and to a lesser extent about PDI. However, given the recent growth of private investments in emerging major economies, it is likely that they will be less averse to PDI particularly when it involves companies from their countries. Developed countries have been traditionally in favour of carbon markets and private direct investments and very skeptical about public investment.

A consensus position is likely to be forced by the Durban Platform since the platform has created a stake for developing countries in mitigation options.

In terms of Table 6.3 the negotiation positions within G20 are likely to be as follows:

Developed countries	
Core Position	Fall Back
(PDI, CM)	(CM, PDI)
Major emerging economies	
Core l position	Fall Back
(P, P)	(P, PDI)

Likely consensus in the post-Durban platform phase

The likely consensus can be (P, PDI) if sub-agreements can be secured on 'IPR issues', 'Business Models' and 'viable partnership systems' between private sector in developed countries with those in emerging and developing countries.

As would be clear from the foregoing discussions, the G20 can be a game changer as far as resource mobilization is concerned partly due to the close nexus the group has to the levers of macroeconomic decision making in all the member countries and partly since the G20 has a moral suasion power on private capital flows. Therefore as discussed in Table 6.3, the G20 can steer the global regime to a stable equilibrium solution of (P, PDI), provided it addresses the intellectual property rights (IPR) issues in emerging/major economies and seeks to promote developed-emerging private sector partnerships that rest on mutually beneficial business models between technology innovators in developed countries and technology developing companies in major economies that can develop and customize technologies to suit developing country contexts. Public investments can, by facilitating technology customization process through demonstration projects in developing and emerging countries, promote rapid technology diffusion. This model can work well in the areas of solar photovoltaic (PV) and clean coal combustion technologies where the risk of technology failure on account of poor technological adaptation in developing country contexts is high. The (P, PDI) equilibrium in Table 6.3, would also overcome the barriers of technical and economic risk barriers associated with carbon mitigation technologies that renders mitigation technologies costlier and risky as compared to conventional adaptation projects that have low technological transformation potential.

Summing Up: Towards an Integrated Framework of Negotiations

The principal thesis advanced in this chapter is about the importance of enshrining the co-benefit principle in the forthcoming climate finance negotiations that will be driven by under the aegis of the Durban Platform of Enhanced Action. At present, adaptation is considered to be a substitute for mitigation and adaptation interventions have a shallow technology base. This situation is not conducive to serious action on climate change. On the other hand, if climate finance negotiators recognize the principle that mitigation action produces the co-benefit on low adaptation costs and accept this principle in the design of carbon markets and current resource allocation systems, it can ensure that the GHG emissions are controlled and the possible rise in global temperature is capped below 2°C. Such a shift in paradigm will also ensure synergistic blending of mitigation and adaptation action besides compelling negotiators to look at issues of IPR protection and possibilities of viable partnership based business models that promote flow of sustainable backstopping technologies between developed, emerging and developing countries.

The chapter considers the G20 as an important forum that can assist the UNFCCC attain the goal of addressing climate change. It advocates public financing as an important factor in overcoming barriers to technology development and diffusion between private sector players from developed and developing countries. Mechanisms such as carbon markets could complement these efforts.

Notes

1. ODA in particular, is stated to be unpredictable as it is subject to the will of legislatures in donor countries. (Muller, 2008)

2. As Muller states at present, all international funding instruments except the recently operationalized Kyoto Protocol Adaptation Fund are replenished through ODA-type bilateral voluntary contributions/ donations (Muller, op.cit). International private flows like FDIs and foreign institutional investors (FIIs) are unpredictable and are dependent on macroeconomic variables (including interest rates), investment climate and capital market trends (UNFCCC, 2008 and Damodaran, 2008).

References

Barrett, S. 2012. 'Negotiating to avoid "Dangerous" Climate Change'. Available at: www.cccep.ac.uk/Events/past/2012/man.

Bryson, B., Z. W. Kundzewics, S. Wu and J. Palutikof, eds. 2008. 'Climate Change and Water'. *Technical Paper of the IPCC*, Geneva: IPCC Secretariat.

Bodansky, D. December 2012. 'The Durban Platform: Issues and Options for a 2015 Agreement'. Centre for Climate and Energy Solutions (C2ES). Available at: www.c2es.org/docUploads/Durban.platform.

Carraro, C. October 17–18, 1998. 'Beyond Kyoto, A Game Theoretic Perspective', Paper presented at the OECD Workshop on Climate Modelling – Background Analysis for the Kyoto Protocol. Available at: http://www.oecd.org/dev/1923135.pdf.

Damodaran, A. 2012. 'The Economics of Coping Strategies and Financing Adaptation Action in India's Semi-arid Ecosystems', *International Journal of Climate Change Strategies and Management* 4(4): 386–403.

_______. October 2010. 'Climate Change Finance and the Global Commons in the Context of the G 20 Process'. *Technical Report – 2/EFGP/2010.* Indian Institute of Management Bangalore: Indian Institute of Management.

_______. 2009. 'Climate Financing Approaches and Systems: An Emerging Country Perspective', *Working Paper 8(E) – 2009.* Russia: Graduate School of Management, St Petersburg University.

_______. 2008. 'Perspectives on Environmental Financing', in *Report and Recommendations of International Conference on Environmental Financing of Global Public Goods- State of Art and Future Challenges.* Bangalore: Indian Institute of Management.

_______. 2006. 'Coastal Resource Complexes of South India: Options for Sustainable Management', *Journal of Environmental Management*, Elsevier 79: 64–73.

Friman, M. and B. Linner. 2008. 'Technology Obscuring Equity: Responsibility in UNFCCC Negotiations', *Climate Policy* 8: 339–54.

Grubb, M. 2008. 'Climate Change Impact, Energy and Development', in *Re-thinking Infrastructure for Development, Annual World Bank Conference on Development Economics, Global 2007*, edited by François Bourguignon and and Boris Pleskovic, 89–130. Washington, DC: The International Bank for Reconstruction and Development / The World Bank.

IPCC. 2007. *Climate Change 2007–Impacts, Adaptation and Vulnerability*, Contribution of Working Group II to the Fourth Assessment Report of the IPCC. Cambridge, United Kingdom and New York, NY, USA: Cambridge University Press.

King, K. 1993. 'The Incremental Costs of Global Environmental Benefits', *Working Paper No 5*. Washington DC: Global Environmental Facility.

Laltanzio, R. K. April 2013. 'International Climate Change Financing: The Green Climate Fund (GCF)', *Congressional Research Service*, 7–500. Available at: *www.crs.gov*, R 41889.

Llewellyn, John and Chaix, Camille. 20 September 2007. *The Business of Climate Change II*. Lehman Brothers Inc. Available at: http://www.llewellyn.co.nz/climatechange2.pdf. Accessed on 18 August 2014.

Muller, B. February 2014a. 'Comments Regarding Policies and Procedures for the Initial Allocation of Fund Resources', *Background Paper GCF/B.06/05*.

Muller, Benito. January 2014b. *How will Green Climate Fund Allocate its Money? All You Wanted to Know but Were Afraid to Ask*. Available at: cdkn.org.

________. June 2008. *International Adaptation Finance: The Need for an Innovative and Strategic Approach*. Oxford Institute for Energy Studies, EV 42.

Ray, D. and R.Vohra. 1997. 'Equilibrium Binding Agreements', *Journal of Economic Theory* 73: 30–78.

Reed, D., G. Pablo, K. Carstensen and D. Pols. January 2009. 'New Mechanisms for Financing Mitigation: Transforming Economies by Sector', *World Wide Fund for Nature (WWF) Discussion Paper*.

Sagasti, F. R., K. Bezangon and F. Prada *et al.* 2005. *The Future of Development Financing: Challenges and Strategic Choice*. Basingstoke, UK: Palgrave, Macmillan.

Saran, S. 2009. *Questions and Answers on India's Position on Climate Change Issues*. New Delhi: Monograph, Prime Minister's Office

Schelling, T. 1960. *The Strategy of Conflict*. Oxford: Oxford University Press.

Stavins, R. October 2007. *A U.S. Cap-and-Trade System to Address Climate Change*. Washington, DC: The Hamilton Project, The Brookings Institution.

Stern, N. 2006. *The Stern Review: The Economics of Climate Change*. Executive Summary. Available at: www.gruene.ch/d/pd/klima_stern_report.pdf.

Sethi, S. 2008a. *Financing Climate Change Fundamentally Different from the Aid Paradigm*. Available at: www.odi.org.uk/events/2009/03/23/439-transcript-mr-Sethi-speech.pdf.

UNFCCC. 2013. *Warsaw Climate Change Conference – November 2013*. Available at: unfccc.int/../7649.php.

UNFCCC. 26 November 2008. *Investment and Financial Flows to address Climate Change: An Update*. Technical Paper. FCCC/TP/2008/7.

World Bank Group. 6 October 2011. 'Mobilizing Climate Finance', A paper prepared at the request of G20 Finance Ministers. Available at: www.imf.org/.../110411 c.pdf.

7 Greening the G20 Agenda: A Way Forward[1]

Parthasarathi Shome and Amrita Goldar

Introduction

Greening of the G20 agenda may be perceived in the context of global governance and, in particular, humane global governance because, greening at a global level or in a global scale is one area that cannot be aspired to, leave along achieved, without high level international recognition of the problem followed by strong cooperation and sacrifices in pecuniary terms. In proposing humane governance, Haq (1999) propounded the most comprehensive of all concepts of governance incorporating economic, political, and civic aspects, though questions of realism persist as to whether such a premise is achievable without a long-term roadmap beyond the familiar ephemeral memories of functioning societies. This becomes obvious from a reading of how humane governance is conceived. To quote Weiss (2000):

> Humane governance involves those structures and processes that support the creation of a participatory, responsive and accountable polity (that is, good political governance) embedded in a competitive, non-discriminatory, yet equitable economy (that is, good economic governance). That requires the resources contributed by people to be ploughed back to serve their own basic human needs, which will in turn expand the opportunities open to them; people must be given the ability to self-organize (that is, good civic governance). Bounded together by such principles as 'ownership', 'decency', and 'accountability', the components of humane governance are inextricably linked. (p. 805)

The issues become somewhat incommodious in the context of global governance. The interconnectedness of individual economies with the inexorable advent of globalization through rapid progress in international trade, telecommunications and finance inarguably characterizes a new industrial revolution. The question that has naturally emerged is, how sustainable is this revolution from the point of view of maintenance of the global environment. This comprises a major cross-border challenge. In turn, it has permeated the G20 development agenda. The Framework for Strong, Sustainable, and Balanced Growth includes a wide agenda comprising objectives, actions and outcomes for the group as a whole (G20, 2009; Hersh, 2010; Ahluwalia, 2011).[2] Thus, despite the group's being primarily set up for cooperation on matters related to the international financial system and its stability, several development pillars were subsequently incorporated in its agenda. The world had quintessentially undergone a metamorphosis and the boundaries of governance had easily crossed national boundaries with global dimensions, in a growing list of concerns with transnational consequences, and energy and environmental issues became important components of that agenda.

Ramifications of the new developments were anticipated by authors such as Cerny (1995) to be the disablement of prevailing frameworks from their ability to provide an already familiar range of public goods (Weiss, 2000). Thus the growing complexity of international markets made state-based collective action for global public goods provision infeasible and unrealistic. This would certainly have been fully observed, if not experienced, by states in the 2008–09 global financial crisis that turned into a global economic crisis. In this context, the G20 emerged as the common platform for global governance. It has to be recognized that the setting up of the G20 has resulted in 20[3] of the most economically powerful countries of the globe coming together to address and discuss issues that supercede national interests that were not necessarily equally successful under the UN system. And, as its agenda widened to include development issues, 'pillars' were incrementally added as their relevance was recognized in the G20 Summits (see Chapter 1). They were:

- infrastructure;
- human resource development;
- trade;
- private investment and job creation;
- food security;
- growth with resilience;
- financial inclusion;

- domestic resource mobilization;
- knowledge sharing; and
- environmental sustainability.

On one hand, the recognition of the pillars challenged the singular focus that had been garnered to address the most crucial fault lines for restoring stability in financial flows. On the other, the broadening of objectives assuaged the developing countries that perceived, in the pillars, their long term structural concerns as a group. The pillar of environmental sustainability forms the focus of this chapter.

What is noteworthy is that, reflecting the interest groups that typically embrace the concern over greening as a way forward, 'international NGO's, grassroots and citizens' movements, multinational corporations and the global capital market' (Weiss, 2000) have been included as relevant actors as implied by their increasing visibility and role. This variegated array of actors poses a set of chastening challenges that are difficult to perceive, leave above resolve, in a cohesive manner in the global context.

Thus, the setting up of G20 resulted in the most economically powerful countries of the globe to recognize and pursue a global development agenda with renewed vigour despite the Group's being primarily set up for cooperation on matters related to the international financial system and its stability. Of the several development pillars that were subsequently incorporated in its agenda, energy and environmental sustainability became important components.

The Main Issues

In their national context, policymakers have to balance four competing objectives in regard to the energy sector – sustaining economic growth, increasing energy access for the poor, enhancing energy security, and improving the environment. Win-win options can help achieve more than one objective at a time, for example, climate mitigation projects can help abate local air pollution through reduced fossil fuel combustion. Other policies may involve a trade-off for which difficult decisions at a national level are called for, for example, reforming domestic fossil fuel subsidy could have deleterious developmental impacts on the energy poor.

Existing literature reveals a direct correlation between economic growth and energy consumption. As developing countries grow, they have the need to provide reliable and affordable energy services to 1.6 billion people without electricity and 2.6 billion without clean cooking fuels (World Bank, 2010). In such a scenario, environmental concerns tend to get superceded by concerns over development and growth, which are given precedence.

Decision-making gets even more complex where global environmental concerns are addressed. Related to the problem of climate change, for example, there are supra-national issues of historical emissions, cross-boundary impacts of disasters such as droughts and floods, technology transfer, carbon leakage and flow of climate finance. It is this 'transnational' nature of environmental issues that has made G20 an important forum for cooperation on potential energy and climate change action as well.

Some of the constituents of the G20 'green' agenda were designed to support initiatives undertaken in other multilateral platforms such as on climate change finance (CCF) and clean energy and energy efficiency (C3E). However, other initiatives taken up by the G20 were novel and taken to a platform possessing effective global reach for the first time. These included issues of fossil fuel subsidy reform, global marine environment protection, and sharpening databases for mapping oil and gas price volatility.

Existing Discussions at the G20

Rationalization of inefficient fossil fuel subsidies

This is one of the priority items within the broad theme of energy and climate change. Studies have found that wasteful fossil fuel subsidies not only add financial burden upon government coffers (especially in times of high energy prices), they damage the environment through increased energy consumption and thereupon global and local pollution. Moreover, since earmarked fuels are often diverted and high-income households have higher per capita energy consumption levels as compared to the poor, the former group benefits disproportionately from such subsidies. According to an international study, the bottom 40 per cent of the population in terms of income distribution receives only 15–20 per cent of the fuel subsidies in developing countries (IEA, OPEC, OECD, World Bank, 2010).

Modelling results provided by the IEA reveal that, if fossil-fuel consumption subsidies in surveyed countries were completely phased out by 2020, global primary energy demand would be cut by 4.1 per cent and CO_2 emissions by 4.7 per cent. The OECD ENV-Linkages global general equilibrium model results reveal that reforms would lead to a 6 per cent reduction in global GHG emissions in 2050 compared with a business-as-usual scenario (IEA, OPEC, OECD, World Bank, 2011). In addition to this, fossil fuel subsidy reform could provide an easily tapped source for climate finance. The IMF estimates that even if reforms resulted in 20 per cent of support being redirected to public climate finance, this could yield $10 billion per year available for climate action (World Bank, IMF, OECD, RDB, IFC, EBRD, ICAO, IMO, 2011).

In this regard, the ongoing efforts by G20 leaders to phase out and rationalize inefficient fossil fuel subsidies as well as prevailing high international energy prices have given a fillip to fossil fuel subsidy reforms across the globe. The IEA estimates that around half of the countries reporting fossil fuel consumption subsidies have either implemented fossil fuel subsidy reforms or announced related plans since the beginning of 2010. On a similar note, many OECD countries have also shown an interest in reforming the support systems for fossil fuel production and consumption, and the taxation of fossil-fuel consumption.

Specifically, over the various G20 summits, member countries have been asked to report the fossil fuel subsidies given by them under different headings and submit a timeline for reform. In each summit following the 2009 Pittsburgh Summit, countries' progress has been monitored with respect to this programme. As mentioned earlier, this was the first instance where G20 members had jointly tackled head-on the tricky issue of fossil fuel subsidies. This issue had been earlier discussed in other multilateral forums such as the UNFCCC[4] and different track-2 academic circles but, on the whole, had not received the same prominence as when recognized by the G20, perhaps due to its political and national sovereignty implications.

The Russian Summit of 2013 initiated a voluntary peer review process for subsidy reforms listed in earlier rounds. Countries were also invited to provide information on the probable impact of subsidy reform from fiscal, economic and environmental standpoints, identify barriers to reforms and existing capacity – technical, analytical and administrative – gaps. The methodology document for the G20 voluntary peer reviews incorporates two interesting aspects into the mix, namely, the possibility of a review of country data against data available from third party sources i.e., relevant international organizations, as well the option of the countries undergoing review to select such material from the review as they would want to make public.

Despite the voluntary nature of the above declarations, there are certain challenges to these reform efforts that should be flagged from a developing country point of view. Some of these emerge at a transnational level, such as the issue of energy poverty and of international energy exporters' welfare. The principles of equity, and common but differentiated responsibilities (CBDR) and respective capabilities under the UNFCCC, recognize the development prerogative of emerging economies. Energy subsidies are often used by them to alleviate energy poverty through access to affordable energy services. Thus, with the reform of subsidies, care should be taken to avoid or mitigate the adverse impact of reforms on the poor through increased social safety nets or redressal schemes. Moreover, the inflationary impact of phasing out consumer subsidies – indirect effect of subsidy reforms – also needs to be addressed by reforming economies, since escalating domestic inflation would require appropriate mitigating policies. For net energy exporting countries, removing subsides in importing countries could have a negative impact on their GDP, despite a positive impact on their export earnings, as energy prices in importing countries rise. OPEC estimates show that, with the phasing out of energy subsidies, the GDP effect on OPEC countries would be an annual average of minus 3.4 percentage points for the first five years (IEA, OPEC, OECD, World Bank, 2011). Recognizing the points above, the St. Petersburg's G20 Leaders' Declaration states '...we ask Finance Ministers to consider, in conjunction with the relevant international institutions, policy options for designing transitional policies including strengthening social safety nets to ensure access for the most vulnerable.' This was strengthened in a 2014 Declaration in Brisbane which recognized '...being conscious of the necessity to provide targeted support for the poor' while rationalising and phasing out inefficient fossil fuel subsidies.

Clean Energy and Energy Efficiency (C3E)

Similar to fossil fuel subsidies, C3E initiatives comprise another area in which the G20 member countries monitor performance. However, in this area, G20 discussions mainly support negotiations held elsewhere i.e., UNFCCC's AWG-LCA,[5] the issues coming under the head of domestic mitigation action and its assessment. Nevertheless, the initiative is important since countries monitor their clean energy deployments and the policy progress made.

Energy efficiency is the lowest cost, largest source for emission reduction and future energy savings from both the energy supply and energy demand sides. Renewable sources, a close second to emission reduction, provide low-to-zero emission fuels for power generation albeit at a comparatively higher cost. Policy promotion in the form of ambitious renewable targets and support policies that stimulate investment in renewable generation has been the overarching trend among G20 countries. Policy has sought to promote greater investment in renewable electricity generation through financing, pricing, fiscal or public bidding policies.

Recent data show that 76 per cent of global hydro-generation is within the G20 Group, and all the growth in hydro-generation over recent years has been emanating from within the G20 countries, notably in China (IEA, 2011). Moreover, 93 per cent of non-hydro renewable generation occurs within the G20 countries, where generation doubled between 2005 and 2010. After hydro, the most dramatic growth has been in the wind and solar PV sectors. In the last five years, a large part of global installed capacity in these two sectors has also materialized within the G20 countries.

Further progress requires putting a price on carbon and providing financial incentives to deploy low-carbon technologies. The price competitiveness of clean energy technologies still lags behind fossil-based technologies due to their lower level of maturity. A mechanism that assigns a price for external environmental impacts/benignity to energy options (e.g. a price on CO_2 emissions) may correct this problem to a large extent. Non-economic barrier removal would, however, require concerted political will and support. These include information, financing, removal of institutional and structural barriers, and regulatory advancement without which investment may not advance in practical terms or may suffer a slowdown.

The C3E working group has noted members' progress in the deployment of clean energy technologies and national policymaking. But it has not attempted to review or evaluate national progress against any set targets or benchmarks. Moreover, no attempt has been made to develop collective goals, for example, G20 deployment progress against pathways needed for achieving renewable energy goals. Instead, the focus in recent summits has been on sharing national experiences or best practices for overcoming barriers to clean technology deployment.

The report on C3E technologies in G20 countries (G20, 2012) prepared by C3E Experts Group for the Mexico Summit has collected voluntarily provided information on member countries' experience on clean technologies (renewable technologies and energy efficiency), policy state of play, and financial requirements for deployment. While a technology discussion is of limited relevance from the viewpoint of the G20 core agenda, a discussion on the budgetary requirements of clean technology, the role of government regulation and public procurement that provides a fillip to a specific technology, and the inclusion of international finance sources in the discussion are no doubt important. G20 members have submitted interesting case studies of their renewable technology and energy efficiency deployment experiences such as Brazil's ethanol policy, India's solar programme and the Middle East's (Saudi Arabia and UAE) experiments with carbon capture and storage (CCS) for enhanced oil recovery (EOR).

Climate Change Finance

The mandate of G20's CCF Working Group is to provide a supporting role to UNFCCC's discussion on climate finance. It seeks to explore the aspect of scaling up climate finance for mitigation and adaptation in developing countries. Subsequently, the G20's Climate Finance Study Group created in the Mexico Summit as part of the CCF discussion seeks to provide a forum for sharing national experiences of climate finance with a strictly defined mandate of not duplicating UNFCCC processes.

The CCF Working Group aims at building upon the work carried out by the UN Secretary General's High Level Advisory Group on Climate Finance. It explores the potential of new and additional fund sources for financing climate change activities in developing countries.[6] Both reports, AGF (2010) and World Bank, IMF, OECD, RDB, IFC, EBRD, ICAO, IMO (2011), draw upon a wide range of sources, including public, private, bilateral and multilateral sources to estimate how the requisite funds would be generated.

The CCF Working Group report states that, in view of the flourishing global private capital markets and growing fiscal challenges in many developed economies, future climate funds would be mainly private in composition (World Bank, IMF, OECD, RDB, IFC, EBRD, ICAO, IMO, 2011). Nevertheless, public policy and finance would continue to play a dual role. It would, on the one hand, establish an appropriate price of carbon, thus providing the incentive framework needed to catalyse private investment; on the other, it would generate public resources for those needs where private flows would not suffice.

The public sector would create an appropriate price of carbon using fiscal instruments such as carbon taxes or tradable emission permits, that ensure that emitters' decisions correctly reflect the associated negative externality so that a social optimal level of production and consumption could be reached. Moreover, these carbon pricing policies could be used for raising additional climate funds and provide incentives for future clean technology development.

Public funds would be needed to address market failures affecting innovation and dissemination of new technologies and to build essential infrastructure. However, market mechanisms such as carbon taxes, or even aviation and maritime bunker fuel charges, should not violate the CBDR principles enshrined under the UNFCCC. The impact on developing countries of charges or taxes should be minimal and should be offset by specially designed compensation schemes.

Through various summits the CCF Working Group has consciously sought to keep a separate identity from the UNFCCC and the negotiating standpoints of individual countries on finance. The circumspect progress report of the Climate Finance Study Group (St. Petersburg Summit) states '…the group could benefit from reviewing several different options for mobilizing climate finance based on national experiences, even if the mobilization of climate finance rests essentially with domestic decisions, and country views differ on which sources to mobilize to that end (G20, 2013a).'

Global Marine Environment Protection (GMEP)

Anthropogenic petroleum pollution of marine waters is caused during the extraction, transportation, and consumption of petroleum. New initiatives of GMEP aimed to close information gaps by sharing best practices to protect marine environment with the final aim of preventing accidents related to offshore exploration and development, and marine transport. For example, new information from the IEA shows that off-shore oil and gas production contributes close to 30 per cent of global petroleum supply and this share would grow in the medium to long-term (GMEP, 2011). Studies also show that biological impacts after an oil spill can encompass alteration of natural habitats, physical smothering effects on flora and fauna, toxic effects on flora and fauna and changes in biological communities resulting from effects on key organisms. The subsequent recovery depends upon both removal of oil, which is toxic or physically smothering, as well as the natural progression of biological processes, e.g. settlement of larvae and growth of seedlings.

The G20's GMEP initiative focused on best practices in all aspects of offshore oil and gas activities, aimed at ensuring safety and environmental protection in offshore oil and gas exploration and development, including prevention of, preparedness for, and dealing with accidents and their consequences. As part of its mandate the Working Group aimed at creating a platform for information exchange and created a central website to compile information from the numerous initiatives related to offshore exploration and development and the protection of the marine environment to facilitate exchange of voluntary best practices. Some countries suggested reviewing and exchanging experience among peers through a non-prescriptive mechanism. In practice, reviewing international regulation of offshore oil and gas exploration, production and transport with respect to global marine environmental protection regulations had occurred at a limited and voluntary level through the GMEP website. There were some discussions of maintaining a database of accidents, their environmental damage and spill responses for GMEP member countries' usage. Nevertheless, it appears that GMEP failed to appear at the 2014 G20 Summit in Brisbane; nor does it appear in the agenda for the 2015 Turkish Presidency of the G20.

Oil Price Volatility

On a similar note, the initiative to track oil price volatility tries to close gaps in crude oil and now natural gas-data reporting and promote greater transparency. It attempts to standardize the reporting process and ensure timeliness to improve predictability of markets and facilitate project planning. The Working Group has made progress to improve the timeliness, completeness and reliability of the Joint Organizations Data Initiative (JODI)-Oil database. The database collects monthly data on seven product categories (crude oil, LPG, gasoline, kerosene, diesel, fuel oil and total oil) and eight flows (production, demand, refinery intake and output, imports, exports, closing stock levels and stock change). Data are collected on all these parameters based on responses by national organizations and administrations responsible for oil statistics through a harmonized questionnaire. The Working Group also works towards improving dialogue between oil producers and consumer countries.

The group explored the idea of extending JODI-Oil to coal and natural gas in its negotiations. As part of its new mandate it has started collecting data for a JODI-Gas database, and is studying the short, medium and long term outlook and forecasts for gas and coal markets. The role of price reporting agencies, such as Platts, for the proper functioning of oil markets is also being examined by the group. Websites have been created for both JODI-Oil and JODI-Gas that provide publicly accessible information on various oil and gas metrics for member countries. While recently launched, JODI-Gas already hosts information for countries that account for 78 per cent of global natural gas supply and 82 per cent of global demand.

G20 Energy and Climate Change Dialogue: New Focus Areas

Under the Mexican presidency, a new item was added in the development – energy and environment – agenda, namely, green growth strategies. The OECD defines green growth as a way to pursue economic growth and development while preventing environmental degradation, biodiversity loss or unsustainable natural resource use. The strategy aims at maximizing the chances of exploiting cleaner sources of growth, thereby leading to more environmentally sustainable growth (OECD, 2010). As compared to the C3E, green growth strategies have a larger mandate since they encompass issues of local as well as global pollution, natural resource use and green technologies.

The policies and approaches used have to be tailored to a country's specific national circumstances. For developing countries, green growth strategies revolve around adaptation policies and sound management of natural resources. It also involves the development of new clean technologies, green industries and jobs, within the framework of their quintessential developmental prerogative of poverty eradication through providing basic amenities to all, as well as the overwhelming dependency of their citizens upon natural resources. Green growth strategies improve climate change resilience among countries and provide an alternative 'greener' trajectory to move along for the same goal. In recent summits, the Group for Green Growth Strategies has encouraged countries to self-report on a voluntary basis their experiences and efforts towards the incorporation of green growth policies in structural reform and sustainable development agendas.

Similar to the C3E initiatives outlined earlier, green growth strategies have market as well as non-market based mechanisms to aid the transition. Market-based instruments include eco-taxes, charges and fees, tradable permits, and removal of environmentally harmful subsidies. Non-market mechanisms would seek to influence the behaviour of firms, households or individuals through command-and-control regulations, pro-green technology policies and innovation.

The Russian G20 Presidency merged a number of energy working groups – Energy and Commodity Markets WG (Working Group), Clean Energy and Energy Efficiency WG, Global Marine Environment Protection WG, excluding Climate Finance issues – into one common G20 Energy Sustainability Working Group to provide greater policy coherence in their specific work settings. Elements of the work on green growth strategies initiated in Mexico were recast into the 'Promoting Investment in Energy Infrastructure' theme while others were absorbed into the 'Inclusive Green Growth' pillar of the Development Working Group. The key messages from both working groups were similar, for example removing obstacles generated by market and government failures, supportive policies for clean technologies as well as reducing barriers to international trade and investment. Clear and predictable domestic policy frameworks and effective regulation were highlighted for host governments seeking to catalyse investment flows in clean energy. Special emphasis was given to the private sector and multilateral development banks for circumventing barriers to clean energy investment.

The November 2014 G20 Summit at Brisbane during the 2014 Australian Presidency saw some progress. The United States announced $3 billion contribution to the UN General Climate Fund that assists developing economies to address climate change. Canada, Germany and Japan also promised financing. However, the subsequent December 2014 Lima Call for Climate Action in Peru witnessed a watered down communique on the climate change agenda itself.

Suggestions for a Way Forward

While the G20 has recognized that energy and environmental issues are inter-related, G20 working groups need to take greater cognizance of the work being done in related working groups and comprehensively incorporate the lessons learnt. To illustrate, fossil fuel subsidies (FFS) reform has been mentioned as one of the most promising options for generating CCF that could thereupon be diverted to fund climate action. The objectives of climate action on which the green funds would be spent are discussed in the C3E working group. Thus, looking at the broader picture and fitting the existing pieces together provide clues to the missing parts that comprise the aspects that need to be incorporated to make the G20 agenda 'greener'.

Carbon taxes vis-à-vis cap-and-trade system

The first issue that G20 needs to weave into its discussion is that of usage of market based instruments and government regulation to achieve environmental aims. Command and control versus market incentives to achieve environmental goals is an old debate among environmental economists. In the current scenario, this debate has taken the form of carbon taxes versus a cap and trade system to achieve emission reduction in countries. Both of these policies provide incentives for private investment and aid innovation in clean energy technologies. These also represent promising avenues for generating additional revenue for funding climate action by nation states, albeit with some disadvantages.

Under a cap-and-trade scheme, governments issue freely tradable emission permits representing a legal right to emit carbon. However, setting limits to emission becomes difficult due to the non-homogenous nature of industrial units and differing marginal costs of fuel switching and energy efficiency. Moreover, setting a limit becomes even tougher if consumption behaviour rather than production is sought to be modified.

For energy taxes, due to imperfect information, there is some associated uncertainty about how much abatement will actually occur for a given tax level. In a situation of an emission cap under a global agreement, a country may need to adjust the tax rate iteratively to keep emissions within the cap. While designing a universal carbon tax, care would need to be taken, in developing countries in particular, that the poor are protected through redistributive policies and that losing industries are adequately compensated, recalling the CBDR Principle.

Climate change and infrastructure

Following from the above, an aspect that has hitherto not received adequate attention in the agenda is the issue of climate change and associated infrastructure needs. The agenda needs to include economic infrastructure not just in the broader sense of roads, bridges or ports, but also of hospitals, coastal embankments, water storage facilities, water-saving irrigation facilities and rain water harvesting, all of which improve the coping capacities of people to climate change.

Funding needs for green investment are relatively modest compared to global infrastructure investment. It is estimated that of the total infrastructure investment needs worldwide ($7 trillion per annum by 2020), only $1.5 trillion is energy related (Project Catalyst, 2010). On a comparative scale, the figures for funds required for mitigation, adaptation, and technology are quite small. In developing countries, mitigation could cost $140 to $175 billion a year over the next 20 years, while adaptation investments could average $30 to $100 billion a year over 2010–50 (World Bank, 2010). Further, comparing these figures with the commitment taken on by developed countries for the Green Climate Fund of $100 billion a year, highlights the inadequacy of funds sought to be raised through multilateral platforms.

Even in the Brisbane G20 Summit, harnessing the benefits of increased public expenditure – as a fiscal policy tool – in green infrastructure was mentioned. Investments made in efficient public transport, smart electricity grids, green buildings and efficient water infrastructure should help solve national infrastructural requirements and, at the same time, promote green growth strategies further. In that light, the relatively low commitment in Lima of just over $10 billion sourced from both developed and developing countries could be viewed as a disappointment.

Water availability and quality

The availability and quality of water are important factors that determine the coping capacities of ecosystems to climate change. The issue of water constraints has so far been discussed only in the context of food security and irrigation water requirement in G20 negotiations. Thus, other crucial aspects of the problem such as limited water availability and competing water requirements (for potable and other uses) need to be discussed, possibly as part of the sustainable development negotiations. The impact of countries' municipal and industrial effluent discharge on water quality should also be taken up in the G20 discussions on energy sustainability in the future summits.

UNEP (2011) estimates that without improvements in water use efficiency, water demand would exceed supply by 40 per cent in 20 years' time. Less than half of this could be addressed by improvement in water productivity and increase in supply through the construction of dams and desalination plants. A major part would, therefore, require infrastructure investment, water policy reform and new technology. The water deficit situation would be further aggravated with climate change. Increased temperature would have an impact on the hydrological cycle through increased evaporation. In most regions precipitation would be both intense and varied, often with longer dry periods in between. With glacier and melting of snow caused by climate change, fresh water supplies would increase initially, but supply would decline over time. The other source of freshwater for human consumption – groundwater – would also diminish in scope since intense precipitation for a short time would not allow groundwater aquifers to recharge fully and this would lead to water tables falling. Thus, the common threat of water scarcity faced at the global level needs to be tackled on a platform that is representative of the global interests it deserves. Such a platform is the G20.

Knowledge and technology dissemination

Another important missing piece is the issue of generating knowledge conditions such that countries can initiate national level projects. This issue has been highlighted and discussed within the G20, albeit for a small component of GMEP. It needs to be scaled up to cover other issues of environmental services and climate technologies, and for both mitigation and adaptation.

As an innovation vehicle, the G20 could begin to discuss ways and means of supplementing the work carried out at UNFCCC's Subsidiary Body for Scientific and Technological Advice (SBSTA)[7]or take forward the Green Growth Knowledge Platform (GGKP).[8] In Australia, the G20 discussed the ways and means to make climate-friendly technologies more accessible, surmount IPR issues and make technology transfers easier. This was covered in a Report of the G20 Climate Finance Study Group that was issued in Australia.

While government regulation, as well as climate funding, provide an enabling environment for the germination of climate friendly projects, their final materialization depends upon availability of technology. As outlined before, due to market failure there is a clear role of government in technology innovation in the initial R&D and demonstration stages. Many important technologies of current relevance have had government backing. These include rail transport, nuclear energy, internet and global positioning systems (GPS).

Green technology development on an international level is trickier with many political economy considerations. The green products market is growing and there are obvious first mover advantages for the country that wins the 'technology race'. Pioneering countries create niche export markets setting the path for future cost reductions through scale economies, and reap benefits from licensing technologies to the rest of the world. Thus, multilateral cooperation on science, technology and innovation is an extremely beneficial approach to address issues related to technical exchanges among countries, funding arrangements, capacity building and international technology transfer. In fact, the Mediterranean Solar Plan is an example of cooperation among countries on the large-scale demonstration and deployment of concentrated solar power. Other diffusion mechanisms such as innovative collaboration mechanisms in intellectual property, for example, patent pools, and networking R&D are also being explored.

Research consortia are well suited to conduct long-term research with economies of scale and economies of learning in carbon capture and storage, third generation photovoltaic, deep offshore wind, second and third generation bio-fuels, and climate-monitoring technologies. However, as technologies come closer to the commercialization stage, the scope for cooperation reduces as the application of IPR becomes a constraint. Concerns over IPR and transfer and innovation of climate-smart technologies should ideally be considered in the World Trade Organization's (WTO's) agreement on Trade-Related Aspects of Intellectual Property Rights (TRIPS) as it establishes minimum legal standards of protection for WTO members.

Patents perform a dual role in this context. They provide an important incentive to invest in innovation by allowing firms to recover their investment costs. However, they prevent developing countries from using the patented invention without the consent of the IPR owner except in the case of compulsory licensing. Thus, when enforcement of IPR is perceived to be weak, foreign firms may not license their most sophisticated technologies for fear of usurpation. It may also lead firms to keep their inventions secret or not patented, which would, in turn, harm diffusion.

Land management and forestry

As regards environmental services, two crucial issues relate to land management and forestry. The combination of land use, and land use change and forestry (LULUCF), could provide the answer to problems of air and water pollution as well as land degradation within countries. Under the item 'commodity markets and food security', the G20 has already discussed the issue of land management. This could be broadened in subsequent G20 rounds to incorporate the environmental ramifications of agricultural practices. Green growth strategies should also cover the issue of land degradation.

Land under permanent snow cover or deserts would fall under the category of naturally degraded land. Anthropogenic land degradation would cover land that has become barren due to industrial effluents and wastes, overgrazing by animals, deforestation and mining. In regard to the limited land availability and high pressures on its use, land management practices become critically important.

Global deforestation is alarmingly high at 13 million hectares per year (UNEP, 2011). While a part of this is addressed by replanting, the new 'forest' provides far less ecosystem services as compared to natural forests. The high rate of felling of trees is primarily driven by demand for wood products and by the pressure of other land uses such as agriculture and pastures. To abate this, opportunity for additional payments for conservation and improved land management may flow from the scheme for Reduced Emissions from Deforestation and Forest Degradation (REDD) under the UNFCCC. REDD could provide a monetary benefit to countries for reducing deforestation and degradation. This would help in the conservation of biodiversity and mitigation of climate change as the programme aims at protecting biologically diverse areas that have high carbon stocks and are at high risk of deforestation.

Green jobs

This is an aspect that fits well into the existing structure of G20 agenda items. With more intensified sustainable patterns of development, green jobs in renewable energy and infrastructure should account for a progressively larger share of total job creation in the future. This aspect should be taken up in greater detail within the 'job creation' item under the agenda item of development. A website serving as a global public-private knowledge sharing platform (Global KSP) on skills for employment has been created under the Russian Presidency and focuses on anticipating training requirements and skills required for green jobs. However, this remained primarily undiscussed in Australia.

Public expenditure should be geared at green industries that generate green jobs. However, in addition to the new jobs created in sectors such as renewable energy and energy efficiency, care needs to be taken to ease tensions caused due to the transition towards a green economy. These require policies to assuage the job loss that occurs with the decline in traditional industry sectors, resulting in shifts in employment structures and an adaptation in job profiles. The creation of green jobs is often constrained by skill gaps; thus, the adaptation of job profiles would require training and skill creation across the existing work force.

Energy trade and related action

Yet another aspect – energy trade and embodied carbon – is an important one that needs to be highlighted further. This issue is already being addressed somewhat under the items of oil price volatility and C3E. It is expected that the item 'green economy' would discuss this issue further.

The issue of trade sanctions stems mainly from competitiveness concerns in countries that are signatories to the Kyoto Protocol. There is the concern that any plan that exempts developing countries from emissions limits would not be effective because carbon-intensive industries would simply shift their operations to one of such exempt countries. This would both undermine the environmental benefits of the Kyoto Protocol and also affect the competitiveness of signatory countries. These concerns have led to proposals for tariff or border tax adjustments to offset any adverse impact of capping CO_2 emissions within national boundaries.

The debate remains divided on whether a tax on embodied carbon is compatible with international trade regulations under the WTO. Trade measures are often justified as a mechanism to ensure compliance with multilateral environmental agreements (MEAs) (World Bank, 2010). The issue in assessing the compatibility of trade measures with climate change policy arises from the application of unilateral measures based on national policies or product standards. With relevance to these border measures, it is stated that the WTO and other trade agreements do allow 'exceptions' for trade measures that might otherwise violate free trade rules but that can be justified as necessary or related to an effort to protect the environment or conserve exhaustible natural resources so long as they are 'non-discriminatory' and 'least trade-restrictive.'

Conclusion

To conclude, plugging gaps in the broader landscape of greening the G20 agenda should be a central activity of future G20 Summits, taking forward the agenda to make it 'greener'. As a first step, aspects of climate financing through subsidy rationalization, adaptation in infrastructure and water, technology sharing and transfer, LULUCF, green jobs and energy trade are needed to be addressed comprehensively.

Since financing appears to be the most crucial issue for meaningful action to be taken and be continued, the discussion taken up in Russia on promoting investment in energy infrastructure needs to be taken forward. Revenue from alternative sources could be used for addressing global objectives of the G20's green agenda in particular because traditional taxes on capital and labour are suffering increasingly from low revenue productivity as international movements of factors of production have increased rapidly.

Recent rounds have developed a softer approach towards the green agenda through greater emphasis on data and knowledge sharing initiatives. The focus has also been on increasing face-to-face interactions among G20 members. Such initiatives need to be taken forward, with data gathering and improving transparency being the first step towards coherent policymaking. The G20 needs to recognize its strength as a pioneering group that defines the economic mood of the global economy. The group as a whole needs to serve the green agenda as well. It needs to set positive benchmarks for climate and environmental action, be it in emission reduction commitments, undertaking investment that supports clean technology or preserving the environment that the world can aspire towards as a shining example of humane global governance.

Endnotes

1 All opinions and views are exclusively those of the authors'.

2 The Framework for Strong, Sustainable, and Balanced Growth was launched in the Pittsburgh G20 Summit. The launch of the Framework and also the Mutual Assessment Process (MAP) were mentioned in points number 5 and 6 of the Leaders' Statement. To elaborate: '5) Framework for Strong, Sustainable, and Balanced Growth. To put in place this framework, we commit to develop a process whereby we set out our objectives, put forward policies to achieve these objectives, and together assess our progress. And 6) We call on our Finance Ministers and Central Bank Governors to launch the new Framework by November by initiating a cooperative process of mutual assessment of our policy frameworks and the implications of those frameworks for the pattern and sustainability of global growth,' in *G20 Leaders Statement: The Pittsburgh Summit*, 24–25 September 2009.

3 Nineteen countries plus the European Union accounting for over 80 per cent of global GDP.

4 United Nations Framework Convention on Climate Change.

5 Ad-hoc working group on long-term cooperative action.

6 Based on the commitments made under the UNFCCC, a flow of funds of $30 billion for the period 2010–12 and $100 billion per year by 2020 need to be arrived at.

7 Subsidiary Body for Scientific and Technological Advice (SBSTA).

8 The GGKP was established in January 2012 by the Global Green Growth Institute, the Organization for Economic Co-operation and Development, the United Nations Environment Programme and the World Bank.

References

AGF. 2010. *Report of the Secretary General's High-Level Advisory Group on Climate Change Financing*. New York: United Nations.

Ahluwalia, M. 2011. The G20: A New Experiment in Global Governance', in *Festschrift in Honour of Prof. Lord Meghnad Desai*. London: Palgrave Macmillan.

Cerny, P. G. 1995. 'Globalization and the Changing Logic of Collective Action', *International Organization* 49(4): 595–625.

G20. 2009. *G20 Leaders Statement*. Pittsburgh Summit, 24–25 September, Pittsburg.

_________. 2012. *Clean Energy and Energy Efficiency Technologies in G20 Countries Report*. Available at: www.hse.ru/en/org/hse/iori/g20doc. Accessed in July 2014.

_________. 2013. *Russia G20: G20 Leaders Declaration*. St. Petersburg Summit. Available at: www.g20.utoronto.ca/summits/2013stpetersburg.html. Accessed in July 2014.

_________. 2013a. *G20 Climate Finance Study Group: Progress report to G20 Leaders*. Available at: www.hse.ru/en/org/hse/iori/g20doc. Accessed in July 2014.

GMEP. 2011. 'Sharing Best Practices to Protect the Marine Environment, to Prevent Accidents Related to Offshore Oil and Gas Exploration and Development, as well as Marine Transportation, and to Deal with Their Consequences', Global Marine Environment Protection Working Group, G20 Cannes Summit Issue paper, France.

Haq, M. 1999. *Human Development in South Asia 1999: The Crisis of Governance*. Human Development Centre. Oxford: Oxford University Press.

Hersh, A. 2010. 'Monitoring Commitments and Compliance of the G20 Framework for Strong, Sustainable, and Balanced Growth'. *New Rules for Global Finance*. 13 January, Washington. Available at: www.new-rules.org. Accessed in July 2014.

IEA. October, 2011. 'Clean Energy, and Energy Efficiency Deployment and Policy Progress', *G20 C3E*. Available at: http://www.iea.org/publications/freepublications/publication/G20_paper.pdf. Accessed in July 2014.

IEA, OPEC, OECD and World Bank. June 2010.'Analysis of the Scope of Energy Subsidies and Suggestions for the G20 Initiative'. Submission to G20 Summit Meeting, Toronto, Canada.

_________. 2011. 'Fossil-fuel and Other Energy Subsidies: An Update of the G20 Pittsburgh and Toronto Commitments'. *Joint Report by IEA, OPEC, OECD and World Bank*. Cannes, France: G20 Summit Meeting.

OECD. 2010. 'Green Growth Strategy: Implementing our Commitment for a Sustainable Future'. *Interim Report*. Paris: Meeting of the OECD Council at Ministerial Level.

Project Catalyst. 2010. *From Climate Finance to Financing Green Growth*. San Francisco: Climate Works Foundation and European Climate Foundation.

UNEP. 2011. *Towards a Green Economy: Pathways to Sustainable Development and Poverty Eradication*. United Nations Environment Programme.

Weiss, T. G. October 2000. 'Governance, Good Governance and Global Governance: Conceptual and Actual Challenges', *Third World Quarterly* 21(5): 795–814, published by Taylor & Francis, Ltd.

World Bank. 2010. *World Development Report 2010: Development and Climate Change*. Washington DC: World Bank.

World Bank, IMF, OECD, RDB, IFC, EBRD, ICAO and IMO. November 2011. 'Mobilizing Climate Finance', Paper Prepared at the Request of G20 Finance Ministers, Cannes, France.

8 Revisiting Fossil-Fuel Subsidies in the Context of Ongoing G20 Dialogue

A Discussion with Special Reference to India[1]

Meeta Keswani Mehra and Divya Datt

Introduction

Background and context

The reliance on energy subsidies by governments worldwide is ascribed to the need to achieve diverse goals of economic development, social equity and environmental protection.[2] In developed and emerging economies alike, there is widespread use of subsidies in both production and consumption of energy, even though the justification provided differs between the two groups of countries. For instance, developed country governments justify energy subsidies in production on grounds of maintenance of local or regional employment (especially during economic recession) or boosting domestic supply of energy. On the other hand, developing and emerging economies mostly attribute subsidies to alleviating energy poverty and ensuring access, especially to populace at subsistence levels of energy consumption. Despite significant reforms toward market-orientation and rationalized regulation in developing and emerging economies, the reliance on energy subsidies remains high.

Notwithstanding their well-intentioned rationale, it is recognized that subsidies tend to distort price signals, and hence induce inefficient choices by producers and consumers. By making a fuel cheaper, subsidies induce overuse or inefficient use of energy, culminating in negative externalities such as excessive natural resource depletion or environmental pollution, including emissions of greenhouse gases. Further, subsidies impose a burden on budgetary resources, and may even crowd out other forms of government investment that may be merited (Saunders and Schneider, 2000).

Arguably, however, provisioning of subsidies is fundamentally country-specific and draws from the sovereign right of each country to develop economic and social policies based on its national circumstances and policy objectives. However, on account of their extension into domains of international trade and the global environment, fuel subsidies occupy an important place in the discussion agenda at international and regional forums such as the WTO, UNFCCC, the G20 leaders' conferences, and Asia Pacific Economic Cooperation (APEC).

At their meeting held during 24–25 September, 2009 in Pittsburgh, USA, the leaders of the G20 nations agreed to ramp up efforts to rationalize and reduce fossil fuel subsidies in a manner that wasteful energy consumption is avoided while, at the same time, the negative consequences for the poorest (as essential services provision) are prevented. Accordingly, individual countries had to develop country-specific implementation strategies and timeframes for a phase-out of such subsidies bearing in mind their specific circumstances and report back to the G20.

The progress in this regard has been affected by several considerations. To begin with, there has been neither an agreement on a common definition of 'subsidy' nor on a specific time frame for their rationalization. While some members have proposed the adoption of an existing definition, such as that used by the IEA or WTO (GSI, 2010), other countries have favoured creating a new definition for the purpose of deliberations in the G20. Production subsidies for crude oil, coal and natural gas have been intensely protected by industry in countries like the US and Canada while consumption subsidies are guarded in India, Indonesia and Saudi Arabia (on social and political grounds), resulting in no clear agreement on a common definition. Furthermore, it is emphasized that the subsidy reform initiatives have to be 'country-owned and country-led.' That is, while it is agreed that both consumer and producer subsidies need to be rationalized, countries can exercise discretion in deciding which subsidies to focus reform efforts on (Lang, 2011).

In this context, the aim of this research is to identify, in general, the rationale and motivation for energy subsidies across OECD and non-OECD countries, the type of subsidy provisioning, and the underlying economic, social, and environmental concerns being raised from an international perspective. This is the subject of discussion in the following section. The rest of the chapter focuses on India. Next the discussion focuses on fossil fuel subsidization in India in the context of the G20 discussions, with an emphasis on concerns of providing energy access and reducing energy poverty. The rationale for continuing with individual fuel-specific subsidies is discussed as well as the reforms initiatives for subsidy rationalization. In the next section, key macroeconomic, efficiency, equity and environmental implications of reforms are highlighted through an analysis of case studies from the individual fuel subsectors.The chapter also presents a discussion on estimation of elasticity of fuel consumption in the household sector, which could then help guide subsidy reforms. The last section offers some concluding remarks.

Motivation for granting energy subsidies

According to economic theory, social welfare is maximized when the price of each good and service is ascertained by the free interaction of buyers and sellers in a set of complete, perfectly competitive and well-functioning markets. In reality, however, market distortions in the form of monopoly structures, input supply constraints, infrastructure bottlenecks, lack of access to demand-side technologies and large utility consumers, abound. Moreover, supply of energy does not fully internalize the environmental and social benefits or costs associated with certain types of energy activities, causing markets to fail due to these externalities. This merits government intervention and regulation of energy markets in the pursuit of economic, environmental and social goals (UNEP, 2004).

The rationale for energy subsidies stems from a myriad of social and economic development imperatives (WEO and IEA, 2010). In detail, these comprise:

- *Macroeconomic growth and development:* Energy is a critical input to all the sectors of the economy – energizing transport, providing electricity to industry, commerce, agriculture, and in provisioning social services such as education and health. Governments rely on energy subsidies to lower relative energy prices so as to spur the growth of specific sectors. Coal, diesel and natural gas subsidization demonstrate this goal.
- *Redistributing natural resource wealth:* In fossil fuel abundant countries, the below market price supply of energy is perceived as a policy tool to redistribute and share more widely the benefits of abundance of indigenous natural resources. These also take the form of fuel subsidies to energy-intensive industries such as petrochemicals, fertilizers and aluminium etc. to enhance their competitiveness and diversify industrial growth.
- *Meeting basic needs and enabling energy transitions:* Fossil fuel subsidies provide a way to expand affordability and accessibility of efficient

and clean fuels to the poorest sections of society thus enabling energy transitions resulting in improved quality of life. The most commonly used is the subsidy on LPG for cooking and kerosene for lighting to reduce the use of traditional biomass fuels.

- *Bolstering domestic energy supplies toward energy security:* National governments stimulate domestic production of energy as means to reduce import dependency. This is achieved by providing higher producer prices, grants or low interest loans, loan guarantees, tax exemptions or reductions, preferential access to mineral resources or land at below market prices to specific companies (IEA, OPEC, OECD and World Bank, 2010)
- *Protecting local or regional environment:* Subsidies on clean energy forms, including renewable energy technologies, are aimed toward the objective of protecting local environment and mitigating climate change.

However, there is a flip side to all this. Energy subsidies tend to use up public finances in resource-constrained economies, which could otherwise be used for other developmental expenditure by the government. These also tend to abet rent-seeking behaviour by lobby groups and militate against both supply-side and demand-side efficiency improvements, and render new forms of renewable energy uncompetitive with adverse environmental consequences (World Bank, 2010). In the rest of this section, specific subsidy estimates in the OECD and non-OECD are compared, followed by a discussion of some of the common concerns that have been raised.

Types of fuel subsidies across G20 countries

Taxonomy of subsidies

Given the widespread support measures offered by governments, a clear-cut definition of subsidy may be difficult to establish. From a practical viewpoint, one could refer to the definition offered by the OECD in that –'a subsidy is a measure that keeps the prices for consumers below market levels, or keeps prices for producers above market levels or that reduces costs for both producers and consumers by giving direct or indirect support.'

Subsidies may take different forms. Some take the form of a direct impact on price, such as grants and tax exemptions, while others work in a more indirect fashion, such as economic regulation that tilts the market in favour of a particular good or government-supported research and development (R&D). Governments provide subsidies either through the budget or off the budget. Accordingly, the classification of subsidies provided in Earth Council (1997) and OECD (1998) could be integrated and adapted to derive the following taxonomy (see Mehra *et. al*, 2004) (Table 8.1).

Table 8.1: Taxonomy of Subsidies

Points of impact	**Effects on government budget**	
	On-budget	**Off-budget**
Direct subsidies	Grants or payments to consumers or producers	Grants or payments to consumers or producers
Indirect subsidies on output	Deficiency payments, sales premiums, preferential sales tax and value added tax (VAT) rates, tax credits, exemptions and allowances	Domestic market price support, price regulation and quantity controls, government procurement policies, government brokered sales contracts, trade-oriented support, border protection (import and tariffs, quantitative import restrictions, non-tariff barriers)
Raw material and intermediate product inputs	Support to material and energy input (e.g. energy, fertilizers, irrigation water), provision of infrastructure and complementary services below long run marginal cost	Materials and services in kind or below long run marginal cost
Capital and labour input or income or profit earnings	Support to non-material and non-energy inputs (e.g. labour and capital equipment), accelerated depreciation allowances, income tax concessions, concessional credit, preferential loans, loan or liability guarantees, debt write-off, provision of infrastructure and services at less than long run marginal cost, support to R&D (e.g. on production techniques, safety and environmental protection) or government R&D expenditures	Concessional credit, royalty concessions, low rate of return requirements, exemptions from certain environmental regulation

Source: Cited in Mehra *et al.*, 2004 (adapted from Earth Council, 1997; OECD, 1998)

The discussion is restricted to review of subsidies listed above. That is, the authors do not address implicit or indirect subsidies that accrue when external costs are not taken into account in the production and consumption decisions of producers and consumers respectively.[3]

Energy subsidies measurement and provisioning across countries

Fuel subsidies prevail in developed and developing countries alike. Although there exist key differences in the reasons for and the manner in which fuels subsidies are provided, the recent international thrust on subsidy reforms, necessitate a rough estimate of energy subsidies across different countries.

Existing cross-country estimates of energy subsidies by OECD (for OECD countries) and IEA (for emerging economies and oil exporting countries) are worked out by using different approaches. The OECD estimates (used for subsidy measurement for 24 OECD countries) refer to a broader measure of 'support' than the usual conception of 'subsidy'. Their approach includes both direct budgetary expenditures and tax expenditures that in some way provide a benefit or preference for fossil fuel production or consumption relative to alternatives.[4] In comparison, the IEA utilizes a price gap approach for the emerging economies and oil exporting countries. The price gap assesses the wedge between the actual (prevailing) and the 'free-market' or benchmark price of a fuel. The price gap method is beset with several shortcomings, such as inefficiencies in border prices due to international market distortions, absence of an obvious benchmark price for non-traded energy commodities, effect of subsidies that is not incorporated in the final consumer price but instead in the structure of supply mix, and finally omission of producer subsidies. The alternate approach to quantifying subsidies that relies on budgetary estimates provided by the governments of economies that subsidize fossil fuels (as the one adopted by OECD) would generate a more precise measure of actual expenditures on subsidies. However, the latter method is not adopted due to paucity of consistent data sets to enable cross-country comparisons.

Turning now to the quantified estimates, the new work at the OECD for 24 countries puts the aggregate support to fossil fuel production or consumption at round $60 billion in 2010. Of this, a bulk go to petroleum (54 per cent), followed by coal (24 per cent) and natural gas (22 per cent). The share allocation across producer and consumer subsidies is roughly 22 per cent and 67 per cent, while the balance is made up by general services support, including those for R&D (IEA/OPEC/OECD/World Bank, 2011).

The IEA estimates, for around 37 developing and emerging economies (including the oil exporting countries) that represent 50 per cent of global fossil fuel consumption, peg the aggregated global fuel subsidy at $409 billion in 2010 (around $100 billion more than in 2009), which mainly covers consumption subsidies on fossil fuels. Amongst these, oil products are estimated to account for the largest share, totalling $193 billion (47 per cent of the total), and natural gas accounting for $91 billion. Subsidies on account of under-pricing of electricity are also significant, reaching $122 billion. Subsidies to coal end-use consumption are put at a smaller level of $3 billion (IEA, OPEC, OECD and World Bank, 2011). The year-on-year fluctuations are largely ascribable to changes in the international oil prices.

Clearly, an accurate multi-country comparative assessment is not possible due to the different estimation approaches of the OECD and IEA. There is a need for developing a robust methodology to facilitate a comparison between these two sets of estimates.

Energy subsidies estimates for OECD countries

According to OECD, energy subsidy levels in terms of direct budgetary expenditure and tax expenditure vary widely across countries (see Table 8.2). As can be seen, in Australia, Canada, France Japan and USA, a bulk is directed to the petroleum sector, while in the UK, natural gas accounts for a major share. In Germany, on the other hand, coal accounts for a predominant share of total subsidies. The experience as regards the share of producer versus consumer subsidies is mixed. For instance, in Australia, France and the UK, it is consumer subsidies that are dominant, while producer subsidies have a larger share in Japan. This mix is more balanced in case of the Canada and USA.

Table 8.2: Subsidy estimates in select OECD countries, 2012 (provisional)

Country	**Unit**	**Coal**		**Petroleum**		**Natural gas**		**Total**
		PSE	**CSE**	**PSE**	**CSE**	**PSE**	**CSE**	
Australia	Million Australian dollars	36.90	NA	596.44	7288.26	112.33	16.82	8050.74
Canada	Million Canadian dollar	20.92	4.21	830.12	1440.05	437.82	460.31	3193.43
France	Million euro	NA	3.00	100.18	2377.71	6.82	266.17	2753.879

Country	Unit	Coal		Petroleum		Natural gas		Total
		PSE	CSE	PSE	CSE	PSE	CSE	
Germany	Million euro	1938.05	560.16	303.38	1714.02	33.90	545.70	5095.22
Japan	Million Japanese yen		NA	12257.56	NA	400.02	124.26	12781.84
UK	Million British pound sterling		81.33	158.75	380.25	121.25	3509.81	4251.39
USA	Million US dollar	631.88	756.61	2445.82	2666.39	2725.42	2392.12	11618.25

Source: OECD, 2013.

Energy subsidies estimates for developing and emerging countries

One finds large variations in the IEA consumption subsidy estimates within the emerging economies and oil exporting group (Table 8.3), although, in general, the subsidies are higher in 2012 than in 2009. The highest absolute subsidies are estimated for oil exporting countries, namely, Iran (at $82.50 billion), followed by Saudi Arabia and Russia at $61.50 billion and $46.2 billion respectively. In the case of Iran and Saudi Arabia these also make up for large share of their GDP, that is, 15 per cent and 8.5 per cent respectively, and are also amongst the highest on a per capita basis. Within the emerging economies, India and China are reported to have the highest fossil fuel subsidization with estimated values at $42.8 billion and $26.9 billion respectively. Notably, however, at 2.5 per cent and 0.3 per cent respectively, subsidies are also amongst the lowest as a per cent of aggregate GDP in the group of countries analysed. Given their large population size, the level of subsidies provided are again the lowest in India and China on a per capita basis.

Table 8.3: Fossil fuel consumption subsidy indicators for select emerging economies and oil exporting countries, (2013)

Country	Total subsidy (billion dollars)	Average subsidization rate (percentage in 2012)	Subsidy per person (dollar/ person in 2012)	Total subsidy as share of GDP (percentage in 2012)
Argentina	11.7	26.5	283.4	2.5
China	26.9	3.4	20	0.3
Egypt	26.2	53.7	324.9	10.2

Country	Total subsidy (billion dollars)	Average subsidization rate (percentage in 2012)	Subsidy per person (dollar/ person in 2012)	Total subsidy as share of GDP (percentage in 2012)
India	*42.8*	*17.6*	*34.5*	*2.5*
Indonesia	26.5	28.3	109.3	3
Iran	82.5	73.8	1102.4	15
Mexico	19	16.2	141.8	1.3
Pakistan	14	37.3	78.6	6
Russia	46.2	19.4	325.5	2.3
Saudi Arabia	61.5	78.9	2189	8.5
South Africa	1.83	4.5	33.7	0.4
Venezuela	28.2	82	944.5	7.4

Source: IEA fossil fuel subsidies database for 2013.

As regards consumption subsidies by fuel type, the highest magnitude of subsidies has been found in the case of oil products, followed by electricity. In the case of the former, as expected, the oil-exporting countries, i.e., Iran ($35.8 billion), Saudi Arabia ($47.1 billion), Venezuela ($20 billion), Egypt ($16.9 billion) and Indonesia ($21 billion) rank the highest within group. Outside this group, significant oil subsidies are found in India ($32.4 billion) (Table 8.4).

Table 8.4: Magnitude of fossil fuel consumption subsidies by fuel, 2013 (billion dollars)

Country	Oil	Natural gas	Coal	Electricity
Argentina	1.1	5.1		5.5
China	12.9	0.5	3.3	10.2
Egypt	16.9	3.1		6.2
India	32.4	3.8		6.6
Indonesia	21			5.5
Iran	35.8	29.6		17.1
Mexico	15.5			3.5
Pakistan	0.6	9.9		3.5
Russia	0	24.6		21.6

Country	Oil	Natural gas	Coal	Electricity
Saudi Arabia	47.1			14.4
South Africa	0.13			1.7
Venezuela	20	4.2		4

Source: IEA fossil–fuel subsidies database for 2013.

In the case of natural gas again, Iran and Russia account for the highest subsidies, at $29.6 billion and $24.6 billion respectively. By comparison, much lower levels of subsidies are provided in China ($0.5 billion), Argentina ($5.1 billion), Egypt ($ 3.1 billion), India ($3.8 billion) and Pakistan ($9.9 billion).

The data on coal subsidies is scanty, to say the least. The magnitude of subsidies is reported only for China, which has a heavy reliance on coal as a source of energy. The level of subsidies granted amount to a $3.3 billion, somewhat higher than the level in 2009.

As for electricity, which accounts for the second highest level of subsidies for the entire group of countries, the largest magnitude prevails in Russia ($21.6 billion), Saudi Arabia ($14.4 billion) and Iran ($17.1 billion), followed by China ($10.2 billion). In case of India these are significantly lower ($6.2 billion).

Several points are noteworthy here. First, besides the above estimates, it is reported by IEA that well over 1.3 billion people across the world have no access to electricity and around 2.7 billion people use dirty fuels for cooking. Energy subsidies are justifiable on grounds of providing this stratum energy access and energy security towards improving their standards of living. Any adverse impact of subsidy removal is felt disproportionately by these groups. Second, in so far as a country is abundant in a fossil fuel resource, the appropriate benchmark price in the calculation of the price gap should be the domestic cost of production, rather than its price on the international markets. Third, domestic prices adjusted for purchasing power parity may be considerably higher than those in the absence of such an adjustment. On these specific grounds, there is the need to revisit and corroborate the price gap assessments of IEA by reviewing national characteristics, also country-level data and statistics for greater accuracy. And finally, there has been growing momentum towards fossil fuel subsidy reforms, in that amongst the countries covered by IEA under the price gap approach, almost half have either already undertaken reforms or announced related plans commencing start of 2010 (IEA, OPEC, OECD and World Bank, 2011).

Concerns with energy subsidies: Developed and developing country standpoint

In the context of the deliberations in G20 countries' forums, several apprehensions have been expressed with regard to energy subsidy provisioning – ranging from inefficiency in consumption and supply and burgeoning government budgetary deficits to adverse distributional and environmental outcomes. Here again, there exists a slight difference in the nature of concerns raised by the OECD countries on the one hand and those in the emerging economies or oil-exporting countries on the other. Clearly, the concerns of each group stem from their national circumstances and associated policy goals. The authors attempt to highlight some of these concerns.

- *Market distortions:* A subsidy, by its very nature, involves a complex set of changes in economic resource allocations through its effect on relative costs and prices. Essentially raised by developed countries, subsidies in production reduce competition and create market distortions in the form of encouraging less efficient producers, suboptimal plant operations and jeopardizing future investments. Such subsidies are commonly operated toward coal mining and oil and gas extraction, allowing less efficient firms to remain artificially competitive against imports and prop up indigenous production. This may pose a barrier to introduction of more productive and cleaner production technologies as new firms enter the market. On the consumption side, concerns that mar economic efficiency relate to low relative prices of select fuels that encourage wasteful consumption and delay actions toward energy efficiency in final or intermediate energy consumption in residential, commercial or industrial operations. For instance, a rise in the price of petrol may induce a switch from the use of private cars to a public mode of transport while a rise in the price of electricity for commercial buildings may encourage diffusion of more energy-efficient lighting and space conditioning devices (WEO and IEA, 2010).
- *Blunting global demand responses:* This is a familiar concern that finds its basic origin in the OECD countries and has a close link with the market distortion argument. By maintaining domestic fuel subsidization in the face of dramatic international price increase (as in case of oil in 2008), there is dulling of market signals in terms of less than efficient response of demand to rise in market prices. This is due to no or less than full pass-through of world price increases to domestic consumers, with governments absorbing the difference through its budgetary support to the energy supply companies.

- *Straining governments' budgetary resources:* Some support measures – such as direct grants, infrastructure provision and tax concessions – are financed directly by the government, and any increase (reduction) of these has an instantaneous negative (positive) impact on the government budget. The reduction/removal of off-budget support also impacts the budgetary deficit, albeit only in the long run, as this works through enhancing the efficiency of resource use in the economy, and hence reducing budgetary deficits (Mehra *et.al.*, 2004). The stress on government's budgetary resources is a matter of concern for the import-dependent emerging economies. Observably, during periods of persistently high energy prices, provisioning subsidies or maintaining lower than market prices for fuels can become financially unsustainable. E.g., given the spate of oil price rise during 2008, (as also the international price hikes prevailing currently), the spending on oil and gas imports rose to high levels of 6 per cent and 3 per cent of GDP in India and China, thus having an unprecedented adverse impact on governments' budgets despite the upward revision of select petroleum products prices in the domestic markets. Notwithstanding the subsequent softening of oil prices, after mid-2008 until recently, the governments did not lower the fuel prices in a bid to reduce subsidization. Moreover, the Indian government and oil marketing companies have been regularly raising select petroleum product prices in a bid to make up for losses on account of the rising world prices of crude oil and, more importantly, a depreciating rupee against the US dollar.
- *Environmental impacts:* Energy subsidies tend to have diverse environmental effects. The adverse environmental outcomes associated with fossil fuel subsidization are closely linked with the market inefficiency argument. The distorted price signals generated by artificially low relative prices of select fuels lead to both inefficient fuel use and suboptimal fuel mix. These market failures culminate in excessive energy use or inappropriate inter-fuel substitution, having negative environmental effects. A counterargument that is posed is that fossil fuel subsidies are not necessarily environmentally damaging. For instance, public funding of R&D in fossil fuel relating activities can lead to positive environmental outcomes in the form of development and use of cleaner fuels or fuel combustion technologies. Subsidies to renewable energy and energy-efficient technologies can lead to reduced fuel use and cleaner fuel mix. In the context of non-OECD countries, there is merit in retaining the subsidies on fuels such as electricity and

LPG for the poor, who would otherwise lack access to cleaner fuels and instead rely on less efficient and polluting biomass fuels such as fuelwood and crop residues. In the context of the global environmental debate, developing countries argue that, the discussion on fossil fuel subsidy reduction should be delinked from concerns of tackling climate change through CO_2 reduction given their very low levels of emissions per capita. For instance, India's per capita CO_2 emissions are about 1.4 tonnes, while the per capita world average is 4.2 tonnes and that for most OECD countries is in the range 10–20 tonnes per capita.

- *Fuel diversion and disproportionate benefit accrual to the rich:* A widespread criticism levelled against fuel subsidies is that these entail unbalanced benefits to the non-targeted or wealthier populace. Thus, in terms of their distributional impact these may turn out to be regressive. A common illustration of this is the undue advantage of very low electricity prices for water pumping in agriculture accruing to the richer farmers in India. Furthermore, in the absence of plugging of supply side leakages, these tend to encourage fuel diversion and adulteration, e.g., a commonly witnessed case in the Indian context is adulteration of diesel with kerosene as the price of latter is substantially subsidized. Arguably, however, the way to contend with these is not to eliminate subsidies but to channelize their flow to the targeted group and plug diversions in the supply chain. There are however implementation challenges associated with targeting the beneficiaries such as through direct cash compensation, as witnessed recently in India and discussed later in the chapter.

The balancing of these concerns remains a challenge. To analyse the progress in subsidy reforms, it is necessary to examine more rigorously as to what a subsidy revamping or rationalization programme might achieve in macroeconomic, social and environmental domains for the individual countries. Some of these impacts are closely linked to the consumers' response to price revisions, often exhibited in terms of price elasticities of fuel demand of households. These aspects constitute the scope of discussion of the next three sections of the chapter, in the specific context of India.

Fuel Subsidization in India – Tracking the Current Thinking

This section provides a focussed discussion on various aspects of fuel subsidization in India – covering the underlying motivation as well as the specific pricing policies and the subsidy reforms that have been underway in the recent years.

Justification for energy subsidies in context of prevailing growth and development objectives

Energy is a key input into the growth and development of an economy, especially of an emerging country like India. India is poised to grow at an annual rate of 8 to 9 per cent over the next two decades (Government of India, 2006a). India's population is likely to reach a level of 1.45 billion by 2030 (WEO and IEA, 2007), with the proportion of urban population rising from the prevailing 30 per cent to 49 per cent in 2030. On account of these economic and demographic changes, it is emerging as an economic giant and a centre for energy use.

The important sources of primary commercial energy in India comprise those obtained naturally (that is, coking and non-coking coal, crude oil, natural gas, and hydro and nuclear power) and those that are derived (namely, petroleum products and thermal power). Of these, coal and lignite and petroleum are the key sources. The total primary commercial energy supply (including imports) in 2006/07 was estimated at 360 mtoe, of which over half (53 per cent or 191 mtoe) was derived from coal and lignite. Of the remaining, 128 mt (36 per cent) was obtained from crude and petroleum products, 29 mtoe (8 per cent) from natural gas and a relatively small amount of 12 mtoe (3 per cent) from power from hydro, nuclear and renewable energy (TEDDY, 2009).

It is important to note the fact that, in 2007, the level of per capita consumption of primary energy in India was a mere 0.53 toe (tonnes of oil equivalent), as compared to the per capita consumption of 1.48 toe in China, 3.48 toe in UK, 7.75 toe in US and 1.82 toe for the world as a whole, India's energy consumption must grow to sustain higher economic growth rates, support developmental priorities, and enhance economic well-being. Further, despite its formidable growth record, poverty and a lack of access to sufficient amounts of clean and efficient energy remain grave concerns and a challenge in India, especially in rural areas (Pachauri and Jiang, 2008). In 2009, India housed nearly 403 million who had no access to electricity (of which 380 million were in rural and another 23 million in urban areas), and there persists an undue 78–80 per cent overall dependence of population on traditional biomass energy forms for its cooking and heating end-uses (WEO/IEA, 2010).

The key rationale provided for subsidization of fuels such as kerosene or electricity finds its origin in ensuring access and affordability of these energy forms for the poorest. Another objective that is accomplished by subsidization of fuels for residential use, namely, natural gas, LPG or kerosene, is substitution of more polluting and inefficient biomass-based energy forms such as fuel wood, crop residue and animal dung (Government of India, 2010). The general approach to energy subsidization is enumerated below:

1. *Cross subsidization of power tariffs*: Power tariffs in India have historically been set on the principle of cross-subsidization, with subsidies to residential and agriculture financed from above-cost supply to railways, industrial and commercial sector consumers. Providing cheap power to agriculture for the purpose of irrigation was a policy in line with promoting the Green Revolution in the country and the residential sector was geared towards enhancing access. Though the intention has been justifiable, much more prudence could have been be exercised in the way it has been implemented (Mehra *et.al.*, 2004).
2. *Regulated prices of domestic coal and gas*: With an overwhelming dependence of India's power generation on coal, linking of coal pricing to import parity will translate into much higher power tariffs, putting the goals of energy poverty reduction and larger access to energy in jeopardy. A similar argument is put forward for administering the price of natural gas at a lower price as inputs for the priority sectors, such as power and fertilizer production (Mercados and GAIL, 2010). However, the Government has recently in principle accepted the recommendation of the Rangarajan Committee (Government of India, 2012) that has suggested mandating a price of domestically produced natural gas at an average of international hub prices and cost of imported liquefied natural gas (LNG). The actual implementation of the formula has, however, been deferred due to the 2014 Lok Sabha elections in the country.
3. *Regulation of imported fuel prices*: Given the international oil price volatility, the adjustment in domestic petroleum prices have been dampened through subsidy measures to insulate the domestic economy from such fluctuations and keep the inflation under check (Government of India, 2010; WEO and IEA, 2010).

Within this overall policy framework, India has been actively reviewing its fuel-subsidization policies in the last few years. In what follows, the authors trace the existing pricing mechanism, allude to available indicators of the extent of subsidies provision and discuss the subsidy reforms that are either underway or are proposed for the individual fuel supply sectors toward greater market-orientation. In the process they raise questions on the feasibility and effectiveness of the transformations in the pricing policy regimes

Lastly, the discussion on fossil fuel subsidy reduction should be delinked from concerns of tackling climate change through CO_2 reduction. This follows from India's position in the international climate change negotiations wherein it would not want to be described as a 'major emitter', with per capita CO_2 emissions of a mere 1.4 tonnes, while the per capita world average is 4.2 tonnes and that for most OECD countries is around 10–20 tonnes per capita.

Given this milieu, an attempt is made to revisit the subsidies debate.

Pricing, subsidization and pricing reforms in individual fuel sectors

According to IEA, energy subsidies in India in 2010 (worked out according to the price gap approach) have been put at an aggregate of $22.29 billion with the average subsidization rate at 13.5 per cent. Of this, a bulk accrue to oil (73 per cent) followed by natural gas (at 10 per cent) and electricity (at 17 per cent) (Tables 8.3 and 8.4). There have been marked year-on-year fluctuations in these, explained by the volatility of world energy prices that have been used as the benchmark for the price gap calculations.

In comparison, domestic estimates of budgetary subsidies for kerosene (through the public distribution system (PDS)) and domestic LPG in 2010–11 have been put at ₹ 930.6 crores ($0.21 billion) and ₹ 1,973.6 crores ($0.44 billion) respectively.[5] These amount to an aggregate of a little over ₹ 2,900 crores ($0.65 billion), much lower than those reported by price gap based IEA estimates.

However, it is important to note that India has been actively reviewing its fuel-subsidization policies in the last few years, which is discussed in the following subsections.

Coal

The pricing of coal in India has historically followed a cost-plus-fair-return principle. Coal production in India is mainly dominated by two public sector companies – Coal India Limited (CIL) and Singareni Colliery Company Limited (SCCL). The price of coal was partly freed up (for the better non-coking coal grades A to D) in 1997, followed by a complete deregulation (of the poorer grades E and F) in January 2000. Most recently, in February 2011, there was a move to import parity pricing for select grades, namely, A and B while a 30 per cent hike in coal prices in E and F grades was effected for sectors like steel, cement, etc. whose outputs fetch market-determined prices. On the other hand, sectors like power, fertilizers, and defence that do not enjoy market pricing for their products have been exempted from the price hike (Hindu Business Line, 27 February 2011).

The principle of cost-plus-pricing has proved to be inadequate in bringing the coal market in equilibrium, with the demand almost always exceeding the supply, entailing growing reliance on coal imports at the margin. It is claimed that the prevailing prices of thermal coal are around 50 per cent of the price of imported coal (WEO and IEA, 2010; Live Mint, 2010). Nonetheless, several points regarding coal pricing are noteworthy:

- There exists a huge difference between the quality and calorific value of Indian versus imported coal; the former being much lower in calorific value (at 3500–4000 kcal/kg) and high in ash content (35–40 per cent) as compared to the latter (around 6200–6500 kcal/kg calorific content and 10–12 per cent ash). Thus, any comparisons or price-gap calculations will have to make explicit adjustments for coal quality and chemical composition.
- Around 80 per cent of total domestic coal production is used for power generation. With rigid price caps on electricity prices for select consumers, especially those that are meant to support the lifeline consumers and provide higher rates of economic growth and enhanced well-being, electricity production can little afford sharp escalations in input coal prices (Rao, 2006). Rationalization of coal process thus cannot be independent of price reforms in the power sector.
- Thermal power plants burn the lowest quality of E, F and G grades of non-coking coal, making them a monopsony buyer of these specific grades of coal that do not find use in alternative sectors, such as steel and cement manufacturing. Furthermore, CIL is a monopoly supplier. Thus, establishing a market mechanism (requiring a large number of buyers and sellers) for pricing coal in India is an arduous task, to say the least.
- Additionally, the power sector has to be supplied coal based on long-term contracts and dedicated point-to-point investment in

transportation and handling, namely, railways and coal handling yards. This deems it necessary to have long-term supply and price contracts between the power and coal industry, as also the Indian Railways.

- The Expert Committee on Road Map for Coal Sector Reforms calculated the free-on-rail price of domestic thermal coal for power plants at pithead (or at mine head) at \$5/million kcal, inclusive of royalty and tax. Add to this freight and handling cost of around \$7–11/million kcal for a distance between 1000–2000 kilometres (from mine head) puts the delivered cost of domestic coal at \$12–16/million kcal. In comparison, the delivered cost, insurance and freight (CIF) price of imported coal is estimated at \$13/million kcal (Government of India, 2005). Platt's coal report puts the prevailing CIF price in 2010 at US \$ 91–105/metric tonne (around \$15–17.5/million kcal at a calorific content of 600 kcal/kg) (Platts International Coal Price Report, 2010). Thus, imported thermal coal is cost competitive only at the coastal locations of Western or Southern India. However, its needs to be kept in mind that the choice between imported and domestic coal is increasingly a function not just of prices but also the availability of domestic coal.

- The Expert Committee also observed that establishing the domestic coal prices on import parity principle (especially the lower quality power grade coal) will not be appropriate for the Indian coal industry because – (1) the price of imported coal may not be the appropriate reference price, since fuel prices should reflect the pattern of use that conform to optimal production with reference to their long-term availability and costs; (2) there does not exist robust competitive price for coal that could be universally accepted as the benchmark; (3) import parity might lead to dependence of domestic consumers on imported coal, thus jeopardizing energy security; and (4) a bulk of Indian coal is of non-tradable variety, thus putting to question the very notion of import parity (Government of India, 2005).

Accordingly, the Expert Committee proposed that a distinction be made as regards pricing of coal for power plants and rest of the consumers. In case of the power sector, it envisaged that a regulated and special price of coal, based strictly on the cost of production subject to efficiency norms and allowable rate of return to the supply sector be maintained to ensure the competitiveness of the Indian industry and affordable supplies to poorer sections of domestic consumers. It also envisaged putting in place a Fuel and Supply Transport Agreement (FSTA) to cover the three parties involved – coal supplier, coal consumer, and the transporter. For the other larger consumers, it proposed that 60 per cent of demand be met through the FSTA, and the remaining market-determined through mechanisms such as e-auctions. The smaller consumers will have to procure their supplies freely from traders, imports or e-auctions. Thus, market mechanisms are increasingly made to play a larger role in coal pricing for select sectors.

More recently, an even more significant change has evolved in government thinking as it has been considering pricing the domestically produced coal on par with global prices, especially with regard to pricing of higher grades of non-coking coal (Live Mint, 2010). This is notwithstanding the fact that such a move may increase the cost of the raw material and lead to a rise in power tariff.

India is also to introduce an auctioning system for its captive coal blocks. This will replace the age-old system of a government committee taking a decision on the allotment from among a list of applicants, a system beset with corruption and absence of transparency. The auctioning mechanism is expected to contribute producing around 125–50 million mt/year of captive coal (Platts International Coal Price Report, 2010).

Oil

At the prevailing higher international price of crude oil and rupee devaluation, the reported levels of under recovery by domestic public sector oil marketing companies (OMCs) as in November 2011 is put at ₹ 10.17/litre for diesel, ₹ 25.66/litre for PDS kerosene and ₹ 260.50/cylinder for domestic LPG. In addition, a subsidy of ₹ 0.82/litre on PDS kerosene and ₹ 22.58/cylinder on domestic LPG has been provided by the government. The OMCs have incurred an aggregate under-recovery of the order of ₹ 37,719 crores, ₹ 13,361 crores and ₹ 13,820 crores on diesel, PDS kerosene and domestic LPG sales during April-September 2011, which amount to an aggregate of ₹ 64900 crores ($12.48 billion) (PPAC website).[6]

The Indian government has actively reviewed and revised its petroleum pricing policy, since price controls of select products in this sector have led to a substantial financial burden on the central government budget and have adversely impacted the finances of the national oil companies.

The administered pricing mechanism (APM) for oil was dismantled following the major pricing reforms in 1997 and 2002 that operationalized the market-determined pricing mechanism. These resulted in free market prices for crude oil, price of petroleum products by indigenous refineries being linked to import parity, consumer prices of all petroleum products (with the exception of LPG and PDS kerosene) being market determined, and flat rate subsidization of LPG and kerosene. The period during 2002 to 2004 witnessed the national oil companies frequently resorting to revisions of petrol, diesel and domestic LPG prices in response to market forces. However, kerosene price were left largely unchanged.

Subsequently, in the period 2004 to 2008, policy changes were introduced with the prime objective of smoothing out oil price volatility in the domestic economy. First, there was the introduction of a price-band mechanism in 2004 that provided partial freedom to the national oil companies to revise the retail prices within the band of +/- 10 per cent of the mean of the rolling average of last 12 months and last 3 months of international cost and freight (C&F) prices. However, the mechanism had to be abandoned in light of very sharp increases in global oil prices. Second, in 2005, with focus on transparency and price stability, the then constituted Rangarajan Committee suggested a formula of trade parity pricing for petrol and diesel at the refinery gate as well as the retail point. The formula utilized a principle of weighted average of import and export parity prices, and suggested a ceiling within which marketing companies would exercise the flexibility to set the actual retail prices of petrol and diesel. The Committee also recommended complete removal of subsidies on LPG and limiting the kerosene subsidy to Below Poverty Line (BPL) families (Government of India, 2006).

Finally, the most recent attempt in this direction has been the setting up of Expert Group on a Viable and Sustainable System of Pricing of Petroleum Products in 2009 to suggest a viable and sustainable system of pricing of petroleum products (Government of India, 2010). The analyses of the Expert Group pertained to four petroleum products, which have been the subject matter of considerable public debate in the context of fuel subsidization, namely, petrol, diesel, kerosene and LPG. (For more discussion on this, see Section 3).

For the year 2009–10, the Expert Group estimated the under recoveries by the oil marketing companies to be of the order of ₹ 46 thousand crores ($10.2 billion), which in 2020–21 could rise to ₹ 157 thousand crores ($34.9 billion) at the international crude price of $80/barrel (bbl) and to as high as ₹ 401 thousand crores ($89.1 billion) at the international crude oil price of $120/bbl.[7] The unit under recovery for PDS kerosene and domestic LPG was estimated at ₹ 20.7/ litre and ₹ 244.4/cylinder respectively at $80/bbl price of international crude oil price. These were worked out to be of the order of ₹ 34.1/litre and ₹ 398.3 if the world crude oil price rises to $120.

At that juncture the financial burden imposed on the state-owned oil marketing companies was being partially made good by issue of discounts, oil market bonds or direct transfers.[8] The Expert Group underscored the need for a change in the existing policy to establish a balance between the capacity of the consumer to bear higher prices and the fiscal stability of the government. The key recommendations made were:

- In case of petrol, the price increase can be easily borne by the motorized vehicle owners, implying eminent merit in market–determined price – both at the refinery gate and retail levels. The spillover effects to other commodities is ruled out in case of petrol in view of its use for final consumption for private transport.
- As for diesel, again the market-determined price at the refinery gate and retail point was suggested. This was justified on the ground that dominant consumers of diesel (trucks and light commercial vehicles or LCVs) typically pass on these costs to higher rental charge collection, while personal sports utility vehicles (SUV) and car owners can afford the higher prices. In case of diesel use for agricultural uses (tractors, thrashers, tillers, harvesters, and water pumps), the burden of higher prices could be accounted for in setting the minimum support prices for crops.
- As for kerosene and LPG, a transparent and effective distribution mechanism through issue of Unique Identification (UID) or Smartcard was emphasized. (This is already under implementation by the Unique Identification Authority of India.) Before its full implementation could be achieved, the suggestion was to rationalize the PDS kerosene supplies in a way as to reduce the all India allocation by 20 per cent, reduce subsidies in small steps and link these to progress of electrification, LPG and piped gas availability for domestic use.
- The LPG supplies to be made at higher prices, with institution of periodic upward revision in line with higher per capita incomes. The subsidy on domestic LPG to be effectively targeted for lifeline consumption by the BPL category.
- The adoption of the above bunch of measures are expected to reduce

the under recoveries from the expected ₹ 45.6 thousand crores to ₹ 15.1 thousand crores in 2009/10.

Indeed, some progress towards rationalization of petroleum prices has led to creation of a more levelled playing field between the state-owned and private sector fuel retailers, whose retail prices were previously higher than those of their state-run rivals, because they were not eligible for the state subsidies. Further, the state-controlled national oil producers are no longer required to provide discounts on crude sales, so they can begin to function more like private companies and will be able to change market-based crude prices (WEO and IEA, 2010). Finally, for better targeting of subsidies, a new mechanism recommended by the Task Force of the Unique Identification Authority of India, which comprises setting up an IT-enabled public distribution system network (PDSN) to provide direct subsidies on kerosene and food to poor, has been approved (in principle) by the Indian government (Government of India, 2011a and Government of India, 2011b). However, on account of administrative concerns, and in response to a Public Interest Litigation (PIL), the Supreme Court of India in September 2013 ruled that Aadhaar or UID is not mandatory to avail essential services from the government, such as subsidized LPG cylinders, admission into private aided schools etc. In a more recent ruling, of March 2014, the Supreme Court asked the Indian government to withdraw all orders making Aadhaar or the UID number mandatory for its residents. Thus, concerns pertaining to effective implementation of lump sum transfer schemes abound.

Natural gas

Over the last two decades, natural gas has emerged as a significant source of energy and feedstock for the Indian economy. The level of production in 2009 was put at around 132.83 million standard cubic meters per day (mscmd), with main producers being Oil and Natural Gas Commission (ONGC), Oil India Limited (OIL), joint ventures (JVs) of Tapti, Panna-Mukta and Ravva and Reliance Industries Limited (RIL) (Krishna-Godavari (K-G D6) basin in Andhra Pradesh). Of the total production, a bulk (nearly 43 per cent) is contributed by RIL, and the remaining 57 per cent by all the others put together. As against this, the Working Group Report for Petroleum and Natural Gas for the Eleventh Plan put the demand in 2009–10 at 225.52 mmscmd, implying a significant shortfall to be made up by imports of LNG. In future, as the demand for gas in power and fertilizer sectors rises, the shortfall in supply will be even higher. Thus, the pricing of natural gas gains considerable significance in light of the prevailing situation of excess demand.

At present, there are broadly two natural gas pricing mechanisms prevailing in India – gas priced under the APM and the non-APM gas whose prices are determined by the free interplay of market forces. The prices under the APM are regulated by the government for priority consumers. The non-APM of free market price gas comes from either the domestic gas from JVs and imported LNG.

The APM of natural gas pricing (currently accounting for around 60 per cent of total gas sold in India) essentially covers gas produced by state-owned corporations – ONGC and OIL. The supplies are directed toward power, fertilizer, consumers covered under court order (such as consumers of city gas) and small consumers with allocations of less than 0.05 mmscmd. The price structure prevailing for these consumers is as under:

Table 8.5: Gas prices under the APM regime

Consumer category	Price ($/million metric British thermal units: MMBTU)
APM – power and fertilizer	1.79
APM – city gas	2.15
APM – northeast power and fertilizers	1.08
APM – northeast city gas	1.29
APM – northeast market price	1.79

Source: Mercados/GAIL, January 2010

Given the large price differential between the regulated price of natural gas and the free market price, government has been announcing upward revisions of the former from time to time. For instance, in 2005 government raised the consumer price for power, fertilizers and other small consumers from ₹ 2800 mscm to ₹ 3200 mscm. The subsequent suggestions of the Tariff Commission indicated a further increase in the producer price (rather than the consumer price) to ₹ 3710/mscm and ₹ 4150/mscm for ONGC and OIL.

The non-APM natural gas under the production sharing contracts of JVs as part of the New Exploration Licensing Policy (NELP) has been typically priced higher, between $3.50/MMBTU to $5.65/MMBTU, and any supplies through the Gas Authority of India Limited (GAIL) to the APM consumers is made feasible by making up for the price differential from the gas pool account.

The pricing of gas derived from the gas fields awarded by the government under the NELP will be based on a pricing formula linked to the crude oil price, and in January 2010 it was put at round US $ 4.20/MMBTU. The price of LNG imported under long-term contracts has been almost entirely prescribed as in the sale and purchase agreements (SPAs) between the LNG seller and the buyer, while spot cargoes are purchased on mutually agreeable commercial terms (Mercados/GAIL, 2010; WEO/IEA, 2010).

In May 2010, through a significant move, the government announced a huge 230 per cent increase in the price of APM gas, from $1.79/MMBTU to $4.20/MMBTU, equivalent to price accruing to RIL for their gas supply from K-G D6 field. This was to make up for the under recoveries by the state-owned companies, ONGC and OIL. In yet another pragmatic move, government has announced that any new gas discoveries by ONGC and OIL in the blocks handed over to them in the APM regime may be sold at the market-driven price (WEO/IEA, 2010). More recently, the government has, in principle, accepted the recommendation of an expert panel on natural gas pricing appointed by the Prime Minister in 2012. The Rangarajan Panel has argued that since there is no market determined arm's length pricing in India nor is it likely for some time, there is a need for a policy on pricing of natural gas. It has suggested mandating a price of domestically produced natural gas at an average of international hub prices and cost of imported LNG. The recommendation has, however, been controversial and therefore the Government has played safe by deferring its implementation till after the 2014 Lok Sabha elections in the country.

Electricity

The retail electricity prices in India have been based on a cost-plus principle since the last 60 years or more. However, given the policy of cross subsidization, with heavy subsidies accruing to select residential and agricultural sectors, the power sector has been finding it difficult to cover its costs of supply. According to a recent analysis by KPMG, the average cost of supply of power in India is worked out to be around ₹ 2.76/kWh in 2007, while the cost recovery through average tariffs charged is ₹ 2.27/kWh (around 82 per cent of the cost) (KPMG, 2009). The electricity prices charged to agricultural consumers are even lower at 26 per cent of the cost of supply. These estimates are derived from the database of Central Electricity Regulatory Commission (CERC).

Table 8.6: Average cost of supply and tariffs for electricity (₹/kWh)

	2005	2006	2007
Cost of supply	2.54	2.58	2.76
Average tariff charged	2.09 (82%)	2.21 (86%)	2.27 (82%)
Agricultural tariff	0.757 (30%)	0.794 (31%)	0.719 (26%)

Figures in parenthesis indicate percentage of recovery of average cost of supply.

Source: KPMG, 2009

An alternative estimate of subsidy put forward by IEA for 2009 is of nominal level of residential tariffs being $0.07/kWh (57 per cent of the OECD average) while industrial consumers pay $0.09/kWh (more or less equivalent to that in OECD) (WEO and IEA, 2010). Notably, however, the Expert Group on Integrated Energy Policy (EGoIEP) of Government of India, which submitted its report in 2006, points toward the fact that, when compared in terms of PPP, Indian tariffs especially those for the industrial, commercial and residential consumers are amongst the highest in the world (Government of India, 2006a). Several other aspects in the context of electricity supply and distribution are noteworthy:

- On the demand side, the Indian government has been striving to provide for the energy consumption of the lifeline consumers in the form of electricity (as also clean cooking fuel). This consumption will need to be subsidized for some consumers till their income levels rise to make it affordable for them. However, it is important to reiterate the need for effective targeting that will ensure that only lifeline level consumption is actually subsidized (Government of India, 2006a).

- Providing cheap power to the agricultural sector for the purpose of irrigation was a policy in line with promoting agricultural productivity in the country. Though the intention has been justified, no prudence is shown in the way it was implemented. At least two significant points need to be highlighted here. First, the operating inefficiencies in generation, transmission and distribution (T&D) activities and inaccuracies in the measurement of agricultural consumption due to diversion for non-agricultural use, pilferage and theft etc. constitute leakages in the subsidy provision chain. Hence, the official estimates of agricultural subsidies are often stated to be an overestimate of the actual levels. Second, the tariff charged to agriculture is not on the basis of actual power consumption, but a lump-sum that is levied on the installed capacity of the irrigation pumps. Since it is typically the large farmers who own these pump sets, the average price of electricity decreases as the consumption of electricity rises. The small and marginal farmers are unable to take advantage of these increasing returns. This runs counter to equity considerations (see discussion in Mehra *et.al.*, 2004).

- At a more macro level, power sector reforms have been under way since the 1990s. There has been the unbundling of the state electricity boards to privatize distribution, and encourage independent power producers in generation. With the enactment of the Electricity Act of 2003, the laws pertaining to generation, transmission and distribution have been consolidated. Each state/union territory has to set up the state electricity regulatory commissions to undertake tariff fixation, and the CERC for bulk tariff setting for the central generating and transmission utilities. Proposals towards tariff rationalization have largely included specific reforms such as a minimum 3 per cent rate of return to each utility, a tariff of no less than 50 per cent of average cost of supply, and agricultural tariffs to rise to this level over a period of time.
- In the meantime, EGoIEP has put forward the proposal for controlling the technical and commercial losses in T&D of state power utilities, to sustain financially the growth of Central and State Public Sector Units (PSUs) and to attract private investment in the power (Government of India, 2006a). In a recent move, the central government has formulated a scheme for financial restructuring of state distribution companies to enable the financial turnaround of the state distribution companies for their long-term viability. The scheme contains measures to be taken by state discoms and state governments for achieving financial turnaround by restructuring their debt with support through a transitional finance mechanism by the central government.[9]

An Analysis of the Implications of the Current Subsidy Regime

The scale of fossil-fuel subsidies and the manner in which these are financed and administered in India has far reaching implications beyond the sector itself. Subsidies impact the economy's fiscal health, developmental spending, external accounts, and possibly employment and growth. Large-scale subsidies can adversely affect investments in the sector, increase the extent of rent-seeking and commercial malpractice, discourage both demand-side and supply-side efficiency improvements, and dampen the growth of renewable energy alternatives. Therefore, it becomes necessary to balance the social benefits of subsidies against the possible economic, social and environmental costs. In what follows, the key economic, social and environmental implications of the subsidy regime in the country are discussed.

Macroeconomic impact

As discussed in Section 2, energy subsidies have visibly contributed to a worsened fiscal balance in the country both due to larger government expenditures and smaller tax revenues. An idea can be gauged from the fact that while the reported fiscal deficit in the crisis year 2008–09 was of 5.86 per cent of GDP, the effective fiscal deficit, including securities issued in lieu of subsidies to oil and fertilizer companies was up to 7.8 per cent (Ministry of Finance, 2010, 2011a). A 2006 study by National Council of Applied Economic Research (NCAER) examining the macro economic impact of an oil price rise on the Indian economy (using Input-Output {I-O} price analysis combined with a computable general equilibrium (CGE) model) points to the need for understanding the wider implications of short-term measures. Specifically, the numerical simulations show a worsening of fiscal deficit and trade deficit following an international price rise of crude, when domestic prices are insulated from international prices based on government's absorption of the price gap in its own budget. This adversely affects future domestic prices as well as output and erodes the competitiveness of the exports. Attempts to reduce the fiscal and trade deficit by reducing other expenditures of the government could also reduce overall output of the economy. It may also have more difficult long-term implications depending on which government expenditures are cut. In fact, the study notes that if the international price rise is passed on to consumers, the effect on GDP from an increase in prices would be lower than when domestic prices are insulated through subsidies. Further, the fiscal deficit remains more stable implying that the potential for further inflationary tendencies is curbed (NCAER, 2006).

In addition to the impacts on the economy's fiscal health, it is evident that the current approach to subsidization has affected the health of the public sector OMCs due to inordinately high under recoveries even as the subsidy sharing burden on the upstream sector reduced private sector participation in the sector. All these, in turn adversely affect the energy security of the country.

Equity implications

There is now substantial evidence, both documented as well as anecdotal, that subsidies that were intended for providing access to the poor to petroleum products have often been poorly targeted, have benefited the rich disproportionately and have resulted in several other distortions in the economy. The regressive nature of petroleum subsidies is glaring in the case of LPG, the consumption of which shows a clear urban-rich bias (see Table 8.6). The 2006 Committee on Pricing and Taxation of Petroleum Products in fact notes that BPL households may constitute as few as 10 per cent of the total domestic LPG consumers (Government of India, 2006b). Analysis of NSSO data also reveals that in urban areas the top three income deciles consume about 40 per cent of the LPG while spending less than 5 per cent of their total expenditure on the fuel (Government of India, 2010)

In the case of kerosene, while the lower middle and poor classes have benefited from the subsidy, its use has been predominantly for lighting and not for cooking (particularly in rural areas) (see Tables 8.7 and 8.8). Also the percentage decline in the total allocation of PDS kerosene has fallen short of the decline in percentage of households using PDS kerosene, indicating its growing diversion to other uses (Government of India, 2010).[10] In particular, the subsidized fuel has found its way to the transport sector where it has been used to adulterate diesel, thus undermining the large investments that have gone into upgrading vehicular emission standards in the country. A study conducted by NCAER also throws up some other interesting observations. While the aggregate gap between annual PDS supply and PDS purchase is as high as 36 per cent, the gap between the estimated household kerosene consumption and PDS supply is of the order of only 18 per cent. Thus, about half of the diverted kerosene ends up with households who either do not possess a ration card or those who buy it at black market prices.[11]

By the same logic, the richer states of the country are the disproportionate beneficiaries of the subsidy on petroleum products on a per capita basis due to higher consumption of the subsidized products. For instance, the average per capita kerosene allocation in high-income states in 2007/08 was 14.1 liters which was 41 per cent higher than that of low-income states. (Chakraborty *et. al.* 2010, Government of India, 2010)

Table 8.7: Percentage of households and average monthly per capita expenditure (MPCE) by primary source of energy for cooking – all-India, 2007–08

Primary source of energy used for cooking	Rural		Urban	
	Percentage of households	Average MPCE (Rupees)	Percentage of households	Average MPCE (Rupees)
Firewood and chips	77.6	707	20.1	780
LPG	9.1	1389	61.8	1764
Dung cake	7.4	713	1.4	801
Kerosene	0.6	945	7.6	1109
No cooking arrangement	1.7	2654	5.7	3033
All*	100	772	100	1472

*includes sources other than those listed in column one

Source: Ministry of Statistics and Programme Implementation, 2010. NSS Report No.530: Household Consumer Expenditure in India, 2007–08; NSS 64th Round.

Table 8.8: Percentage of households and average MPCE by primary source of energy for lighting – all India, 2007–08

Primary source of energy used for lighting	Rural		Urban	
	Percentage of households	Average MPCE (₹)	Percentage of households	Average MPCE (₹)
Kerosene	38.6	604	5.1	716
Electricity	60.2	886	93.8	1518
No lighting arrangement	0.6	576	0.3	1010
All*	100	772	100	1472

*includes sources other than those listed in column one

Source: Ministry of Statistics and Programme Implementation, 2010. NSS Report No.530: Household Consumer Expenditure in India, 2007–08; NSS 64th Round.

Successive expert groups on petroleum pricing have highlighted the need for a gradual phase out of subsidy on kerosene and LPG (particularly the latter) and improved targeting. As noted earlier, the Government of India has constituted the Task Force for Direct Transfer of Subsidies In order to evolve a suitable mechanism for direct subsidies to individuals/families who are entitled to kerosene, LPG and fertilizer and to evolve a model of direct transfer of subsidies on these items by re-engineering existing systems, processes and procedures (Government of India, 2011a). A new mechanism suggested by the Task Force included setting up an IT-enabled PDSN to provide direct subsidies on kerosene and food to poor, has already got in principle approval by the Indian government. Such a mechanism will help the beneficiaries to exercise choice in receiving their entitlement in kind or cash and at their most preferred location and help to check corruption, pilferage and diversion in the PDS (Government of India, 2011a and Government of India, 2011b).

Efficiency and environmental implications

By distorting price signals given out to economic agents, price controls and subsidies create inefficiencies that result in misallocation of resources in the economy. The fossil-fuel sector provides several glaring examples of such inefficiencies. First, subsidizing domestic consumers eliminates any incentive to economize on the use of petroleum products even in times of international price rise. In fact, when prices of crude rose in international markets, the demand for petroleum products such as petrol and diesel recorded double digit growth in India – even higher than the country's GDP growth – on account of artificially low domestic prices and increases in personal incomes (Government of India, 2010). As noted earlier, this trend is unsustainable from the point for the country's fiscal and trade balance.

The higher taxation of petrol vis-à-vis diesel is contrary to the worldwide trends where the excise levies on both products are more or less equal. The contrarian trend in Indian economy has had several adverse outcomes such as less emphasis on efficiency in road transport carriage as well as in agricultural and off-road applications and the spawning of diesel passenger vehicles with adverse environmental outcomes (Government of India, 2006a). In fact, the subsidy on diesel (along with cross-subsidization of passenger movement by freight movement by the railways) is one of the factors that has encouraged growth in freight movement by trucks rather than rail, which consumes around 1/4th as much diesel per net tonne kilometre as trucks (Government of India, 2010). India's roads account for a higher share of freight traffic compared to other continental-sized countries like the US and China (Figure

8.1), despite the fact that a large part of India's freight traffic comprises bulk material and moves over long distances that can be more economically served by rail and waterways (McKinsey, 2010). Further, the higher dependence on road transport is adverse for the environment as emissions from road transport are higher than emissions from rail and waterways.

Figure 8.1: Freight transport in India – dominated by roads

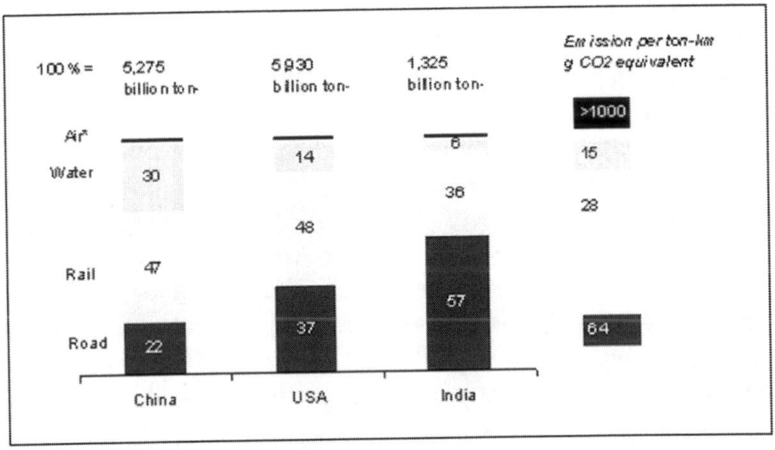

Source: As compiled by McKinsey 2010

Again, as noted earlier, the price differential between diesel and kerosene has resulted in large amounts of subsidized PDS kerosene – over 35 per cent – being diverted for unauthorized purposes including adulteration of diesel and use in standby generating sets. A consequence of this diversion is that the more than ₹ 20000 crore of investment in producing Euro III and Euro IV diesel would be negated to large extent.

Moving to the electricity sector, the cross-subsidization of agricultural and household sectors discourages energy-efficiency while providing an incentive for theft of power by industrial and commercial consumers. High electricity prices charged to industry also stimulates self-generation using inefficient diesel-powered generators. International experience suggests that the rate of diffusion of energy-efficient technologies is positively impacted by higher energy prices or lower capital costs (Bhattacharya and Cropper, 2010). Empirical evidence from US for instance suggests that higher energy prices have encouraged the adoption of energy-efficient room air-conditioners, central air-conditioners, and gas water heaters. While the effect of tariff reform in the electricity sector on appliance purchases has not been formally studied, there is qualitative evidence that consumers consider electricity prices when purchasing major appliances (Bhattacharya and Cropper, 2010). In the same vein, policies that heavily subsidize electricity use for farmers have contributed to poor energy-efficiency of agricultural pump sets in the sector in addition to encouraging overexploitation of groundwater resources. Again, subsidies to specific energy forms and technologies can undermine the development and commercialization of other technologies that might ultimately become more economically and environmentally attractive.

While these are some inferences that can be drawn on the efficiency and environmental impacts of fossil fuel subsidies (and hence the potential benefits of reducing them), a rigorous assessment of the economic and environmental impacts of fossil fuel subsidy reform is complex since subsidies come in different forms and are not always transparent and also since subsidy removal may have a multiplier effect across sectors. Ellis (2010) from the International Institute for Sustainable Development reviews six major studies that have been undertaken since the early 1990s to assess the economic, environmental and, in a few cases, the social impacts of fossil fuel subsidy reform at a global level. All these multi-country, multi-fuel studies include India and point to significant environmental and economic benefits that would result from the reform of fossil fuel subsidies.

The economic benefits arise from the more productive use of resources across countries, with concomitant terms-of-trade effects and savings in government expenditure which can be channelized into alternative social programmes. The focus of environmental impacts in these studies is reductions in emissions of either GHGs or only CO_2. For instance Burniaux *et al.* (2009) examined both unilateral and multilateral energy subsidy removal. They find that in the absence of any other mitigation measure, the emission of all GHGs in India would fall by about 7.2 per cent by 2020 and 25 per cent by 2050 relative to the BAU scenario due to multilateral removal of energy subsidies in non-OECD countries. On the other hand, the country's GDP can be expected to rise by 1.2 per cent and 3.1 per cent relative to the business-as-usual (BAU) in 2020 and 2050 respectively. Notwithstanding these expected trends, a discussion on the impacts of fossil fuel subsidy reforms in India will be driven primarily by local environmental concerns.

Assessing the local environmental benefits of subsidy removal is more complex given the nature of these impacts as well as the data required to understand and isolate them. For instance, while reducing fossil fuel subsidies may bring down their consumption and hence associated emissions, it may be argued that the sudden removal of subsidies for cooking fuels could increase the reliance on biomass for cooking, increasing pressure on forests and negatively affecting indoor air quality. This issue would need to be examined in greater detail.

Thus, while some assessments of the effect of phasing out of fuel subsidies on the macro-economy, public finance, equity, and local and global environment are available, a comprehensive analysis in this respect remains to be undertaken. Moreover, there has been deficient focus on the efficiency implications of moving from a regulated to a market-determined fuel pricing regime, in terms of conservation in fuel use and inter-fuel substitution possibilities that it may bring about. All of these aspects require careful analyses.

Fuel Expenditure and Price and Expenditure Elasticities in Household Sector

Most studies that assess the social or economic impact of subsidy removal or subsidy reform rely on partial- or general-equilibrium analyses to capture the impacts on consumer fuel expenditure and government tax expenditure on subsidies. Estimates of baseline fuel consumption pattern as well as fuel demand elasticities form important inputs into analyses of these impacts. This constitutes the focus of this section. Without getting into an impact assessment of subsidy reforms, this section focuses on the basic descriptive analysis of fuel use in rural and urban households in India and provides an assessment of fuels' own- and cross-price demand elasticities as well as responsiveness of fuel demand to changes in aggregate expenditure of households.[12] The analysis is based on NSSO's consumer expenditure surveys of households spanning the period 2005–10. The surveys do not report prices of fuels, therefore prices were estimated as the ratio of total expenditure on each fuel and the quantity consumed at the household level. A better understanding of these elasticities can help improve targeting of subsidy reforms by sector and end-use, rather than resorting to the limiting assumptions of zero elasticity of demand.

In what follows, the authors describe the data set, provide the basic descriptive statistics of the important variables, and discuss the estimates of elasticities inferred from the data. This sections ends with some policy implications that can be drawn from preliminary analysis of the survey data.

Data set

The analysis in this section draws upon the data collected periodically by the NSSO on consumer expenditure and covers three such rounds of survey, namely, the 62nd Round (July 2005–June 2006), the 64th Round (July 2007–June 2008) and the 66th Round (July 2009–June 2010). With these three rounds put together, the total number of households surveyed equals 190,588, with the composition across rounds of survey and the rural-urban mix as in Table 8.9.

Table 8.9: Distribution of surveyed households across rounds and sector (rural-urban)

Round	Frequency	Percentage
62nd	39436	21%
64th	50297	26%
66th	100855	53%
Total	190588	
Sector	**Frequency**	**Percentage**
Rural	109784	58%
Urban	80804	42%
Total	190588	

Source: Compiled from NSSO Consumer Expenditure Survey for Rounds 62nd, 64th and 66th.

The key variables on which data were extracted included quantity of fuel purchased and the expenditure incurred, as well as economic and demographic variables such as household monthly per capita expenditure and household size. The fuels covered included fuel wood, kerosene (from PDS and other free-market sources), LPG, electricity, petrol and diesel.[13] For their purpose, the authors only focussed on fuels that were used predominantly for cooking and lighting end-uses, leaving out petrol and diesel, which are primarily used for transportation or motive power.

The data for the three rounds of the survey were pooled and stacked together as a cross-section. The time-related changes have been captured by introducing time-indexed variable for the three survey rounds.

Basic descriptive statistics of key variables

Table 8.10 provides the basis descriptive statistics for the important variables that are used for working out the elasticity estimates.

Table 8.10: Descriptive statistics for the variables

Variable	Number of observations	mean	Standard deviation
Household size	190587	4.73	2.46
Monthly per capita expenditure	190588	1417.11	1403.36
Fuel wood			
Qty. (Kg)	116485	139.54	149.21
Value (₹)	116485	210.50	182.73
Kerosene PDS			
Qty. (litres)	106775	3.27	2.42
Value (₹)	106777	34.56	22.53
Kerosene (non-PDS or other)			
Qty. (litres)	39892	3.06	4.14
Value (₹)	39892	66.57	77.06
LPG			
Qty. (Kg)	83829	11.36	8.63
Value (₹)	83829	257.62	113.63
Electricity			
Qty. (kWh)	155239	84.33	520.16
Value (₹)	155263	206.32	241.85

Note: Qty. represents the physical units of quantity purchased during a month, while value refers to the expenditure over a month, both based on a 30-day recall period of the respondent.

Source: Compiled from NSSO Consumer Expenditure Survey for Rounds 62, 664 and 66.

As can be seen, the fuel basket of households is quite diverse in terms of the mix of fuels used by them. While modern fuels such as LPG, kerosene and electricity are present, the dependence on traditional fuels, such as fuel wood (as also charcoal, coke and animal dung) continues to persist in a significant way.

Regression results and discussion

The regression analysis was carried out by major fuels and purpose of use (cooking, lighting, and mixed end-use) for rural and urban areas separately.

In general, a log-log relationship was postulated in demand and price variables, such that the estimated coefficients of own and other fuel prices would directly represent the own- and cross-price elasticities of demand. The explanatory variables were taken to be the price of the fuel as well as that of potential complement and substitutes, in addition to a dummy for the survey round, household size, and monthly per capita expenditure. In general, the regressions results showed an overall good fit of the model to the data, as indicated by a significant F statistic though the R^2 varied from low to moderate, which is reasonable given a large cross sectional dataset. The key results are discussed below while the detailed tables can be found in Annexure 8.1.

Regressions for cooking fuels – rural

The first regression estimation was that for fuel wood which is largely used for cooking or water heating (Table 1, Appendix 1). The analysis confirmed that fuel wood demand was negatively related to its own price, and positively related to the prices of substitute fuels such as PDS kerosene and LPG. The own price elasticity is worked out to be -0.789, while the cross elasticities are 0.123 and 0.40 for PDS kerosene and LPG.[14] Interestingly, the price of electricity and price of non-PDS kerosene were found to be statistical insignificant determinants of fuel wood demand.

The demand is also positively related to the survey round, household size and monthly per capita expenditure, although all these coefficients are small in magnitude.

The next estimation was for LPG demand – used for cooking (Table 2, Appendix 1). Evidently, there exists a statistically significant dependence of LPG demand on all of the variables considered – own price, price of fuel wood, price of electricity, price of PDS kerosene, household size and monthly per capita expenditure The own price elasticity is negative and high (at -1.027, the demand is elastic), while cross-price elasticity with respect to fuel wood is low but negative (-0.102) indicating that it is a complement fuel for LPG. Other fuels, namely, electricity, PDS kerosene and non-PDS kerosene are substitutes in consumption, with cross-price elasticity of the order of 0.076, 0.293 and 0.245 respectively. Thus, demand for LPG is much more elastic with respect to own price than of other fuels. As expected, the responsiveness of LPG demand is positive in respect of household size and monthly per capita expenditure. The time index capturing the survey round was not found to be significant and hence left out of the regression estimation.

Regressions for cooking fuels – urban

For cooking and water heating, regressions similar to the rural sector were run for the urban households (Tables 3 and 4, Appendix 1).

The own price elasticity of fuel wood demand is found to be negative and high at -0.80, with both PDS kerosene and LPG as substitutes in consumption. The cross-price elasticity with respect to the two is found to be 0.14 and 0.20, both low but statistically significant substitutes. The coefficients of index of survey round, household size and monthly per capita expenditure have a positive sign; albeit low in magnitude. As in the rural case, both electricity and non-PDS kerosene prices showed up as insignificant explanatory variables and were dropped from the regression estimation.

The other regression equation that is estimated is that of demand for LPG. The own price elasticity is negative and high at -0.944, while both fuel wood and PDS kerosene are found to be substitutes, with PDS kerosene being a closer substitute (elasticity of 0.358) than fuel wood (elasticity of 0.058). The magnitude of the coefficients attached to household size and monthly per capita expenditure is small but significant with plausible signs. Variables that turn out to be insignificant explanators, and hence left out of the equation, are electricity, non-PDS kerosene and index for survey round.

Regressions for lighting fuels – rural

The demand for electricity for lighting (and other) end-uses, the regression analysis throws up a high and negative own price elasticity of demand (at -0.876). PDS kerosene is found to be significant substitutes reflected in the magnitude of elasticity (at 0.377), while non-PDS kerosene is a complement, albeit a weak one (with elasticity at -0.081). Demand for electricity has increased over time as depicted by a positive sign of the coefficient. Both household size and monthly per capita expenditure have a direct effect on electricity demand, although the coefficients for both are small (Table 5, Appendix 1).

Regressions for lighting fuels – urban

In the urban households the demand for electricity , for lighting (and other) end-use was found to be negatively correlated with own price – own price elasticity of demand is negative and significant although it the demand is less elastic (elasticity at -0.692) in case of urban households than the rural ones, as expected. PDS kerosene is a substitute, but with low elasticity of 0.110. While the demand for electricity is positively related to household size and monthly per capita expenditure, the latter has a much smaller effect at the margin than the former. Price of non-PDS kerosene and index of survey round are found to be insignificant explanators of demand for electricity, and hence excluded from the regression analysis (Table 6, Appendix 1).

Regression for mixed end-use – rural

To begin with, for PDS kerosene, all other fuels, with the exception of non-PDS kerosene, showed up as insignificant and, therefore, were dropped from the regression equation. The own price elasticity is found to be negative, at -0.6, and non-PDS kerosene is a complement although with a low elasticity estimate of -0.125. The coefficient of monthly per capita expenditure is positive but again low, while a negative relationship is found with time, captured by a negative coefficient of index of survey round (Table 7, Appendix 1).

For non-PDS kerosene, prices of both electricity and fuel wood were found to be insignificant and, hence, dropped. The own price elasticity was found to be lower, at -0.21. Moreover, PDS kerosene turns out to be a complement while LPG is a substitute. The cross price elasticity with respect to PDS kerosene is estimated to be higher (at -0.33) than own price elasticity. The coefficient of monthly per capita expenditure is again low (Table 8, Appendix 1).

Regressions for mixed end-use – urban

In case of PDS kerosene, all variables other than the price of non-PDS kerosene show up as insignificant and, hence, excluded. The own price elasticity of demand for PDS kerosene is negative and very high at -1.956, while non-PDS kerosene is found to be a complement (elasticity at -0.121). A positive relationship with the household size and monthly per capita expenditure is also found, although the magnitude of both the coefficients is small. A negative association is estimated with respect to the index of survey round (Table 9, Appendix 1).

As for non-PDS kerosene, both fuel wood and LPG prices were found not to be significant and were left out of the estimation. PDS kerosene and electricity are found to be complementary in use. The cross-price elasticity with PDS kerosene is very high (at -1.753), which was much higher than the own price elasticity (at -0.376).

There was a positive relationship found with respect to household size and monthly per capita expenditure albeit the coefficients are again low, while an inverse association is found with respect to time, implied by a negative coefficient of index of survey round (Table 10, Appendix 1).

The notable inferences that can be drawn from the above estimations can be summed up as follows:

- First, the relationships amongst some fuels (i.e., complements versus substitutes) are not entirely straightforward, as observed from the regression results. For instance, in the fuel wood demand regressions for rural areas, PDS kerosene shows up as a substitute, however in the PDS kerosene consumption regressions for rural households, fuel wood price is an insignificant explanatory factor. A similar relationship between LPG and fuel wood is found in rural areas. Clearly, other factors that influence inter-fuel relationships need to be understood. In the above case, it might be inferred that for households that have switched from fuel wood to cleaner and more modern fuels (kerosene and LPG), that is, moved up the energy ladder, fuel wood is no longer a substitution option. For households that are in the process of transition, prices and hence the level of subsidy available on cleaner fuels, will be an important determinant. In general, with the exception of fuel wood demand equations, the constant term is found to be very large and highly significant, explaining the presence of omitted variables from the model or presence of heterogeneity.
- PDS kerosene emerges as a substitute for electricity as a lighting fuel in both urban and rural areas, however, its use as a cooking fuel is not ruled out since it emerges as a substitute for both fuel wood and LPG in rural and urban areas. The use of non-PDS kerosene especially in urban areas is not clear (since it shows up as insignificant in both the lighting and cooking equations in urban areas). In rural areas, it shows up as a substitute to LPG and complement to electricity. Once again, any subsidy reform would need to clearly understand the factors that determine the multiple uses that a fuel is put to as well the cross-price relationships amongst fuels across these uses.
- Moreover, in the non-PDS kerosene consumption equations, the authors find that the magnitude of own price elasticity is lower than that of the cross-price elasticity with respect to PDS kerosene in both urban and rural areas, indicating a strong complementarity in use between the two sources of kerosene supply (PDS and non-PDS). However, by and large, the regressions for kerosene consumption (both PDS and non-PDS sources) are weaker with much lower R^2 values. Further, the coefficient for the index of survey round for all PDS and non-PDS kerosene consumption equations is found to be negative (although

rather small in magnitude) but significant. This points out that the consumption of these fuels is slowly reducing over time. These findings also corroborate the observation from other studies about diversion of kerosene to other sectors and end-uses, and the need for better targeting of kerosene subsidy.

- In general, monthly per capita expenditure is found to be a significant determinant of demand for individual fuels, although the estimated coefficients are small in magnitude.

The important policy implications that flow out of the above analyses can be summarized as follows:

- The own and cross-price elasticity of demand for the chosen fuels are generally found to be high, albeit close to or less than *one in most cases.* These elasticity estimates could be used in the assessment of impact of subsidy reforms on fuel demand, rather than relying on the restrictive assumption of zero elasticity of demand (Table 8.11).

Table 8.11: Summary of elasticity estimates

Fuel	**Rural**	**Urban**
Fuelwood	–0.789	–0.80
LPG	–1.027	–0.944
Electricity	–0.876	–0.692
PDS kerosene	–0.6	–1.956
Non-PDS kerosene	–0.21	–0.376

Source: Author's estimates

- On the one hand, from a pure economic efficiency perspective, Ramsey rule for efficient commodity taxation implies that tax levels across commodities or the price-cost margins should be inversely proportional to their price elasticity of demand in order to minimize the distortion in consumption. Given the author's estimates, this rule can form the basis for targeting subsidy reforms to those fuel uses where the elasticity of demand is the lowest. This will also be able to take care of the revenue considerations of the subsidy reform endeavour.

- It is found that non-PDS kerosene (in both rural and urban areas) and electricity (in urban areas) demonstrate amongst the lowest elasticities, while elasticity in case of PDS kerosene is high, especially in urban areas. Thus, from a purely efficiency perspective, non-PDS kerosene and urban electricity supply may form the candidates for subsidy rationalization.

- On the other hand, however, excessive reliance on the Ramsey principle will entail a higher burden of subsidy removal on those consumers that have the least elastic demand for a specific fuel (for instance, consumers of kerosene in rural or urban areas or consumers in urban areas in general), some of whom may be lifeline consumers with little or no room to manoeuvre due to absence of access to substitute fuels. Thus, equity considerations may support some differentiation in tax levels across products (e.g., lower tax levels on products consumed more by the poor, such as kerosene and domestic LPG). This would necessitate more disaggregated elasticity estimation by income/ expenditure class to be able to recommend a more nuanced approach to fuel price changes and subsidy targeting.
- In utilizing the elasticity estimates, a clear balancing across the objectives of efficiency, equity and revenue will have to be achieved so that any subsidy reforms initiative finds wider support and acceptability from diverse stakeholders.

Conclusion

In the context of the deliberations in the G20 countries' group, many reservations have been put forward about energy subsidy provisioning – from encouraging inefficiency in consumption and supply to escalating government budgetary deficits, from adverse distributional outcomes to local and global environmental concerns. The differences in the motivation and perception of concerns raised by the OECD and non-OECD country groups stem from the sovereign nations' individual circumstances and policy goals. However, it needs to be said at the outset that a meaningful comparison of subsidy estimates between these two groups of countries is not possible given the difference in assessment methods.

In the OECD countries, energy subsidies in the form of consumer subsidies (mainly on petroleum products) and producer subsidies on fossil fuels or nuclear power continue to prevail. The goal of the subsidies has been to provide protection to local industries from competition and from imports for reasons of regional employment or energy-supply security, or both. To the contrary, subsidies in the non-OECD developing countries, such as India, are aimed at keeping the price of basic goods and services (that use energy as a key input) at affordable levels and ensure access clean and modern fuels to the lifeline consumers for end-uses such as residential cooking and lighting. Moreover, since a bulk of energy production and supply is state–owned, the state utilities are usually treated as public service entities and are not required to maximize profits (UNEP, 2004).

Based on the earlier discussions the authors draw up the following specific conclusions towards revamping fuel subsidies in the specific context of India.

Coal

- Around 80 per cent of total domestic coal production is used for power generation. Thus, rationalization in coal prices cannot be undertaken independently of reforms in the power sector. However, there is the need to critically assess the cost of coal per unit of useful heat value so that any regressive anomalies in the relative pricing structure are ruled out.
- In the absence of large number of sellers and buyers for coal, and need for long-term supply and price contracts as well as point-to-point investment in the handling and transport network, establishing a free market mechanism for pricing coal in India remains an arduous task.
- Recent thinking seems to favour the regime of linking domestic coal prices to the price of imported coal. However, unlike petroleum products, there are no robust competitive prices for imported coal which could be universally accepted as benchmarks. Caution will thus have to be exercised in selecting appropriate benchmarks.

Oil products

- Given the country's rising dependence on oil imports as well as the general trend of increasing oil prices, it is fiscally unsustainable and economically inefficient for the government to insulate the consumers from price rise and bear a rising burden of subsidies. In line with what has been reasoned by all expert groups on the subject, domestic prices of petroleum products have to reflect international prices. The government should also allow OMCs some flexibility in fixing retail prices subject to stipulated guidelines on price ceiling.

- There is justification for continuing with subsidies on social grounds. However, it has to be ensured that the subsidy takes into account the profile of fuel consumers and is appropriately targeted. Given that both LPG and petrol is consumed by the economically better-off, there is no basis for continuing subsidies on these two fuels. As regards PDS kerosene, the government needs to ensure that the allocation of subsidy across states is based on a standard measure of people below the poverty line (such as one used by the Planning Commission) and that it is targeted to benefit only these groups. In this context, it may be said that studies find that the PDS has an impressive rural penetration, thus, the question for reforms is whether the same delivery machinery can be used to achieve the same reach at lower cost. The proposal to use or direct transfers or IT enables smart cards for the disbursement of the subsidy should be pursued in earnest.
- Where the government deems it necessary to subsidize consumers, the burden should be borne by it and explicitly and transparently shown in the budget. The earlier practice of relying on instruments such as the oil-bonds only postpones the resolution of the issues while compounding the economic and financial costs to producers/suppliers.

Natural gas

- The differential pricing of gas by sector and geographical location may have to continue for a while. The price of natural gas for priority sectors, such as power and fertilizer, will remain regulated in view of the regulated end-user prices for their products. However, in its recent moves, significant price increases for gas supplied by state-owned companies have been announced to put them at par with the private suppliers.
- Recently, the study by Mercados for GAIL has come up with an innovative gas pricing mechanism based on sectoral pooling of prices for the power and fertilizer sectors, for achieving price stabilization. The other sectors (such as compressed natural gas or CNG users for transportation and domestic gas users who have alternatives in LPG) could access their supplies from out-of-pool import contracts, smaller domestic gas sources and spot LNG (Mercados and GAIL, 2010). The government also needs to minimize the influence of populist politics on LNG pricing reforms.

Electricity

Electricity reforms are lagging behind given the massive future investment requirements and the critical role of the power sector in sustaining growth. One of the main reasons for this has been the lack of political will to revise electricity tariffs to economic levels and reduce subsidies and cross-subsidies. As noted, the country currently has some of the lowest and most uneconomic average electricity tariffs in the world, which are unsustainable, hamper much needed investments, encourage inefficient use of resources, and are not targeted at the poor. In fact, subsidies for agriculture have been disproportionately appropriated by richer famers and water-intensive crops. Thus, these subsidies have proved to be counterproductive both from the equity and resource–conservation point of view. Thus, lifeline metering and supply-side measures with explicit subsidies that are more carefully targeted are needed. Consumers prefer reliable supplies over subsidized and unreliable supplies. The evidence in India itself clearly suggests that better performing States have more economic pricing (till they reach a threshold level) and lower cross-price subsidies and distortions in tariffs (with industrial supply price ratio to domestic tariffs rationalized). Better tariff setting thus goes hand-in-hand with better economic performance (Ministry of Finance, 2011b).

In general, it is observed that the recently developed energy subsidies databases of IEA have an exclusive reliance on the price-gap approach for estimation of subsidies for developing and emerging economies. India's own estimates of energy sector subsidies fall significantly short of IEA estimates and, it is important that for India a re-assessment of subsidy estimates be carried out by utilizing national and state-level data for greater accuracy to capture the level of budgetary subsidies and tax expenditures for this purpose.

Appendix

Detailed results of fuel-specific regression analyses for rural and urban areas

Legend

lnfuelwd_kg : Log of fuelwood consumption (in kg)

lnlpg_kg : Log of LPG consumption (in kg)

lnelec_kwh : Log of electricity consumption (in kwh)

lnskopds_lit: Log of PDS-kerosene consumption (in lit)

lnskooth_lit: Log of Non-PDS-kerosene consumption (in lit)

lnfuelwd_uv: Log of unit value of fuelwood

lnlpg_uv: Log of unit value of LPG

lnelec_uv: Log of unit value of electricity

lnskopds_uv: Log of unit value of PDS Kerosene

lnskooth_uv: Log of unit value of Non-PDS Kerosene

round: NSS Round

hhsize: Household isze

mpce: Monthly per capita expenditure

cons: Constant term

Table 8.12: Fuel wood consumption by rural households

Source	SS	df	MS	
				Number of obs = 9595
				F(6,9588) = 729.79
Model	2458.0022	6	409.667034	Prob > F = 0.0000
Residual	5382.19883	9588	0.561347395	R-squared = 0.3135
				Adj R-squared = 0.3131
Total	7840.20103	9594	0.817198356	Root MSE = .74923

lnfuelwd_kg	Coef.	Std. Err.	t	P>|t|[	95% Conf. Interval]	
lnfuelwd_uv	-0.7896741	0.0135047	-58.47	0.000	-0.8161461	-0.7632021
lnskopds_uv	0.1231878	0.055978	2.20	0.028	0.013459	0.2329165
lnlpg_uv	0.4000199	0.0462545	8.65	0.000	0.3093513	0.4906885
round	0.0266244	0.0053801	4.95	0.000	0.0160783	0.0371705
hhsize	0.0937167	0.0028529	32.85	0.000	0.0881245	0.099309
mpce	0.0000533	4.85e-06	10.99	0.000	0.0000438	0.0000629
cons	0.8284722	0.3747349	2.21	0.027	0.0939126	1.563032

Table 8.13: LPG consumption by rural households

Source	SS	df	MS		
				Number of obs =	429
				F(7,421) =	18.28
Model	41.4976925	7	5.92824179	Prob > F =	0.0000
Residual	136.524537	421	0.324286312	R-squared =	0.2331
				Adj R-squared =	0.2204
Total	178.02223	428	0.415939789	Root MSE =	0.56946

lnlpg_kg	Coef.	Std. Err.	t	P>|t|	[95% Conf. Interval]	
lnlpg_uv	-1.027115	0.1068672	-9.61	0.000	-1.237175	-.8170552
lnfuelwd_uv	-0.1021175	0.0468746	-2.18	0.030	-0.1942549	-0.0099801
lnelec_uv	0.0764728	0.0347873	2.20	0.028	0.0080943	0.1448513
lnskopds_uv	0.2931628	0.1477507	1.98	0.048	0.0027418	0.5835838
lnskooth_uv	0.2446143	0.1066533	2.29	0.022	0.0349749	0.4542537
hhsize	0.0311976	0.0088075	3.54	0.000	0.0138854	0.0485098
mpce	0.0000721	0.0000192	3.75	0.000	0.0000343	0.0001098
cons	3.578304	0.4955055	7.22	0.000	2.604331	4.552277

Table 8.14: Fuel wood consumption by urban households

Source	SS	df	MS		
				Number of obs =	3414
				F(6,3407) =	252.57
Model	910.894869	6	151.815812	Prob > F =	0.0000
Residual	2047.87019	3407	0.601077249	R-squared =	0.3079
				Adj R-squared =	0.3066
Total	2958.76505	3413	0.866910359	Root MSE =	0.77529

lnfuelwd_kg	Coef.	Std. Err.	t	P>|t|	[95% Conf. Interval]	
lnfuelwd_uv	-0.7993383	0.0223749	-35.72	0.000	-0.8432079	-0.7554688
lnskopds_uv	0.1409238	0.0800406	1.76	0.078	-0.0160088	0.2978563
lnlpg_uv	0.1984148	0.0696724	2.85	0.004	0.061811	0.3350186
round	0.055259	0.0083639	6.61	0.000	0.0388603	0.0716578
hhsize	0.0835452	0.005309	15.74	0.000	0.073136	0.0939543
mpce	0.0000431	0.0000105	4.09	0.000	0.0000224	0.0000637
cons	-0.5276499	0.5646943	-0.93	0.350	-1.634824	0.5795238

Table 8.15: LPG consumption by urban households

Source	SS	df	MS	
				Number of obs = 3414
				F(5,3408) = 175.27
Model	238.84879	5	47.769758	Prob > F = 0.0000
Residual	928.863488	3408	0.27255384	R-squared = 0.2045
				Adj R-squared = 0.2034
Total	1167.71228	3413	0.342136618	Root MSE = 0.52207

lnlpg_kg	Coef.	Std. Err.	t	P>|t	[95% Conf.	Interval]
lnlpg_uv	-0.9441625	0.0464928	-20.31	0.000	1.035319	-0.8530059
lnfuelwd_uv	0.0567326	0.0149316	3.80	0.000	0.0274569	0.0860083
lnskopds_uv	0.3585341	0.0537283	6.67	0.000	0.2531911	0.4638771
hhsize	0.0637465	0.0035731	17.84	0.000	0.0567409	0.0707521
mpce	0.0001012	7.05e-06	14.35	0.000	0.0000874	0.0001151
cons	3.665292	0.1829546	20.03	0.000	3.30658	4.024004

Table 8.16: Electricity consumption by rural households

Source	SS	df	MS	
				Number of obs = 4072
				F(6,4065) = 926.90
Model	1734.45293	6	289.075488	Prob > F = 0.0000
Residual	1267.76137	4065	0.311872416	R-squared = 0.5777
				Adj R-squared = 0.5771
Total	3002.2143	4071	0.737463595	Root MSE = 0.55846

lnelec_kwh	Coef.	Std. Err.	t	P>|t|	[95% Conf.	Interval]
lnelec_uv	-0.8758935	0.0121378	-72.16	0.000	-0.8996903	-0.8520968
lnskopds_uv	0.3769048	0.0556562	6.77	0.000	0.2677882	0.4860214
lnskooth_uv	-0.0811063	0.0314635	-2.58	0.010	-0.142792	-0.0194207
round	0.037226	0.00629	5.92	0.000	0.0248941	0.0495578
hhsize	0.0427047	0.0031952	13.37	0.000	0.0364404	0.0489691
mpce	0.0001812	0.0000121	14.94	0.000	0.0001574	0.0002049
cons	1.099583	0.4049112	2.72	0.007	0.3057349	1.89343

Table 8.17: Electricity consumption by urban households

Source	SS	df	MS	
				Number of obs = 25249
				F(4,25244) = 5058.66
Model	7663.0787	4	1915.76968	Prob > F = 0.0000
Residual	9560.17582	25244	0.378710815	R-squared = 0.4449
				Adj R-squared = 0.4448
Total	17223.2545	25248	0.682163123	Root MSE = 0.61539

lnelec_kwh	Coef.	Std. Err.	t	P>|t|	[95% Conf. Interval]	
lnelec_uv	-0.6924262	0.0058084	-119.21	0.000	0.703811	-0.6810413
lnskopds_uv	0.1103083	0.0261242	4.22	0.000	0.0591033	0.1615133
hhsize	0.109255	0.0017357	62.94	0.000	0.1058529	0.1126571
mpce	0.0002881	4.15e-06	69.34	0.000	0.0002799	0.0002962
cons	3.528852	0.0607964	58.04	0.000	3.409687	3.648016

Table 8.18: Consumption of PDS kerosene by rural households

Source	SS	df	MS	
				Number of obs = 11012
				F(5,11006) = 332.88
Model	303.411899	5	60.6823799	Prob > F = 0.0000
Residual	2006.32544	11006	0.182293789	R-squared = 0.1314
				Adj R-squared = 0.1310
Total	2309.73734	11011	0.209766355	Root MSE = 0.42696

lnskopds_lit	Coef.	Std. Err.	t	P>|t|	[95% Conf. Interval]	
lnskopds_uv	-0.59666	0.0295162	-20.21	0.000	-0.6545172	-0.5388029
lnskooth_uv	-0.1250569	0.0158074	-7.91	0.000	-0.1560422	-0.0940716
lnskooth_uv	(omitted)					
round	-0.0078432	0.0028601	-2.74	0.006	-0.0134494	-0.0022369
hhsize	0.0539055	0.00159	33.90	0.000	0.0507887	0.0570223
mpce	0.0000726	7.50e-06	9.69	0.000	0.0000579	0.0000873
cons	2.902348	0.1846513	15.72	0.000	2.540398	3.264297

Note: Variable lnskooth_uv omitted because of collinearity

Table 8.19: Consumption of non–PDS kerosene by rural households

Source	SS	df	MS	
				Number of obs = 926
				F(6,919) = 37.22
Model	71.9027276	6	11.9837879	Prob > F = 0.0000
Residual	295.8848	919	0.321963874	R-squared = 0.1955
				Adj R-squared = 0.1902
Total	367.787528	925	0.397608138	Root MSE = 0.56742

lnskooth_lit	Coef.	Std. Err.	t	P>|t|	[95% Conf. Interval]	
lnskooth_uv	-0.20962	0.0706146	-2.97	0.003	-0.3482046	-0.0710353
lnskopds_uv	-0.3347966	0.1095879	-3.06	0.002	-0.5498682	-0.119725
lnlpg_uv	0.1200584	0.0866622	1.39	0.166	-0.0500204	0.2901373
round	-0.0601647	0.0136184	-4.42	0.000	-0.0868915	-0.033438
hhsize	0.0703933	0.0065618	10.73	0.000	0.0575155	0.0832711

mpce	0.0001184	0.0000166	7.14	0.000	0.0000858	0.0001509
cons	5.021054	0.872265	5.76	0.000	3.309191	6.732916

Table 8.20: Consumption of PDS kerosene by urban households

Source	SS	df	MS	
				Number of obs = 4079
				F(5,4073) = 260.94
Model	517.335017	5	103.467003	Prob > F = 0.0000
Residual	1614.98229	4073	0.396509279	R-squared = 0.2426
				Adj R-squared = 0.2417
Total	2132.31731	4078	0.522883107	Root MSE = 0.62969

lnskopds_lit	Coef.	Std. Err.	t	P>|t|	[95% Conf.	Interval]
lnskopds_uv	-1.956739	0.0601095	-32.55	0.000	-2.074586	-1.838891
lnskooth_uv	-0.1209602	0.0351137	-3.44	0.001	-.1898022	-.0521182
lnskooth_uv	(omitted)					
round	-0.0273686	0.0060315	-4.54	0.000	-.0391936	-.0155435
hhsize	0.0486761	0.0044043	11.05	0.000	.0400412	0.057311
mpce	0.0000999	0.0000143	7.01	0.000	.0000719	0.0001278
cons	7.673579	0.3894531	19.70	0.000	6.910038	8.43712

Note: lnskooth_uv omitted because of collinearity

Table 8.21: Consumption of non–PDS kerosene by urban households

Source	SS	df	MS	
				Number of obs = 4079
				F(5,4073) = 181.49
Model	616.940668	5	123.388134	Prob > F = 0.0000
Residual	2769.00525	4073	0.679844156	R-squared = 0.1822
				Adj R-squared = 0.1812
Total	3385.94591	4078	0.830295712	Root MSE = 0.82453

lnskooth_lit	Coef.	Std. Err.	t	P>|t|	[95% Conf.	Interval]
lnskooth_uv	-0.3765681	0.0459784	-8.19	0.000	-0.466711	-0.2864252
lnskopds_uv	-1.753645	0.0787084	-22.28	0.000	-1.907957	-1.599334
round	-0.0350306	0.0078978	-4.44	0.000	-0.0505145	-0.0195466
hhsize	0.0502931	0.0057671	8.72	0.000	0.0389865	0.0615998
mpce	0.0002454	0.0000187	13.15	0.000	0.0002088	0.000282
cons	8.155237	0.5099565	15.99	0.000	7.155443	9.15503

Endnotes

1 The authors acknowledge the support provided by the Indian Council for Research on International Economic Relations (ICRIER) for this chapter. They would also like to thank the officials of the Department of Economic Affairs, Ministry of Finance, Government of India, for their feedback and comments that helped improve the research. The authors would like to gratefully acknowledge the invaluable comments and insights provided by Rakesh Kacker on the article.

2 The authors focus in this chapter on fossil fuel subsidies. Hence throughout the discussion the term energy subsidies should be understood in this context.

3 External costs imply costs imposed by an activity of one agent that causes an uncompensated for welfare loss to another agent.

4 Tax expenditures are to be interpreted as relative to the benchmark tax structure of the country.

5 The rate of exchange used is ₹ 45= $1.

6 The rate of exchange used is ₹ 52= $1.

7 ₹ 1 crore = ₹ 10^7. Further, the conversion to dollars is made assuming the prevailing rate of exchange of $1= ₹ 45.

8 The issue of oil bonds has been discontinued since 2009–10 and the government has been meeting a part of subsidy from the national budget, which entails a more explicit reporting of the same.

9 http://powermin.nic.in/whats_new/pdf/Financial_restructuring_of_State_Distribution_Companies_discoms_Oct2012.pdf

10 NSSO surveys of household expenditure during 1999–2000 to 2005–06 reveal that around 53 per cent of households in high income states have exited PDS kerosene since 1999–2000, as compared to 24 per cent in low income states. Against this, the actual reduction in kerosene allocation has been much less, around 13 per cent (Government of India, 2010).

11 The 2005 NCAER study titled 'Comprehensive Study to Assess the Demand and Requirement of SKO' was based on a sample survey of urban and rural households. These households were asked questions about their use of kerosene, the price they paid, the use to which it was put, and the source of supply. The estimate of diversion comes from comparing the volumes of kerosene supplied by the government with estimates obtained by aggregating the purchases reported by households. The report is titled The finds cited above are from an article by Suman Bery (Whither the public distribution system?) which appeared on January 10, 2006 in the Business Standard.

12 While the own-price elasticity provides the proportionate change in demand due to proportionate change in fuel's own price, cross-price elasticity assesses this sensitivity in response to price of related fuels that may be substitutes or complements in use.

13 The other fuels covered by the NSSO household survey included coal, coke, animal dung, and charcoal, which were excluded from the authors' analysis since data on these fuels was too scanty to allow any meaningful analysis.

14 The demand is also positively related to the survey round, household size and monthly per capita expenditure, although all these coefficients are small in magnitude.

References

Bhattacharya, S. and M. L. Cropper. 2010. 'Options for Energy Efficiency in India and Barriers to Their Adoption', *Resources for the Future*. Discussion Paper No. 10–20.

Burniaux, J. M., J. Chanteau, R. Dellink, R. Duval and S. Jamet. 2009. 'The Economics of Climate Change Mitigation: How to Build the Necessary Global Action in a Cost-effective Manner', *OECD Economics Department Working Papers No. 701*.

Burniaux, J. and J. Chateau. 2011. 'Mitigation Potential of Removing Fossil Fuel Subsidies: A General Equilibrium Assessment', *OECD Economics Department Working Paper No. 853*. OECD Publishing. Available at: http://www.oecd–ilibrary.org/docserver/download/fulltext/5kgdx1jr2plp.pdf?expires=1304233828&id=id&accname=guest&checksum=2B32CDB218D849F5472E0715A66CCD0D.

Business Standard. 4 October 2011. 'Oil Bonds to Offer OMCs Less Value as Yields Move Up.'

Chakraborty, P., *et al.* 2010. 'Interstate Distribution of Central Expenditure and Subsidies', *Working Paper Number 2010–66*. National Institute of Public Finance and Policy. Available at: http://www.nipfp.org.in/newweb/sites/default/files/wp_2010_66.pdf. Accessed on 3 May 2011.

Coady, D., RG. Robert, O. Rolando, P. John, T. Shamsuddin and J. Tyson. 25 February 2010. 'Petroleum Product Subsidies: Costly, Inequitable, and Rising' Staff Position Note, SPN/10/05. International Monetary Fund, Washington, DC.

Earth Council. 1997. *Perverse Incentives: Subsidies and Sustainable Development*. Geneva.

Ellis, J. 2010. *Untold Billions: Fossil fuel Subsidies, their Impacts and the Path to Reform. The Effects of Fossil-Fuel Subsidy Reform: A Review of Modelling and Empirical studies.* Global Subsidies Initiative. Available at: www.globalsubsidies.org/files/assets/effects_ffs.pdf.

Global Subsidies Initiative. October 2009. 'Achieving the G20 Call to Phase Out Subsidies to Fossil Fuels', Policy Brief, International Institute for Sustainable Development, Geneva.

_______. 2010. 'Relative Subsidies to Energy Sources: GSI Estimates' Available at: www.globalsubsidies.org/files/assets/relative_energy_subsidies.pdf.

Government of India. December 2005. *Report of the Expert Committee on Road Map for Coal Sector Reforms*. New Delhi: Ministry of Coal, Government of India.

_______. 2006a. *Integrated Energy Policy: Report of the Expert Committee*. New Delhi: Planning Commission.

_________. February 2006b. *Report of the Committee on Pricing and Taxation of Petroleum Products*. New Delhi: Planning Commission.

__________. February 2010. *Report of the Expert Group on a Viable and Sustainable System of Pricing of Petroleum Products*. New Delhi: Planning Commission.

________. June 2011a. *Interim Report of the Task Force on Direct Transfer of Subsidies on Kerosene, LPG and Fertilizer*. New Delhi: Planning Commission.

_________. October 2011b. *Report of the Task Force on an IT Strategy for PDS and an Implementable Solution for the Direct Transfer of Subsidy for Food and Kerosene*. New Delhi: Planning Commission.

GSI. March 2010. 'Defining Fossil-fuel Subsidies for the G20: Which Approach is Best?' Policy Brief. Geneva: The Global Subsidies Initiative of the International Institute for Sustainable Development. Available at: www.globalsubsidies.org/files/assets/pb5_defining.pdf.

Hindu Business Line. 27 February 2011. 'Coal India Raizes Prices 30 per cent for Key Sectors'. Available at: http://www.thehindubusinessline.com/companies/article1495614.ece.

IEA. 2009. *Petroleum Prices, Taxation and Subsidies in India*. Paris: OECD.

IEA, OPEC, OECD and World Bank. 2010. 'Analysis of the Scope of Energy Subsidies and Suggestions for the G20 Initiative', prepared for submission to the G20 Summit Meeting, Toronto, 26–27 June 2010.

IEA, OPEC, OECD and World Bank. 2011. 'Joint Report by IEA, OPEC, OECD and World Bank on Fossil-fuel and Other Energy Subsidies: An Update of the G20 Pittsburgh and Toronto Commitments', prepared for the G20 Meeting of Finance Ministers and Central Bank Governors, Paris, 14–15 October 2011 and the G20 Summit, Cannes, 3–4 November 2011.

Koplow, D. August 2009. *Measuring Energy Subsidies using the Price-Gap Approach: What Does it Leave Out?* Manitoba, Canada: International Institute for Sustainable Development.

KPMG. 2009. *Think BRIC: Key Considerations for Investors Targeting the Power Sectors of the World's Largest Emerging Economies*. India Advisory. KPMG Interntional, a Swiss Cooperative.

Lang, K. 2011. *The First Year of the G20 Commitment on Fossil-Fuel Subsidies: A Commentary on Lessons Learned and the Path Forward*. Switzerland: GSI of the International Institute for Sustainable Development.

Live Mint. June 2010. 'Government Considering Import Parity Price for Domestic Coal', *The Wall Street Journal*. Available at: http://www.livemint.com/2010/06/01142523/Govt-considering-import-parity.html

McKinsey and Company. 2010. *Building India. Transforming the Nation's Logistics Infrastructure*. India.

Mercados and GAIL. January 2010. 'Study on Common Pool Mechanism for Natural Gas Industry in the Country' Report Prepared by Mercados Energy Markets India Private Limited for Gas Authority of India Limited.

Mehra, M. K., M. Sinha and S. Sahu. 2004. 'Trade-Related Subsidies – Bridging the North–South Divide: An Indian Perspective'. Discussion Paper of International Institute for Sustainable Development (IISD). Canada.

Ministry of Finance. 2010. 'Indian Public Finance Statistics 2009–2010', New Delhi, India: Government of India.

_______. 2011a. *Medium Term Fiscal Policy Statement, Union Budget 2011/12*. New Delhi: Government of India.

_______. 2011b. *Economic Survey 2010–11*. New Delhi: Government of India.

Ministry of Petroleum and Natural Gas (MoPNG). 2010. 'Basic Statistics on Indian Petroleum and Natural Gas 2009/10'. New Delhi, India: Government of India.

NCAER. 2006. 'Study of Macroeconomic Impact of High Oil Prices'. National Council of Applied Economic Research. Supported by Petroleum Federation of India. New Delhi.

OECD. 1998. 'Improving the Environment through Reducing Subsidies'. Paris, France.

________. 2011. 'Inventory of Estimated Budgetary Support and Tax Expenditures for Fossil Fuel. Preliminary Report'. Paris, France.

Pachauri, S. and L. Jiang. 2008. 'The Household Energy Transition in India and China', *Interim Report IR-08-009*. Vienna, Austria: International Institute for Applied Systems Analysis.

Platts International. 2010. *Platts International Coal Price Report*. Available at: http://www.platts.com/IM.Platts.Content/ ProductsServices/Products/intlcoalreport.pdf.

Petroleum Planning and Analysis Cell (PPAC). website. http://ppac.org.in. Accessed on 15 November 2011.

Rao, S. L. July 31, 2006. 'Confusion in Pricing of Energy Products', *Telegraph*. Kolkata.

Saunders, M. and K. Schneider. 2000. 'Removing Energy Subsidies in Developing and Transition Economies', *Conference Paper No 2000.14*. Canberra, Australia: Australian Bureau of Agricultural and Resource Economics.

TERI. 2009. *TERI Energy Data Directory and Yearbook, 2009*. New Delhi, India.

UNEP. 2004. *Energy Subsidies: Lessons Learned in Assessing the Impact and Designing Policy Reforms*. Geneva: United Nations Foundation.

World Energy Outlook and International Energy Agency (WEO/IEA). 2008. *World Energy Outlook 2008*. Paris: OECD.

________. 2009. *World Energy Outlook 2009*. Paris: OECD.

________. 2010. *World Energy Outlook 2010*. Paris: OECD.

________. 2010. *World Energy Outlook*, Energy Subsidies Database. Available at: www.worldenergyoutlook.org/ subsidies.asp

World Bank. 2010. 'Subsidies in the Energy Sector: An Overview', Background Paper for the World Bank Group Energy Sector Strategy, 2010. Washington DC.

9 Should India Join the International Energy Agency?

Prodipto Ghosh

Introduction

India's membership of the G20, a grouping of major nations set up by expanding the original G8 of the world's largest economic powers, to deliberate upon, and where possible, cooperate on issues of global concern, both enhances India's role in world affairs, as well as imposes possible constraints on policy actions by India.

One of the significant issues before the G20 is the issue of global energy security, which at the present time revolves around the twin poles of security of global petroleum supplies, and the sharing of burdens for mitigation of climate change. In respect of security of petroleum supplies, a key player, hitherto comprising solely present OECD members, is the IEA. There have been suggestions that it is now time for India, China, and possibly Russia to become members of the IEA, on account of their increasing salience in the global oil market. However, the costs and benefits of such membership must be carefully weighed, before a decision is taken to avail of the responsibilities of such membership.

This chapter discusses the pros and cons of India joining the IEA, including possible governance reform of the IEA as a prerequisite of such membership.

The chapter discusses the IEA's origin, mandate, and core mission. It also presents the long-term global oil supply outlook as well as discusses an important emerging global energy option, shale gas. The following section gives an account of India's energy challenges, discusses the prospects of admission of new members to the IEA, summarizes the pros and cons of membership, as well as governance reforms that could be insisted upon as prerequisite to membership of India (and China). It also discusses India's options for cooperation with the IEA without formal membership.

IEA's origin, mandate and core mission

The IEA was established following the first oil price shock of the 1970s; to coordinate emergency supply measures and improve the governance of long-term energy issues. Its core mission is to ensure secure energy supply for its members (presently: advanced industrial countries comprising the OECD).

Background to setting up of IEA: First part

Existing international energy institutions may be divided into: (1) those created by and for petroleum-exporting states (e.g. Organization of the Petroleum Exporting Countries or OPEC); and (2) those created by and for petroleum consuming states (e.g. IEA).[1] There is no major international energy organization with global membership.[2], [3] IEA was formed in November 1974 following the first oil price shock of 1973–74,[4] originally with 16 members, since expanded to 25 members, all of whom are also OECD members.[5] In 2009, the IEA members collectively accounted for 60–70 per cent of global energy consumption,[6] the share, however, declining with time.

The need for an energy-focused organization for OECD members arose from the fact that the existing machinery, the OECD Committee Structure, '*was perceived as too rigid and incapable of taking decisive action*'[7] Despite the formation of the IEA the OECD never gave up the mandate to address energy policy issues, and the G20[8] also has a mandate to address energy policy coordination.[9]

The Agreement on an International Energy Programme, signed by the initial 16 Member states[10] on 18 November 1974, reflected the conviction that the programme should be established in an international treaty rather than in an instrument of lesser legal standing. The most compelling reason for the treaty approach was the need to establish the Agency's Emergency Sharing System,[11] in absolutely binding terms from a legal standpoint. In situations of oil supply disruptions presenting high economic and political stakes, it is possible that countries might take actions, which are not sufficiently consistent with the collective interests of the group, because of internal as well as external forces acting on the countries. At times the costs of compliance with a system of oil sharing might be high. In some situations there also could be pressures by oil producers on selected members or compliance might jeopardize other political objectives, leading member countries toward introverted policies rather than cooperative sharing actions.

Since such divisive factors were clearly at work in various degrees during the 1973–74 crisis, the founders wished, in sharing the available oil supplies, to minimize those potential risks to the integrity of the new emergency response system. During the 1973–74 crisis, experience with non-legally binding arrangements had not been particularly favourable. In particular, the European members of the OECD had not delivered adequately on their political commitments taken in the OECD Stocks Recommendation to maintain oil stocks for emergency purposes. Nor had it proved possible for those members to find the political will to activate the loosely structured OECD Oil Apportionment Decision applicable to the European members of OECD. Accordingly, effective sharing arrangements on a wider basis could not be put in place during the crisis. Thus it was evident that voluntary systems based on recommendations, declarations, or other non-legally binding, imprecise or insufficiently developed arrangements could not be expected to function properly in times of crisis. Since a system of commodity sharing in times of crisis is inherently one that distributes the burdens, no country could reasonably be expected to carry out a costly cooperative action unless it were satisfied that the strongest measures were in place to ensure that the other participants in the system would accept their shares of the overall burden and carry out their commitments under the system.

The founders were clear that they could not allow such difficulties to undermine the objectives of the new agency. The IEA's sharing system could not function unless all members respected their oil stocking and demand restraint commitments and carried out their oil sharing obligations fully and promptly when they arose under the IEA decisions. The founders accordingly concluded that it was necessary to use legally binding provisions on the *key elements* of the system and to embody those provisions in an international treaty, thus making the commitments as formal, visible and convincing as possible. A treaty could also be expected to assist members with their own constituencies in times of crisis. The adoption of legal undertakings would have the advantage of placing them within the international legal system and subjecting them to incentives for compliance. Monitoring and administration would also be greatly facilitated, particularly with the advantage of the IEA reporting, reviewing and performance assessment capabilities. The programme would be much more effective than it might have been if established on political formulations with less formal standing than the legal arrangements which were adopted in the treaty.

Mandate and core mission

The IEA has two major functions, i.e. (1) to maintain and improve systems for managing oil supply disruptions; and in case of oil supply disruptions, to distribute oil allocations to its members; and (2) the development of policy, information sharing, and technology transfer. During the long periods without oil supply crises, the second ('non-core') function is its principal function. The IEA is one of the few international public organizations whose decisions are legally binding on its members. None of the other (regional, net importer) energy organizations have such powers.

Specific binding requirements include: (1) creation of national strategic oil reserves by its members; and (2) allocation decisions, including releases from national strategic oil reserves, in the event of an international oil emergency. These requirements would permit decisions (on both aspects, but principally with regard to the latter) on differentiated criteria across member countries, and given the nature of political decision making by such bodies, the criteria for differentiation, should circumstances warrant it, would reflect the respective voting strengths in the governing board.

The need to coordinate creation of national strategic oil reserves arose from the experience of the 1973 oil crisis, when OECD members competitively stockpiled oil, further enhancing oil prices to the detriment of all. The IEA has, since its formation, required each of its members to maintain a petroleum reserve, computed in terms of a specified number of days of net oil imports of the member country. The level of reserves was originally set at 60 days of net imports, later increased to 70 days, and still later, to 90 days, the last remaining unchanged for over 30 years.

Releases of national strategic oil reserves has been authorized by the IEA twice so far: the first during the 1991 US-Iraq War, and the second, following Hurricane Katrina, which disrupted domestic US oil supplies through damage to oil installations in Mississippi and Louisiana.[12]

Governance and membership

The distribution of the votes on the governing board is based on the net imports of oil by the members in 1973, which has not changed since inception of the IEA. Each member is given three votes, plus a number in proportion to their net oil imports in 1973. The decision-making procedure requires a majority (of votes allocated by the above formula), in particular where specific obligations are to be imposed on the members (Article 61.1) although consensus is the norm in practice.[13] The structure of votes, even of the existing members, would be very different if based on current net oil imports. While the more general procedures are provided in Article 73,[14] Articles 62.5 and 62.6 of the 1974 Agreement permit adjustments of voting powers periodically based on changes in oil consumption patterns. Despite several attempts in the 1990s, this has not happened so far.

The votes assigned to the 16 original and 25 current IEA members are given in the Appendix.

In the presentation of empirical results later in the chapter, data and projections from the US Energy Information Administration (EIA) have been used. These have been supplemented with other data/projections, where relevant.

Long-term Global Oil Supplies

The discussion below represents the 'Reference Case' of the EIA's 'International Energy Outlook, 2010' (IEO 2010). The Reference Case makes the following assumptions:

- Generally assumes current laws and regulations, and excludes potential future laws and regulations.
- Provisions with sunset clause as specified in law (e.g., expiry of renewable tax credits).
- Includes technologies that are commercial or reasonably expected to become commercial over the next decade or so.
- Includes projected cost and efficiency improvements due to technology improvements, as well as cost reductions linked to cumulative deployment levels.
- Does not assume revolutionary or breakthrough technologies.

Projections of global oil prices till 2035 generated by the model are given below in Figure 9.1.

Figure 9.1: Projections of global oil price till 2035

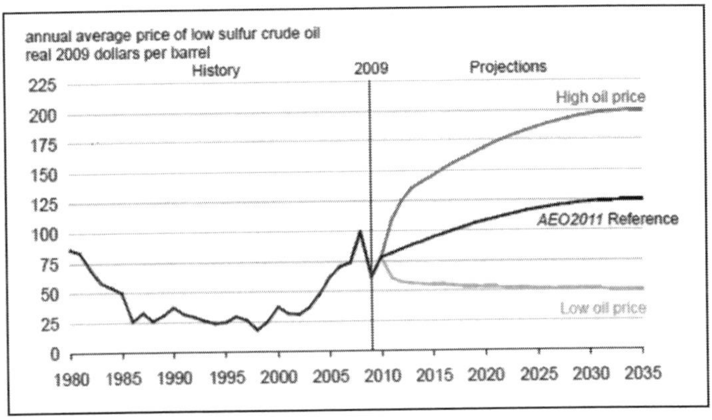

Source: EIA: Annual Energy Outlook 2011.

Oil prices rise in the Reference Case and the 'High Oil Price' case, but moderates in the 'Low Oil Price' case.

Economic activity and population drive increases in oil use; while energy intensity improvements moderate this trend as shown in Figure 9.2.

Figure 9.2: Changes in population, per capita GDP, energy intensity, oil intensity, and oil use in different global regions, 2007–35

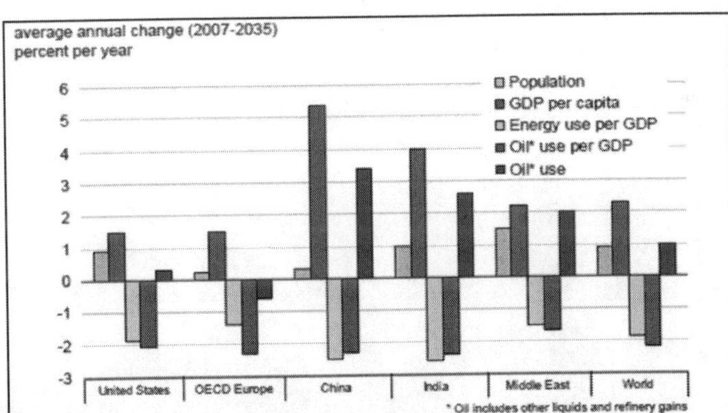

Source: EIA: Annual Energy Outlook 2011.

It may be noted that India's average annual population growth rate (1 per cent) is virtually at par with the global average, while the rate of per capita GDP growth (4 per cent) is next only to that of China (5.4 per cent). Oil use increases at 2.7 per cent per annum, again, next only to that of China. However, India's fall in both energy and oil intensity is the highest in the world (-2.6 per cent and -2.4 per cent respectively), followed closely by China.

Oil use by non-OECD countries exceeds that of OECD countries by 2020, in line with the projections in growth of oil use in China and India, as well as of other developing countries as shown in Figure 9.3.

Figure 9.3: Trajectories of oil use by OECD and non-OECD countries, 2007–35

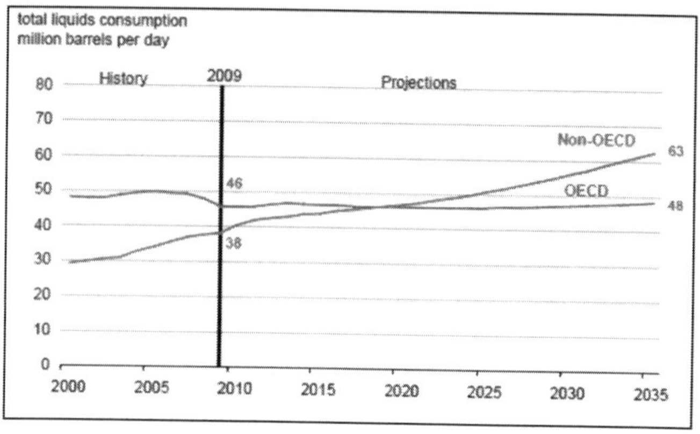

Source: EIA: Annual Energy Outlook 2011.

What are the sources of the increased supply of oil? Within OPEC, the increased supply would be from Saudi Arabia, Iraq, and other Middle East countries as shown in Figure 9.4.

Figure 9.4: Changes in conventional oil production till 2035 from different OPEC sources

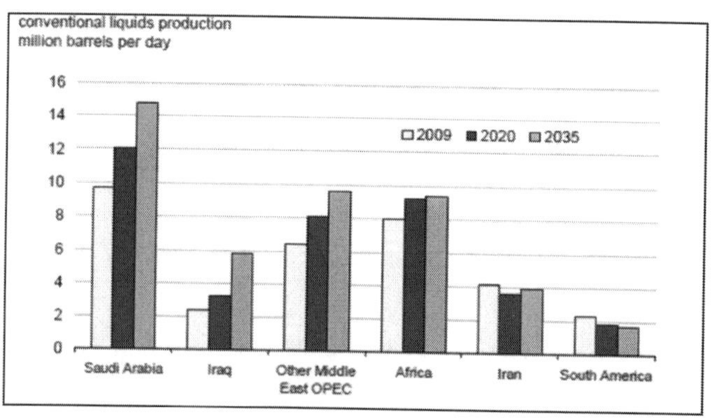

Source: EIA: Annual Energy Outlook 2011.

Brazil, Russia, the United States, and Kazakhstan lead increases in non-OPEC conventional supplies as shown in Figure 9.5.

Figure 9.5: Changes in conventional oil production till 2035 from different non-OPEC sources

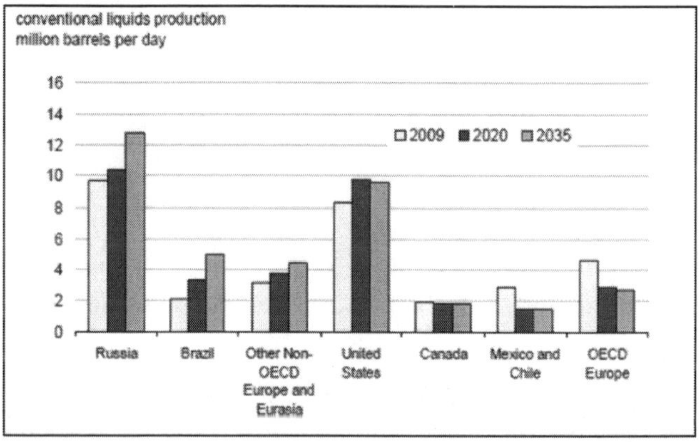

Source: EIA: Annual Energy Outlook 2011.

In addition to conventional oil, production of liquid fuels from non-conventional sources is also likely to increase. Canadian oil sands and biofuels from Brazil and the US would account for 65 per cent of the supply of unconventional liquid fuels as shown in Figure 9.6.

Figure 9.6: Production of unconventional liquid fuels till 2035

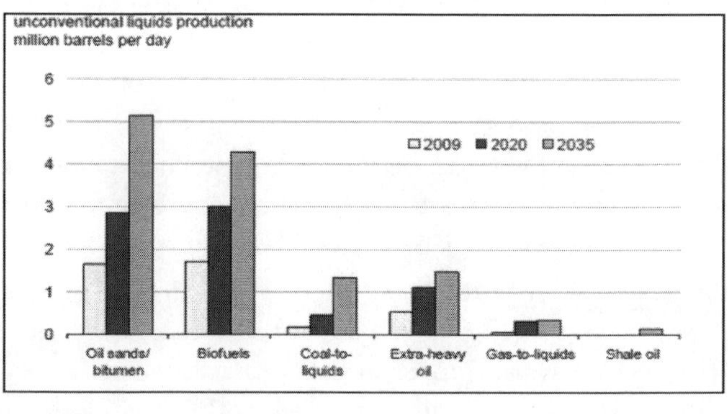

Source: EIA: Annual Energy Outlook 2011.

'Peak Oil': What are the prospects of the much talked about (and feared) 'Peak Oil', characterized by rapidly rising oil prices and falling supply? Earth's endowment of conventional reservoirs of crude oil, though large, is clearly limited. Most of earth's prolific oil basins are already identified; most of these are partially to nearly fully exploited, and production has peaked and declined in some of the most prolific basins. While the EIAs modeling results, even in the high oil price scenario, does not indicate actual falling oil supplies, and consequent runaway increase in oil prices, it would clearly be prudent, while considering policy options, to allow for the possibility of 'peak oil' in the near to medium-term, and certainly well within the present century.

Conventional oil supplies may be supplemented by unconventional liquids: tar sands, oil shales, or created liquids: gas-to-oil, coal-to-oil, biofuels. However, there are major environmental concerns associated with mined unconventional oil; climate change concerns with coal-to-liquid; and food security concerns with respect to biofuels. It is unlikely that individually or collectively, the presently available unconventional liquids would be serious alternatives to conventional oil in the near future.

However, there is a 'new kid on the block', which may yet help realize global energy security in the short to medium term, until renewable energy technologies reach technical and commercial maturity, and may be deployed on a scale that is large enough to replace conventional fossil fuels.

'New Kid on the Block': Shale Gas

Shale gas is natural gas produced from shale. Shale gas has become an increasingly important source of natural gas in the United States over the past decade, and interest has spread to potential gas shales in Canada, Europe, Asia, and Australia. Shale has low matrix permeability, so gas production in commercial quantities requires fractures to provide permeability.

Shale gas has been produced for years from shales with natural fractures; the shale gas boom in recent years has been due to modern technology in hydraulic fracturing ('fracking') to create extensive artificial fractures around well bores. Figure 9.7 illustrates the geology of conventional natural gas and shale gas.

Estimated global resources, together with current production and consumption, are given in Table 9.1. To put this shale gas resource estimate in some perspective, world proven reserves of natural gas as of 1 January 2010 are about 6,609 trillion cubic feet and world's technically recoverable gas resources are roughly 16,000 trillion cubic feet, largely excluding shale gas. Thus, adding the identified shale gas resources to other gas resources increases total world technically recoverable gas resources by over 40 per cent to 22,600 trillion cubic feet.

Figure 9.7: Geology of natural gas and shale gas

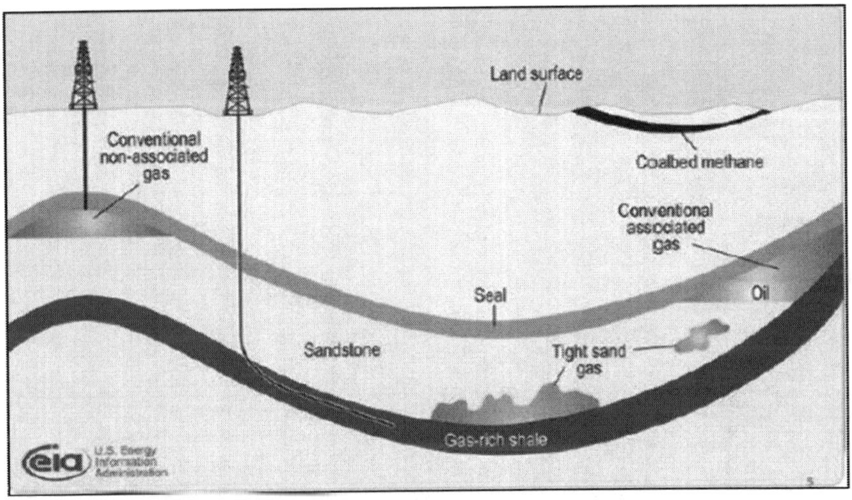

Source: US Energy Information Administration

Table 9.1: Estimated global natural gas resources and technically recoverable shale gas resources

	2000 Natural gas market(1) (trilion cubic feet, dry basis)			Proved natural gas reserves(2) (trillion cubic feet)	Technically recoverable shale gas resources (trillion cubic feet)
	Production	**Consumption**	**Imports (exports)**		
Europe					
France	0.03	1.73	98%	0.2	180
Germany	0.51	3.27	84%	6.2	8
Netherlands	2.79	1.72	(62%)	49.0	17
Norway	3.65	0.16	(2,156%)	72.0	83
U.K.	2.09	3.11	33%	9.0	20
Denmark	0.30	0.16	(91%)	2.1	23
Sweden	-	0.04	100%	-	41
Poland	0.21	0.58	64%	5.8	187
Turkey	0.03	1.24	98%	0.2	15
Ukraine	0.72	1.56	54%	39.0	42
Lithuania	-	0.10	100%	-	4
Others(3)	0.48	0.95	50%	2.71	19

	2000 Natural gas market(1) (trilion cubic feet, dry basis)			Proved natural gas reserves[(2)] (trillion cubic feet)	Technically recoverable shale gas resources (trillion cubic feet)
	Production	Consumption	Imports (exports)		
North America					
United States(4)	20.6	22.8	10%	272.5	862
Canada	5.63	3.01	(87%)	62.0	388
Mexico	1.77	2.15	18%	12.0	681
Asia					
China	2.93	3.08	5%	107.0	1,275
India	1.43	1.87	24%	37.9	63
Pakistan	1.36	1.36	-	29.7	51
Australia	1.67	1.09	(52%)	110.0	396
Africa					
South Africa	0.07	0.19	63%	-	485
Libya	0.56	0.21	(165%)	54.7	290
Tunisia	0.13	0.17	26%	2.3	18
Algeria	2.88	1.02	(183%)	159.0	231
Morocco	0.00	0.02	90%	0.1	11
Western Sahara	-	-		-	7
Mauntania	-	-		1.0	0
South America					
Venezuela	0.65	0.71	9%	178.9	11
Colombia	0.37	0.31	(21%)	4.0	19
Argentina	1.46	1.52	4%	13.4	774
Brazil	0.36	0.66	45%	12.9	226
Chile	0.06	0.10	52%	3.5	64
Uruguay	-	0.00	100%	-	21
Paraguay	-	-	-	-	62
Bolivia	0.45	0.10	(346%)	26.5	48
Total of above areas	53.1	55.0	(3%)	1,001	6,622
Total world	106.5	106.7	0%	6,609	

Source: US EIA: Annual Energy Outlook 2011

It is clear that global technically recoverable resources of shale gas represent a significant accretion to currently known conventional natural gas resources. However, several environmental concerns are associated with shale gas extraction: the shale hydraulic fracturing process involves pumping large quantities of water, benzene (highly carcinogenic), and trade secrets protected proprietary chemicals into the shale rock from the horizontal bores, which shatters the shale rock and enables the gas to flow. Unless there is adequate recovery and reuse of wastewater, shale gas extraction in arid regions would cause significant stress on water resources. Although fears have been expressed regarding contamination of groundwater due to chemicals use, since shale rock is located several hundred metres below the surface, well below aquifers, the possibilities of contamination of groundwater are minimal. However, use of chemicals would require greater transparency, and stronger regulation.

Extraction of large quantities of shale gas requires large numbers of wells separated by a few kilometres, and associated connectivity of gas pipelines. This fact would rule out shale gas extraction in sensitive ecosystems such as dense natural forest.

India's Energy Challenges

India's principal energy challenges arise from the twin imperatives of poverty eradication,[15] given that a key attribute of poverty is use of traditional biomass fuels, on which c. 70 per cent of the population remain dependent, and that of supporting annual GDP growth rates of c. 8–9 per cent. India's per capita energy consumption in 2006 was just 510 kgoe (kilogram, oil equivalent), among the lowest in the world. About 404 million persons had no access to electricity in 2008, and the per capita electricity consumption was just 503 kilowatt hours (KWh) per year (2006). The energy intensity of the economy in 2006 was 4.7 kgoe per $PPP, also a low figure relative to many industrialized countries, signifying that the country was relatively efficient in its use of energy for production activities.

In 2006, India was the fourth largest oil consumer in the world, after the United States, China, and Japan, with total commercial energy consumption of 566 mtoe, an annual rate of increase of 5.2 per cent during 2005–09. Despite the global financial crisis, India's energy demand continues to rise. In terms of end-use, energy demand in the transport sector is expected to be particularly high, as vehicle ownership, particularly of four-wheel vehicles, is forecast to increase rapidly in the years ahead, as also the household sector, as millions of poor families attain middle-class status.

India lacks sufficient domestic energy resources and imports much of its growing energy requirements. In addition to pursuing domestic oil and gas exploration and production projects, India is also stepping up its natural gas imports, particularly through imports of liquefied natural gas.

Coal/lignite accounts for nearly 40 per cent of India's total energy consumption, followed by nearly 27 per cent for traditional biomass sourced from fuel wood and animal residues, and crop waste. Oil accounts for nearly 24 per cent of total energy consumption, natural gas 6 per cent, hydroelectric power almost 2 per cent, nuclear nearly 2 per cent, and other renewables less than 0.5 per cent. Although nuclear power comprises a very small percentage of total energy consumption at this time, it is expected to increase in light of international civil nuclear energy cooperation deals. At present, nearly 30 per cent of India's total energy needs are met through imports.

Figure 9.8: India's fuel mix in 2007

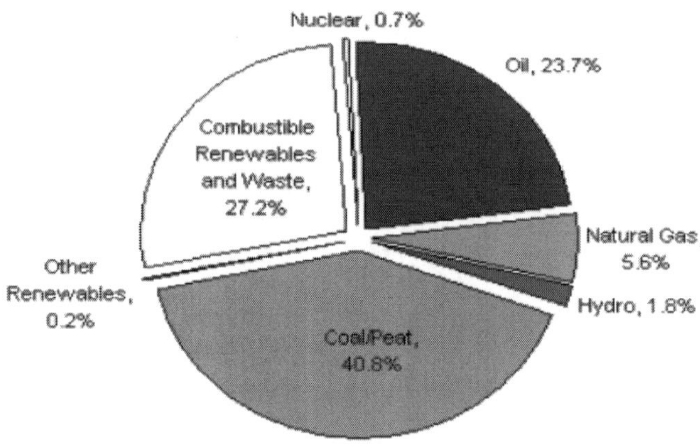

Source: IEA

In 2008 electrification rates for India were nearly 65 per cent for the country as a whole. In urban areas, 93 per cent had access to electricity compared to rural areas where electrification rates were approximately 50 per cent.

India's Oil Situation

India's oil situation

India had approximately 5.6 billion barrels of proven oil reserves as of January 2010, the second largest amount in the Asia Pacific region after China. India produced roughly 880,000 barrels per day (bbl/d) of total oil in 2009 from over 3,600 operating oil wells. Approximately 680,000 bbl/d was crude oil and the remainder comprised other liquids and refinery gain. In 2009, India consumed nearly 3 million bbl/d, making it the fourth largest consumer of oil in the world. It is likely that annual consumption growth till 2012 would be c.100,000 bbl/d.

Figure 9.9: India's oil production and consumption, 1990–2009

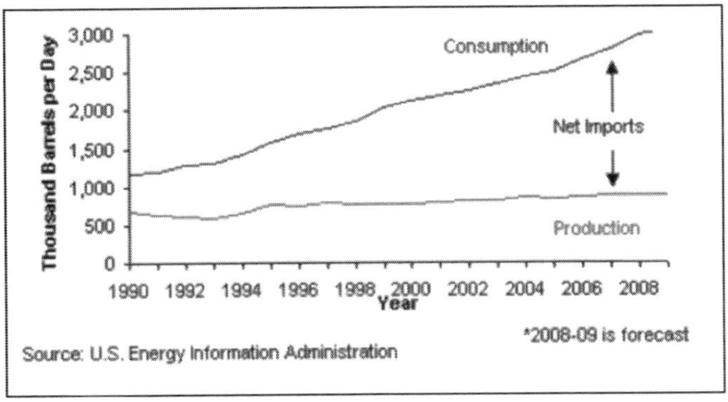

Source: US EIA

The combination of rising oil consumption and relatively flat production has left India increasingly dependent on imports to meet its petroleum demand. In 2009, India was the sixth largest net importer of oil in the world, importing nearly 2.1 million bbl/d or about 70 per cent, of its oil needs. It is expected that India would become the fourth largest net importer of oil in the world by 2025, after the United States, China, and Japan.

Nearly 70 per cent of India's crude oil imports come from the Middle East, primarily from Saudi Arabia, followed by Iran. It is expected that this import dependence would rise in light of limited prospects for domestic production.

Figure 9.10: India's crude imports by country in 2009

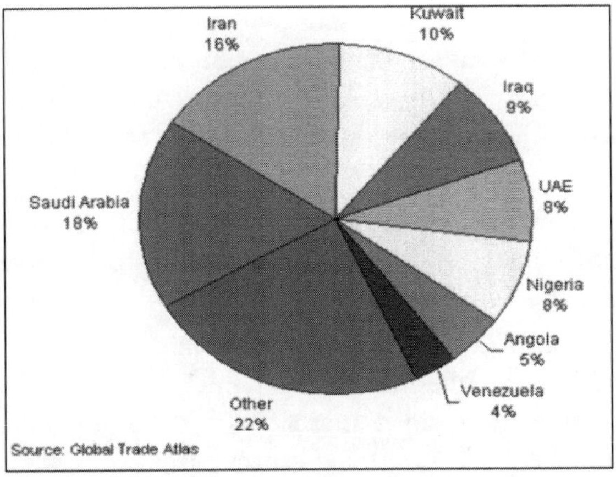

Source: Global Trade Atlas

Most of India's crude oil reserves are located offshore, in the west of the country, and onshore in the northeast. Substantial reserves are also located offshore in the Bay of Bengal and in Rajasthan. India's largest oil field is the offshore Mumbai High field, located northwest of Mumbai and operated by ONGC. Another of India's large oil fields is the Krishna-Godavari basin, located in the Bay of Bengal. Block D6 in the Krishna-Godavari basin, operated by Reliance Industries, began oil production in September 2008.

The primary mechanism through which the Indian government has promoted new exploration and production (E&P) projects has been the NELP framework, involving competitive bidding for shares in the oil extracted, after accounting for exploration and production costs.

In recent years, Indian national oil companies have increasingly looked to acquire equity stakes in E&P projects overseas. The most active company abroad is ONGC Videsh Ltd. (OVL), the overseas investment arm of ONGC. OVL conducts oil and natural gas operations in 13 countries, including Vietnam, Myanmar, Russia (Sakhalin Island), Iran, Iraq, Sudan, Brazil, and Columbia. One of OVL's most high profile investments is its share in the Greater Nile Petroleum Operating Company (GNPOC), which has engaged in E&P work in Sudan since 1997. OVL acquired a 25 per cent equity stake in the company in 2003, with the balance held by the China National Petroleum Company (CNPC, 40 per cent), Petronas (30 per cent), and the Sudan National Oil Company (Sudapet, 5 per cent). The GNPOC acreage in Sudan holds proven crude oil reserves of more than one billion barrels with current production levels at roughly 300,000 bbl/d from 10 fields. In addition to the upstream activities, the GNPOC companies operate a 935-mile crude oil pipeline that pumps oil to Port Sudan for export. OVL also holds a 20 per cent stake in the ExxonMobil led consortium that operates the Sakhalin-I project in Russia. According to company estimates, the oil fields associated with Sakhalin-I hold recoverable crude oil reserves of 2.3 billion barrels.

In addition to ONGC, other Indian companies are also actively involved in E&P projects abroad. OIL, for example, is working on projects in Libya, Gabon, Nigeria, and Sudan.

India had 2.8 million bbl/d of crude oil refining capacity at 18 facilities as of January 2010, i.e., the fifth largest refinery capacity in the world. In 2009, Reliance Industries added another refinery to its Jamnagar complex to raise the entire complex's refining capacity from 660,000 bbl/d to 1.24 million bbl/d, making the Jamnagar complex the largest oil refinery complex in the world. Other key refinery projects include Essar Oil's Vadinar refinery expansion of 110,000 bbl/d in 2011, 120,000 bbl/d green-field refinery in Bina in 2011 by a joint venture between Bharat Petroleum Corporation Limited and Oman Oil Company Limited, a 180,000 bbl/d grassroots refinery in Bhatinda in 2014 by Hindustan Petroleum Corporation Limited, and Indian Oil Corporation's (IOC) Paradeep refinery of 300,000 bbl/d in 2015. India is slated to add 840,000 bbl/d of refining capacity by 2015 based on currently proposed projects.

Due to expectations of higher demand for petroleum products, further investment in the Indian refining sector is likely. As part of the Eleventh Five Year Plan (2007–12), the government aims to promote India as a competitive refining destination.

Natural gas

India had approximately 38 trillion cubic feet (Tcf) of proven natural gas reserves as of January 2010. India produced approximately 1.4 Tcf of natural gas in 2009, a 20 per cent increase over 2008 production levels. The bulk of India's natural gas production comes from the western offshore regions, especially the Mumbai High complex, though the Bay of Bengal and its KG fields are proving productive. The onshore fields in Assam, Andhra Pradesh, and Gujarat are also significant sources of natural gas production.

In 2009, India consumed roughly 1.8 Tcf of natural gas, almost 300 billion cubic feet (Bcf) more than in 2008. Natural gas demand is expected to grow considerably, largely driven by demand in the power sector. The power and fertilizer sectors account for nearly three-quarters of natural gas consumption in India. Natural gas is expected to be an increasingly important component of energy consumption as the country pursues energy resource diversification and overall energy security.

Despite the steady increase in India's natural gas production, demand has outstripped supply and the country has been a net importer of natural gas since 2004. India's net imports reached an estimated 445 Bcf in 2009.

The outlook for India's upstream natural gas sector is more positive than its upstream oil sector, although the US IEA forecasts that Indian natural gas production would peak between 2020 and 2030.[16]

There have been several large natural gas finds in India over the last several years, predominantly offshore in the Bay of Bengal. ONGC announced a find in late 2006 in the Mahanadi basin off the coast of Orissa, with an

Figure 9.11: India's natural gas production and consumption, 1995–2009

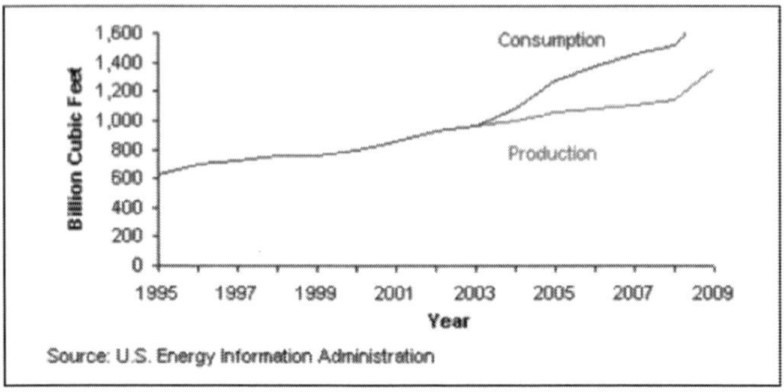

Source: US Energy Information Administration

estimated three to four Tcf of reserves in place. In December 2006, ONGC announced a find of an estimated 21 to 22 Tcf of natural gas in place at the KG-DOWN-98/2 block off the coast of Andhra Pradesh in the KG basin. In addition, Gujarat State Petroleum Corporation (GSPC) holds an estimated 1.8 Tcf of natural gas reserves at the KG-OSN-2001/3 block in the K-G area. Reliance Industries' KG-D6 block holds estimated reserves of 11.5 Tcf and came online in April 2009. Of the nearly 1.4 Bcf/d of initial production, nearly half went to gas based power plants, the rest to fertilizer, LPG plants, and city gas distribution entities. After reaching a production peak of 2.8 Bcf/d in December 2009, Reliance decided in July 2010 to cap production of KG-D6 at 2.1 Bcf/d pending resolution of infrastructure and field maintenance issues.

The power sector continues to receive the lion's share of production allotments. Production from the KG basin is expected to double the country's current natural gas output in coming years.

Natural gas imports

India's natural gas import demand is expected to increase in the coming years. To help meet this growing demand, a number of import schemes including both LNG and pipeline projects have either been implemented or are being considered.

Iran-Pakistan-India pipeline

India has considered various proposals for international pipeline connections with other countries. One such scheme is the Iran-Pakistan-India (IPI) Pipeline, which has been under discussion since 1994. The plan calls for a roughly 1,700 mile, 5.4 Bcf/d pipeline to run from the South Pars fields in

Iran to Gujarat. While Iran is keen to export its abundant natural gas resources and India is in search of projects to meet its growing domestic demand, a variety of economic and political issues have delayed a project agreement. India has made it clear that any import pipeline crossing Pakistan would need to be accompanied by a security guarantee from Islamabad. Due to the uncertainties involving this pipeline, the Eleventh Five Year Plan does not project any gas supply from this route or the two pipelines discussed below:

Turkmenistan-Afghanistan-Pakistan-India pipeline

India has worked to join the Turkmenistan-Afghanistan-Pakistan Pipeline (TAP or Trans-Afghan Pipeline). With the inclusion of India, the project consists of a planned 1,050-mile pipeline originating in Turkmenistan's Dauletabad natural gas fields and transporting the fuel to markets in Afghanistan, Pakistan, and India. In 2008, all parties agreed to induct India as a full member into the project, thereby renaming the pipeline TAPI (Turkmenistan-Afghanistan-Pakistan-India). TAPI is envisioned to have a capacity of 3.2 Bcf/d, but work has not yet begun on the project. Concerns about the project have included the security of the route, which would traverse unstable regions in Afghanistan and Pakistan. Furthermore, a review of the TAPI project raised doubts as to whether Turkmen natural gas supplies are adequate to meet proposed export commitments.

Imports from Myanmar

A third international pipeline proposal envisions India importing natural gas from Myanmar. In March 2006, the governments of India and Myanmar signed a natural gas supply deal. Initially, the two countries planned to build a pipeline crossing Bangladesh. After indecision from Bangladeshi authorities, India and Myanmar studied the possibility of building a pipeline that would terminate in the eastern Indian state of Tripura and not cross Bangladeshi soil.

In March 2009, Myanmar signed a natural gas supply deal with China sourced from a field invested in by GAIL and ONGC, putting the India-Myanmar pipeline deal in question.

LPG

India began importing LNG in 2004. In 2008, India imported 372 Bcf of LNG, nearly 75 per cent of it from Qatar, making it the sixth largest importer of LNG in the world. India imports LNG through both long-term contracts and spot shipments. Currently, India has two operational LNG import terminals, Dahej and Hazira. India received its first LNG shipments in January 2004 with the start-up of the Dahej terminal in Gujarat. Petronet LNG, a consortium of state-owned Indian companies and international investors, owns and operates the Dahej LNG facility with a capacity of five million tonnes per year (mtpa) (975 Bcf/y). India's second terminal, Hazira LNG, started operations in April 2005, and is owned by a joint venture of Shell and Total. The facility has a capacity of 2.5 mtpa (488 Bcf/y), which may be expanded to 5 mtpa (975 Bcf/y) in the future. The five mtpa (975 Bcf/y) LNG processing plant in Dabhol continues to face delays. In addition, Petronet LNG has begun construction of a 2.5 mtpa (488 Bcf/y) LNG import facility at Kochi. The facility is expected to be completed in the first quarter of 2012 and has secured a 1.5 mtpa (293 Bcf/y) supply from Australia's Gorgon LNG project. In order to secure supply of natural gas to India and meet growing demand, India is currently looking to invest in liquefaction projects abroad. For example, ONGC and the Hinduja Group are considering service contracts in Iran to supply five mtpa (975 Bcf/y) of LNG to India. It is also exploring the possibility of investing more in the Sakhalin I LNG project.

Long-term growth in demand for LNG remains unclear however, as price is an issue of contention in India and increasing domestic natural gas production is expected from eastern offshore fields. Industry analysts note that Indian companies appear unwilling to commit to long-term LNG supply contracts at international prices. While negotiations are currently underway for several long-term LNG supply deals, whether or not India's bids will be accepted is questionable. Instead, India is becoming an important destination for spot LNG cargoes.

Electricity

In 2007, India had approximately 159 gigawatts (GW) of installed electric capacity and generated 761 billion kilowatt hours. Nearly all electric power in India is generated with coal, oil, or gas.

Conventional thermal sources produced over 80 per cent of electricity in 2007. Hydroelectricity, a monsoon dependent power source in India, accounted for nearly 16 per cent of power generated in 2007. Finally, nuclear energy produced roughly 2 per cent of electricity during the same year, while geothermal and other renewable sources accounted for approximately 2 per cent. In July 2010, India and Bangladesh signed a 35 year power import deal whereby India will import up to 500 megawatts beginning in late 2012. India also imports some electricity from Bhutan and Nepal. However, these electricity imports are not likely to prove sufficient to make up for India's lack of electric generation capacity.

Figure 9.12: Electricity generation in India by technology type, 1990–2008

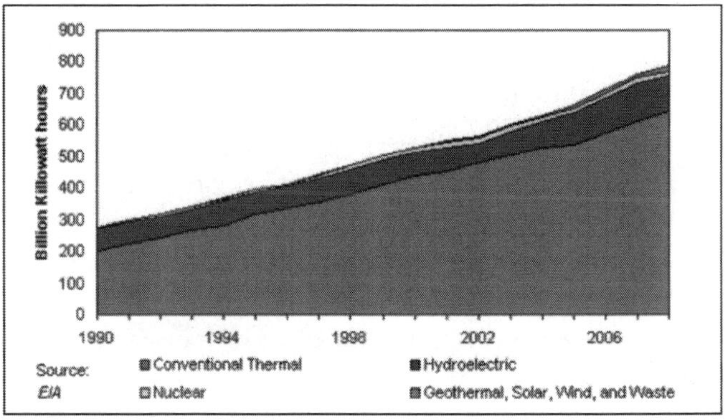

Source: EIA

India suffers from a severe shortage of electricity generation capacity. In addition, blackouts are a common occurrence throughout the country's main cities. Almost 470 million people do not have access to electricity. Further compounding the situation is that total demand for electricity in the country continues to rise and is outpacing increases in capacity. Additional capacity has failed to materialize in India owing to market regulations, insufficient investment in the sector, difficulty in obtaining environmental approval, and funding for hydropower projects. In addition, coal shortages are further straining power generation capabilities.

In order to address this shortfall, the Indian government continues to work towards adding capacity. India's Eleventh Plan set an ambitious goal of adding nearly 79,000 MW by 2012. The country also grapples with electricity efficiency issues. In order to improve efficiency standards, the Energy Conservation Act was passed in 2002, which established the Bureau of Energy Efficiency and has sought to promote efficient use of energy and labeling of energy-intensive products.

Conventional thermal power generation

Conventional thermal-generated power accounted for 80 per cent of electricity in India in 2007. Of these sources, coal is by far the most important fuel source for power generation, with roughly 70 per cent of electricity generated in coal-fired power plants. India is both the third largest consumer and third largest producer of coal in the world, and though the country supplies the bulk of its needs domestically, it is currently a significant net coal importer. In spite of the electric sector's heavy reliance on coal, natural gas is becoming increasingly important due to environmental considerations, quality concerns pertaining to the steel industry, and supply constraints surrounding coal.

Nuclear power generation

India has developed the capability to build and operate nuclear power plants observing international standards of safety. The current installed capacity of nuclear power plants is 3360 MW, accounting for 2.34 per cent of the total installed capacity of the country. The NPCIL (Nuclear Power Corporation of India Ltd) proposes to increase the installed capacity to 9935 MW by 2011/12. The future strategies focus on a three-stage nuclear power programme for the optimal utilization of the available nuclear energy resources (see below).

India has established a civil nuclear cooperation deal with the United States, as well as with Russia, France, and Japan. The government has set its nuclear generation target at 40,000 MW by 2020. India currently has 14 nuclear reactors in commercial operation with more planned.

Closed cycle three stage nuclear power programme

India has limited availability of uranium resources (about 70,000 tonnes), but has one of the largest resources of thorium in the world, amounting to 360,000 tonnes. Therefore, right from inception of its nuclear power programme, India has adopted an approach that would maximize the energy yield from these materials. This is the three stage nuclear power programme. The first stage of nuclear power generation is based on PHWR (pressurized heavy water reactor) technology using indigenous natural uranium. The second stage is based on FBR (fast breeder reactor) technology using plutonium extracted by reprocessing of the spent fuel obtained from the first stage. The third stage consists of using thorium resources.

A 500 MW fast breeder reactor is under construction and was expected to go on stream in 2012. A 300 MW advanced heavy water reactor (AHWR) has been designed. Its construction was due to begin in the Eleventh Plan. The projected installed nuclear power by Department of Atomic Energy (DAE) is shown in Figure 9.13 below:

Figure 9.13: Nuclear power generation projections upto 2050

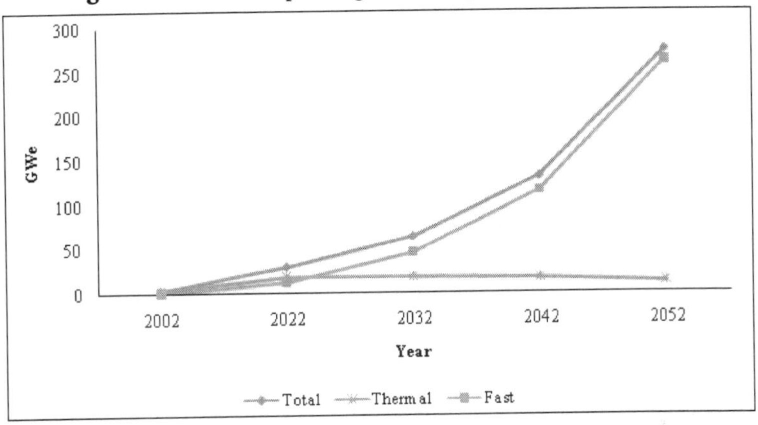

Source: DAE

For sustainability of nuclear energy in the long term, it is important to close the nuclear fuel cycle. In this way one can produce several times more energy from the existing uranium resources if the plutonium from the spent fuel is recycled in fast breeder reactors and this potential can be increased by another order of magnitude by closing the nuclear fuel cycle with thorium. The closed fuel cycle, in comparison to the once-through cycle, also reduces the volumes of radioactive waste requiring treatment and disposal. The FBRs are a potentially important source of energy in the next 50 years.

Hydropower and other renewables

As part of India's goal of diversifying its sources of electric power generation and increasing the country's capacity, increased use of hydroelectric power is also included in the government's plans. However, lack of reliability and environmental and local community concerns make it difficult to fully capitalize upon this domestic energy resource. Nevertheless, an additional 50,000 MW of hydropower capacity is supposed to be installed by the end of the Twelfth Five Year Plan (FYP).

Geothermal, solar, and wind power currently hold little importance in electric power generation in the country. However, the government would like the share of renewables in electricity production to increase, and has put in place an ambitious national solar mission to increase solar power generation to 20 GW by 2022, as well as other measures, for example, renewable portfolio standards and tradable renewable energy certificates.

India's commercial energy balance for 2010–11 is given below in Table 9.2:

Table 9.2: India's commercial energy balance, 2010-11, million tonnes of oil equivalent

	Primary energy						Secondary energy												
	Coal and Lignite	**Hydro-power**	**Nu-clear power**	**Renew-able energy sources**	**Natu-ral gas**	**Crude oil**	**LPG**	**Naph-tha**	**Motor gaso-line**	**Avia-tion turbine fuel**	**Kero-sene**	**High-speed diesel**	**Light diesel oil**	**Fuel oil**	**Other petro-leum products**	**Total pe-troleum products**	**Ther-mal power**	**Total power**	**Total energy**
Supply																			
Production	212.82	9.85	2.26	3.45	46.17	37.71	-	-	-	-	-	-	-	-	-	-	-	15.56	312.27
Imports	44.79	-	-	-	8.05	163.59	5.07	2.22	2.26	0	1.43	2.07	0	0.71	4.39	18.14	-	0.48	234.58
Exports	2.64	-	-	-	-	0	0.18	11.47	14.53	4.77	0.04	21.07	0.09	6.47	9.47	68.07	-	0.01	70.72
Stock changes	-2.82	-	-	-	-	4.85	0.33	1.9	-0.51	-0.02	-0.18	0.31	-0.02	-3.5	-0.20	-1.90	-	-	0.13
Availability	252.15	9.85	2.26	3.45	54.22	206.15	-	-	-	-	-	-	-	-	-	-	-	-	476.26
Petroleum refining	-	-	-	-	2.90	206.15	8.52	18.85	27.96	10.19	8.05	80.78	0.55	19.7	21.83	196.44	-	-	196.44
Own use	0.16	-	-	-	1.63	15.87	-	-	-	-	-	-	-	-	-	-	-	-	-
LPG extraction	-	-	-	-	2.45	-	2.45	-	-	-	-	-	-	-	-	2.45	-	-	-
Power generation	150.07	9.85	2.26	3.45	25.56	-	-	0.55	-	-	-	5.06	0.13	1.24	-	6.98	182.61	198.18	198.18
Conversion loss in power generation	104.5	-	-	-	14.99	-	-	-	-	-	-	2.91	0.08	0.71	-	3.7	123.19	123.19	123.19
Auxiliary consumption in power stations	3.78	0.07	0	0.22	0.27	-	-	-	-	-	-	0.09	0	0.04	-	0.13	4.18	4.47	4.47

contd.

Supply																			
Transmission and distribution losses	-	-	-	-	-	-	-	-	-	-	-	-	-	-	-	0	-	16.73	16.73
Flaring of Natural gas	-	-	-	-	0.87	-	-	-	-	-	-	-	-	-	-	0	-	-	0.87
Coal washery rejects	2.64	-	-	-	-	-	-	-	-	-	-	-	-	-	-	-	-	-	2.64
Conversion	150.07	-	-	-	33.42	206.15	10.97	18.3	27.96	10.19	8.05	75.72	0.42	18.46	21.83	191.91	127.36	144.38	147.89
Net availability	99.28	9.78	2.26	3.24	20.8	190.28	16.19	10.94	15.19	5.41	9.26	57.03	0.31	9.2	16.55	140.08	55.25	54.27	314.42
Consumption	99.28	-	-	-	20.8	-	16.19	10.94	15.19	5.41	9.26	57.03	0.31	9.2	16.55	140.08	-	54.27	314.42
Agriculture	-	-	-	-	0.17	-	0	-	-	-	-	7.59	0	0.07	-	7.66	-	10.87	18.7
Industry	96.74	-	-	-	1.31	-	0.67	0	-	-	-	6.65	0.12	4.1	16.55	28.1	-	20.57	146.72
Transport	-	-	-	-	0.36	-	0	-	15.19	5.41		40.54	0	0.75	-	61.89	-	1.15	63.39
Residential	-	-	-	-	0.33	-	15.45	-	-	-	9.11	-	-	-	-	24.56	-	13.35	38.24
Commercial	-	-	-	-	0.36	-	0	-	-	-	0	-	-	-	-	0	-	5.5	5.85
Other energy uses	2.53	-	-	-	1.87	-	0.07	0.17	-	-	0.15	2.25	0.17	4.28	-	7.09	-	2.84	14.33
Non-energy uses	-	-	-	-	16.39	-	0	10.78	-	-	-	-	-	-	-	10.78	-	-	27.17

Source: TERI Energy Data Directory and Yearbook (TEDDY) 2013/14, The Energy and Resources Institute (TERI)
Note: Conversion factor for coal used for power generation adjusted
LPG – liquefied petroleum gas

Long-term energy use projections

A multi-model projection of India's energy use in the 30 year period 2001–31 reveals that in 2031, without significant additional steps (essentially aimed at cutting the growth of greenhouse gas emissions), India would remain substantially reliant on coal and oil, with an increasing share for natural gas[17] (Figure 9.14):

Figure 9.14: India's primary energy requirements in 2031

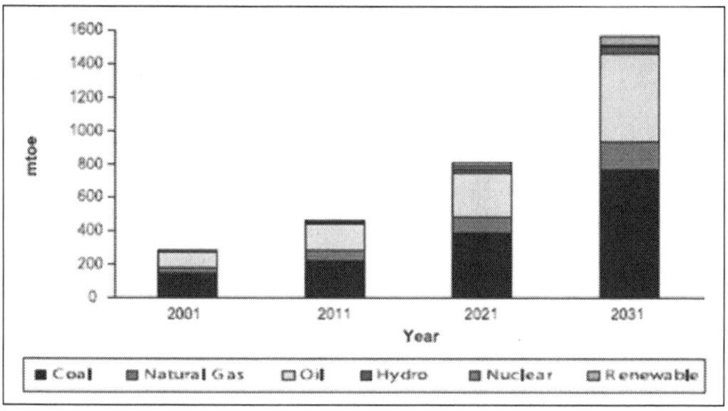

Source: India's GHG emissions profile, results from five models, MoEF, 2009

The shares of different primary energy sources are given below (Figure 9.15):

Figure 9.15: Shares of primary energy sources till 2031

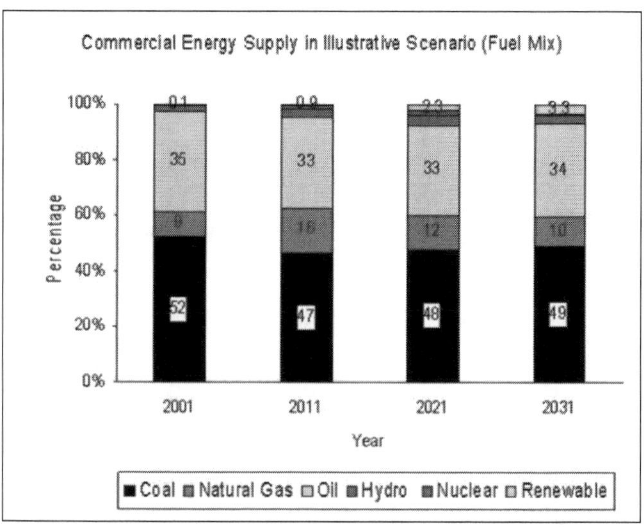

Source: India's GHG emissions profile, results from five models, MoEF 2009

The share of oil hardly declines (from 35 to 34 per cent of the total), and since there is a nearly three-fold increase in aggregate energy, the consumption of oil also increases by a similar magnitude.[18]

While aggregate energy use continues to rise, the energy intensity of the economy, already among the world's lowest, continues to decline (Figure 9.16):

Figure 9.16: Change in India's commercial energy intensity, 2001–31

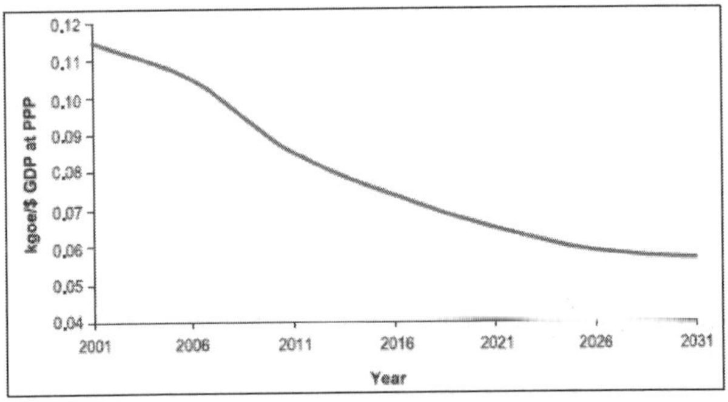

Source: India's GHG emissions profile, results from 5 models, MoEF, 2009

India's policy options for petroleum sector

India's key energy vulnerability till the 2030s is the continued reliance on petroleum, which, given limited national petroleum reserves, must necessarily be largely imported from a volatile global market. Petroleum, in turn, is largely used in the transportation (33 per cent in 2007–08) and industrial (15.6 per cent in 2007–08) sectors, as well as for household energy (16.1 per cent in 2007–08), chiefly kerosene and LPG.[19] Coal imports for power generation may also increase, but the global market for coal is much less volatile than for petroleum, given much broader global distribution of coal resources.

Without any surprise large-scale finds of petroleum within the country or its offshore areas, what are India's policy options in this sector?

One, of course, is increased investment in equity oil abroad. Apart from projected increases in oil output from Saudi Arabia, Iraq, and other Middle East OPEC countries (excluding Iran), significant increases are also projected from Russia, Kazakhstan, Brazil, and Africa. Obtaining equity oil is not simply a matter of commercial bidding, but diplomacy too plays an important part. Fortunately, India has no political issues with any of these countries, and indeed a positive record of diplomatic relations. Nevertheless, translating a general state of good political relations to actual commercial benefits, particularly in situations of intense competition, calls for serious diplomatic leg-work. Necessary diplomatic support to efforts by Indian oil companies, whether state or non-state, to secure equity oil in these countries should thus be a clear task assigned to India's diplomatic establishment.

Second, one needs to look at large-scale substitution possibilities of oil by other, less problematic, energy sources. The author notes in this context the prospects of large-scale shale gas production in India, and the three-stage nuclear power cycle. The lead time for significant yields of shale gas is c. 10 years, while that for thorium based power is longer, perhaps c. 30–40 years. The Indian railways, a major consumer of oil in the transportation sector, have already embarked upon a programme of electrification of its entire track length of c. 63,000 km. However, during the Eleventh Plan about 3500 km of track will be electrified which while nearly double the Tenth Plan achievement of about 1800 km, indicates that it is clearly necessary to accelerate the pace of railway electrification. The electricity required may be generated from coal, natural gas, as well as to an extent, nuclear sources. Given the likely flat time-of-day electricity demand curve for railways, dedicated base-load power plants may be set up in each railway zone.

Urban bus transport has already demonstrated that a fully CNG powered fleet is feasible (in Delhi), and this, rather than diesel should be the preferred fuel for expansion and fleet modernization in other cities as well. The technology for use of CNG in passenger cars has also been sufficiently demonstrated, and with a policy of scaling back on fuel subsidies, there would be an impetus to switch (including by retrofitting the existing stock of petrol cars) to CNG in case of passenger cars as well.

In respect of the household sector, the supply of subsidized kerosene to BPL households for lighting, has enabled large-scale diversion of kerosene to adulterate diesel and petrol. An innovation of subsidizing solar lamps to BPL households, rather than kerosene, would also contribute to energy security. Further, supply of subsidized LPG for cooking to households has taken on the colour of a merit-good for all societal classes. However, where piped CNG has been provided, households have switched entirely to CNG, owing to greater reliability of supply, and the fact of CNG (unsubsidized) being price competitive with LPG (subsidized). The constraint in this respect is the pace of laying CNG distribution lines for households – it is necessary to accelerate this programme, in preference to expanding subsidized supply of petroleum based LPG.

With respect to industry, virtually all uses of petroleum products, even in respect of non-energy use such as naphtha for feedstock in the fertilizer industry, may be substituted by natural gas. This would, of course, require rectification of prices of petroleum products, increased supply (whether by domestic production or imports) of natural gas, as well as accelerated investment in gas pipelines, storage facilities, and import terminals.

Substitution of petroleum based products with CNG would be facilitated by major investment in shale gas extraction (see above). While a pilot project in Durgapur has been initiated, it is essential to quickly scale up the level of effort, so that this new source makes an increasingly important contribution to domestic natural gas supplies. The large-scale extraction of shale gas in the US has already had a stabilizing effect on global trading prices for natural gas, and the prospect of such stability in the future, as more countries, especially China, invest heavily in shale gas supplies makes this fuel preferable to petroleum fuels, even if at the margin it continues to be imported.

To summarize, India's petroleum consumption is likely to increase threefold between 2001 and 2031, while import dependence is likely to increase further, unless urgent steps are taken to substitute petroleum for other less problematic fuels. Possibilities of full electrification of the railways, relying on coal, gas, or nuclear power generation; and substitution of petroleum by natural gas in other transport, industry, and the household sector, exist, and must be realized expeditiously.

Possible Inclusion of New Members in the IEA: India, China, Russia

The effectiveness of the IEAs actions would clearly depend upon the response of the global oil market to releases from the national strategic oil reserves, decided by the Governing Board. To the extent that IEA members' share of global oil trade falls (or increases) over time, its effectiveness would decrease (or alternatively, increase). Since the 1970s, given the enhanced share of global oil trade of China and India (see Figure 9.17), the inclusion of these countries would result in the IEA's interventions gaining in salience in the oil market. Accordingly, the US has suggested their inclusion,[20] and so has the Executive Director of the IEA.[21] The IEA has also actively sought collaboration with Russia,[22] although the reasons are somewhat different in its case.

Figure 9.17: Oil imports of selected countries, 1995–2008[23]

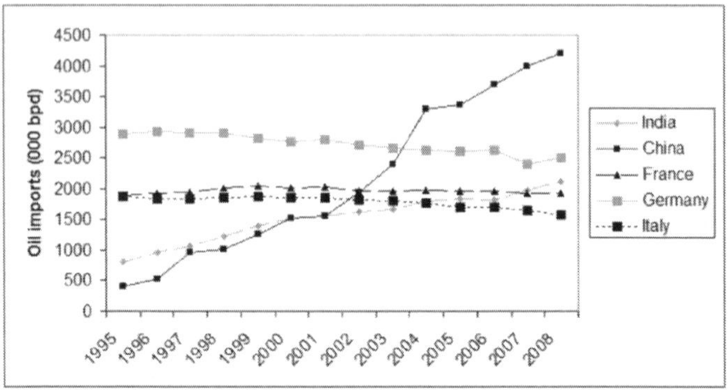

Source: Cogan, Jeff ibid.

Strategic oil reserves of India and China

India's strategic oil reserve

India has commenced the building up of a national strategic oil reserve. The Indian Strategic Petroleum Reserve Ltd (ISPRL), owned by the Oil Industry Development Board, has engaged a consortium comprising firms from Iran, Japan, and China, for constructing the underground caverns for the reserve. The government plans to build such facilities, at three locations in southern India to meet demand for 14–15 days in case of emergencies. The planned facilities would be in underground rock caverns near the east and west coasts of the country so that they are easily accessible to the refining sector. The first strategic oil reserve facility in Visakhapatnam is expected to be completed by October 2011, with an initial capacity of 1.33 million tons, while the second facility will be built at Mangalore by November 2012, and will have a capacity of 1.5 million tonnes. A third facility with a capacity of 2.5 million tonnes will be built at Padur by December 2012.[24]

Based on 2005 prices, ISPRL had estimated an investment of ₹ 2397 crore (c. $540 million) for the facilities. The cost has now gone up to more than ₹ 3000 crores (c. $675 million). In addition, the cost of the oil would have to be taken into account, valued at more than $ 100 per barrel on date, i.e., c. $3.9 billion, or a total of c. $4.58 billion.

The size of the Indian reserve (in 2005) would be close to 200 million barrels if the IEAs norms of 90 days requirement were to be met. The costs of storage caverns for such capacity would likely be c. ₹ 15,360 crores, (c. $3.5 billion) while that of the reserve (at $ 100 per barrel) would be

c. $20 billion, a total of $ 23.5 billion. In addition, there would be operations and maintenance (O&M) costs in each case, roughly proportional to the respective sizes of the reserves. As India's oil imports grow, the capital, O&M, and inventory costs of the strategic oil reserve would increase in step.

China's strategic oil reserve

China plans to spend 100 billion yuan ($15.3 billion) to establish its strategic oil reserve project by 2020. The project will be built in three phases. When completed in 2020, it will have a reserve capacity of 90 days' crude oil imports. The first phase of four reserve bases has been completed and was put into operation in 2009. These bases are located in coastal provinces – Zhenhai and Zhoushan in Zhejiang province; Huangdao in Shandong province; and Dalian in Liaoning province, with a total oil reserve capacity up to 16.4 million cubic meters or 102 million barrels, which is equivalent to the amount of 21 days' oil imports. The second phase, which is expected to have total reserve capacity of up to 26.8 million cum, or 168 million barrels, is under construction, but the locations have not been officially revealed. The third phase is under programming. The total size of the reserve in 2020 is likely to be c. 685 million barrels. At an average of c.$ 100 per barrel, the cost of the oil would be c. $68.5 billion. The total cost of the planned Chinese strategic oil reserve is accordingly, c. $83.8 billion, together with O&M costs.

China had started the national strategic oil reserve discussion since 2003 when the country first turned into a net crude oil importer, and the first batch of projects started construction three years later.[25]

Membership of Russia

Russia is a major oil and gas exporter, not importer, and clearly benefits from OPEC cartel actions, even though it is not a part of OPEC.[26] Its interests would thus appear, as regards oil and gas markets, to be misaligned with those of the majority of IEA members, (the majority of whom are oil importers, and whose mandate is the stabilization of oil prices and ensuring adequate supplies to its members). Nevertheless, there are at least two reasons why IEA membership (or at least collaboration) with Russia have been urged.

One, following the collapse of the Soviet Union, there has been a transformation in Russia's strategic relationships. It is possible, that unlike in the Soviet era, it is perceived by several of the OECD (and by extension, the IEA) members, that a broad front strategic engagement with Russia should also include issues of global energy security. Second, in particular the European IEA members, may be seeking the IEA as an additional political forum to address their perennial gas pricing and supply disputes with Russia, (in which the latter could be placed on the defensive, being in a clear minority), unlike existing bilateral forums.

Nevertheless, the fundamental asymmetry of interests between Russia and the majority of IEA members, in that its interests would likely be opposed to price stabilization measures in case of future oil price shocks, could remain a stumbling block to greater cooperation, even if it led to full membership in due course.

Membership of India (and China)

Membership of the IEA would clearly involve significant direct economic costs for India, which may be quantified by the difference in costs of creation and maintenance of a national strategic oil reserve between what it is prepared to do on its own and the norm of the IEA. While in India's case this could be c. $15.9 billion in capital costs, with O&M costs in addition, China seems prepared to incur the direct economic costs, since its strategic reserve by national political decision equals that required under the IEA mandatory requirement. The benefit would be greater effectiveness of IEAs coordinated steps to stabilize the global oil market, in the event of a future oil crisis.

There is, however, the important question of perceived or actual loss of sovereignty in relation to energy security decision-making.

The current basis of distribution of voting power in the IEA governing board, i.e., reflecting respective oil imports in 1973, if applied to Indian and Chinese membership would result in allocation of votes to them at large variance (much lower) with their present levels of participation in the global oil market, or alternatively, share of GDP of IEA members. Moreover, any attempt to redistribute votes at the IEA Governing Board on a new formula would inevitably result in increase of votes to some at the expense of others – a zero sum game. In particular, if the votes were redistributed, even without admission of India and China, on the basis of (say) 2005 relative oil imports, the US, UK, and Canada would lose significant votes (Figure 9.18). This loss would be greater if the formula were applied upon the admission of China and India (Figure 9.19). There is little incentive among the states that currently dominate the IEA to acquiesce in loss of their voting power in either instance.[27]

Figure 9.18: Net change in IEA Votes of current members, if based on 2005 oil consumption[28]

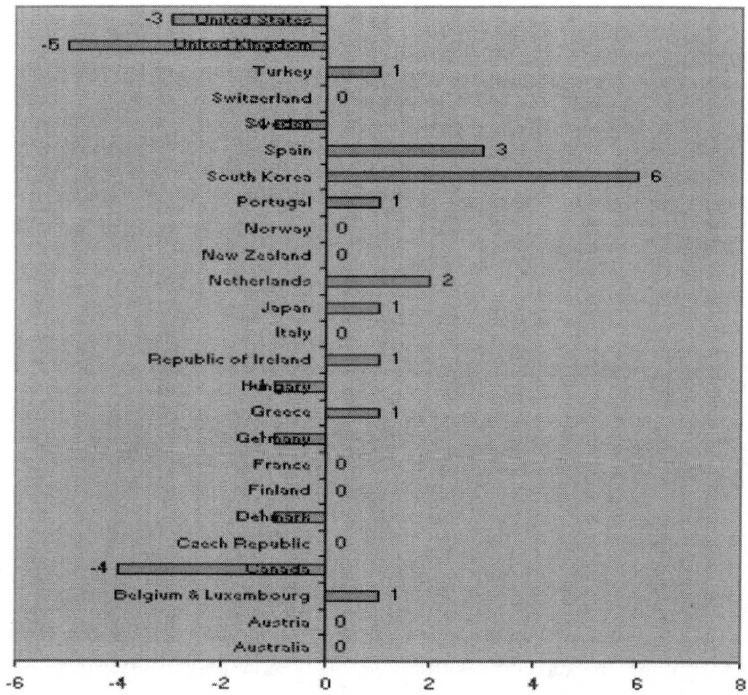

Source: Cogan, Jeff: Ibid.

Figure 9.19: Votes of IEA members upon admission of India and China on the basis of 2009 net oil imports[29]

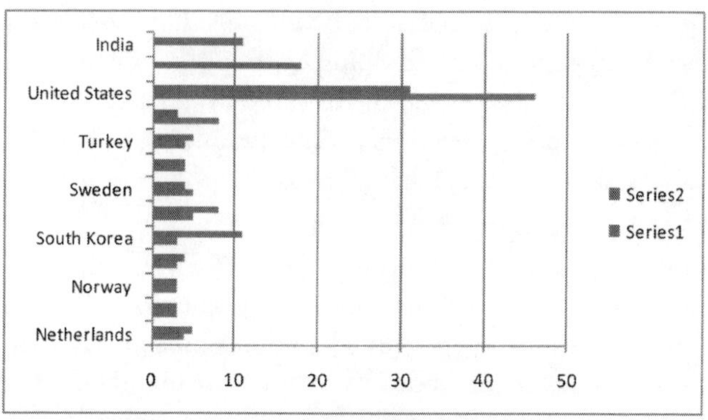

Note: Series 1 is current votes and Series 2 is prospective votes

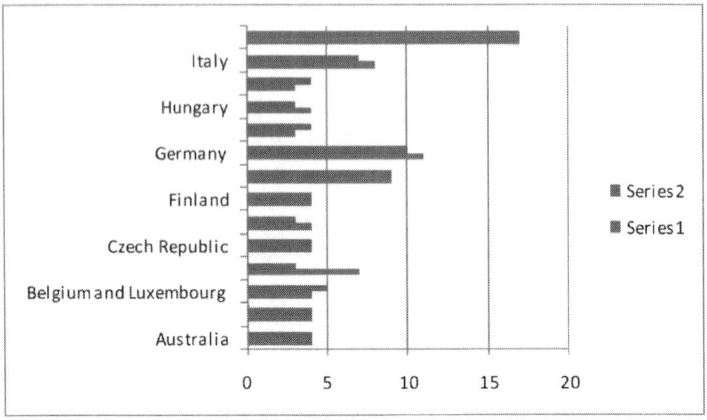

Note: Series 1 is current votes and Series 2 is prospective votes

Source: Own calculations based on US Energy Information Administration 2010 data. Marginal adjustments have been made due to some cases of missing 2009 data; these do not materially alter the results.

Would China and India find it worthwhile to join the IEA under the existing formula for sharing votes (i.e. based on 1973 oil imports)? The point is that releases of oil by the IEA members from their strategic reserves would stabilize global oil prices, albeit somewhat less effectively, even if China and India were not participants. This would benefit India and China, even without their joining the IEA, i.e., these countries are able to free-ride on the benefits of IEA actions without undertaking the costs of IEA membership (mainly creating and maintaining strategic oil reserves under the IEA norms in case of India). This would be in addition to loss of national decision-making power over petroleum policy in situations of emergency, in case of both India and China – to recollect, the IEA governing board's decisions are legally binding on all members). The option of free-riding, without IEA membership, would ensure that their national strategic oil reserves would remain available for release under national policy decisions, while continuing to benefit from the IEA's actions in stabilizing the global oil market.

Another major stumbling block is the present requirement that new members must first become members of the OECD. The question of IEA membership, thus, becomes entangled with the question of whether India (and China) should seek or accept OECD membership. This is a issue outside the scope of the present chapter, but suffice it to note that the OECD also has a set of obligations for members, and it would be necessary to first consider the benefits and costs to OECD membership.[30]

Finally, the IEA imposes significant data and information requirements of its members, including oil market reporting requirements, and proprietary information of private corporations. Responding to this requirement is a non-trivial legal and policy question.

Possible governance reforms

A possible way of addressing India's fears of loss of sovereignty over oil policy in the event of global oil supply emergencies, is to remedy the present governance structure of votes in the IEA Board, which takes decisions that are legally binding on all members.

The present formula for apportioning votes among IEA members involves giving each member three fixed votes, plus a variable number of votes representing its (rounded) share of oil imports aggregated over all members. 'Distortions' in the governance structure of the IEA, i.e. divergences between members' votes and their perceived significance to the global oil market arise in two ways: First, in freezing the votes assigned to members on the basis of their respective oil imports in 1973. While the current shares of oil imports of members (and India and China) is already at large variance from that in 1973, the divergence will be further enhanced in the next two decades, as oil imports from China and India increase faster than from the current IEA members. Second, in the large number of fixed votes collectively held by European members of the IEA, arising from the large number of members from this region (20 out of 25), which magnifies the voting power of this region far out of proportion to its actual share of oil imports of the IEA members. It may be noted that almost all the OECD Europe members are also EU members, which presents a ready-made forum for arriving at common positions on issues before the IEA.[31]

Two possible scenarios for reform of the IEAs Governance structure, with membership of India and China are presented below. In both scenarios, the variable votes assigned to each member vary with its share of oil imports by all IEA members (including India and China). However, while in the first scenario, the fixed votes of each member remain at three, in the second, each member is assigned a fixed vote of one.

Table 9.3 gives projections till 2035 of oil imports of IEA members, India, and China.[32]

Table 9.3: Estimated net oil imports

Region/Country	History			Projections				
	2005	2006	2007	2015	2020	2025	2030	2035
United States	12.5	12.2	12.2	10.3	10	10.2	10.6	10.7
Canada	-1.0	-1.1	-1.1	-2.0	-2.4	-3.0	-3.6	-4.4
OECD Europe	10.0	10.3	10.1	10.5	10.3	10.5	10.7	10.8
Japan	5.2	5.1	4.9	4.1	4.2	4.2	4.1	4.0
Australia and New Zealand	0.5	0.5	0.4	0.5	0.6	0.6	0.7	0.7
China	2.7	3.2	3.6	6.2	7.6	9.0	10.6	12.1
India	1.6	1.8	1.9	2.2	2.6	2.8	3.2	3.5
Total	**31.6**	**32.0**	**32.0**	**31.8**	**32.9**	**34.3**	**36.3**	**37.4**

Source: International Energy Outlook, 2010, US EIA.

Table 9.4 gives the projected (rounded) voting rights, keeping the fixed votes of each member at three, and adjusting the variable votes in line with the respective shares of oil imports.

Table 9.4: Projected (rounded) voting rights with fixed votes of each member = 3

Country	2005	2006	2007	2015	2020	2025	2030	2035
United States	43	41	41	35	33	33	32	32
Canada	3	3	3	3	3	3	3	3
OECD Europe	35	35	35	36	34	34	32	32
Japan	19	19	18	16	16	15	14	14
Australia and NewZealand	5	5	4	5	5	5	5	5
China	12	13	14	22	26	29	32	35
India	8	9	9	10	11	11	12	12
Total	125	125	124	127	128	130	130	133

Source: Author's estimates

Table 9.5 gives the projected (rounded) voting rights with fixed votes of each member = 1, and adjusting the variable votes in line with the respective shares of oil imports.

Table 9.5: Projected (rounded) voting rights with fixed votes of each member = 1

Country	2005	2006	2007	2015	2020	2025	2030	2035
United States	41	39	39	33	31	31	30	30
Canada	1	1	1	1	1	1	1	1
OECD Europe	33	33	33	34	32	32	30	30
Japan	17	17	16	14	14	13	12	12
Australia and New Zealand	3	3	2	3	3	3	3	3
China	10	11	12	20	24	27	30	33
India	6	7	7	8	9	9	10	10
Total	**111**	**111**	**110**	**113**	**114**	**116**	**116**	**119**

Source: Author's estimates

The percentage shares of voting rights of members vary dramatically between the two scenarios.

Figure 9.20: Shares of projected oil imports of IEA members, India and China till 2035

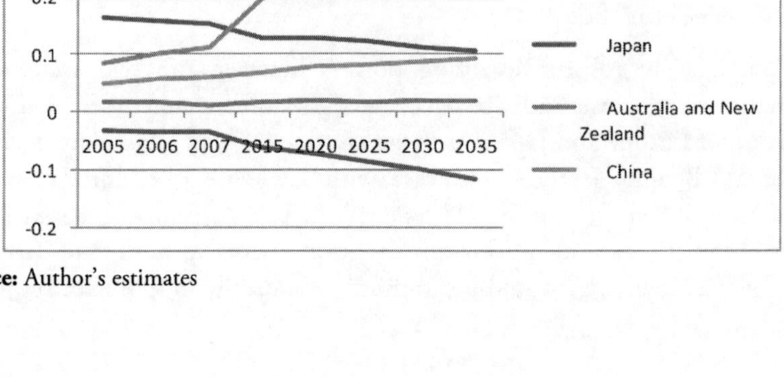

Source: Author's estimates

Figure 9.21: Projected percentages of voting rights with fixed votes of each member = 3, variable votes adjusted in line with projected oil imports

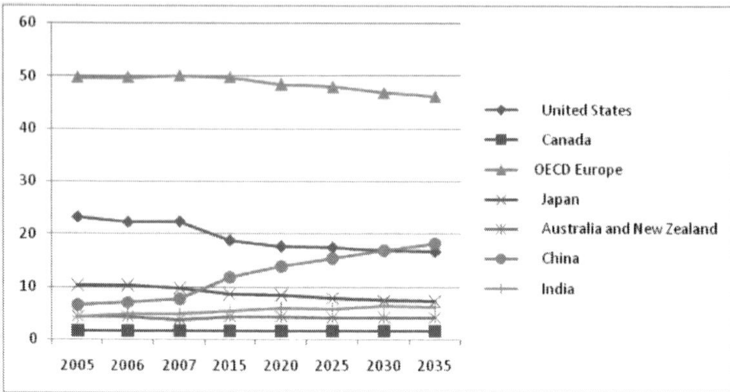

Source: Author's estimates

Figure 9.22: Projected percentages of voting rights with fixed votes of each member = 1, variable votes adjusted in line with projected oil imports

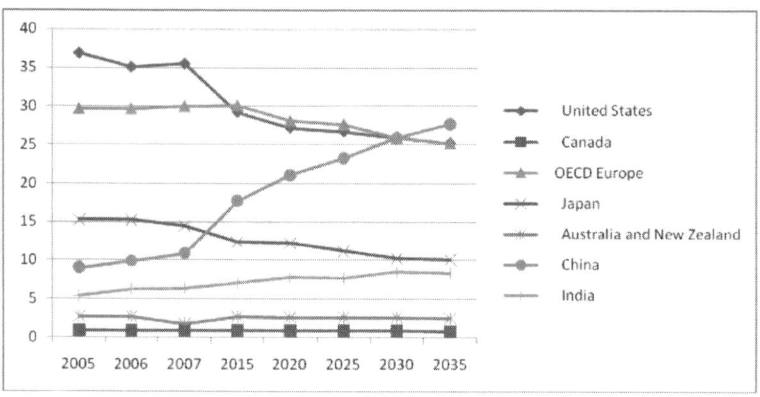

Source: Author's estimates

The changes in respective voting powers between the two scenarios is dramatic: In the case with fixed voting rights of each member as three, a coalition of Europe and Japan, *even without the US*, can dictate the decisions of the IEA Board.[33] In the second case, with fixed votes of each member as 1, a coalition of Europe and the US may still dictate decisions till about 2015, but from that time on, no obvious coalition is able to dominate. (In each case, the variable votes would be adjusted periodically in line with projected oil imports).

Would the present IEA members agree to such governance reform? This question has to be answered with reference to similar moves for governance changes in other multilateral organizations, the UN, the World Bank, the IMF, regional development banks, and so on, and is beyond the scope of this chapter.

Options for India for Cooperation with the IEA Membership

If the economic and political costs of IEA membership are unacceptable to India (and China), and/or serious governance reform is unattainable, what alternatives may be explored for mutually beneficial collaboration?

Collaboration with IEA

In the absence of membership, regular and systematic consultation by India (and China) with the IEA is one possibility. Potential avenues for such collaboration are as follows:

Exercises of Coordinated Emergency Response Measures (CERM)

The IEA regularly conducts mock exercises of the CERM, at which, if invited, observers from India may participate. While such invitations have been sent by IEA in the past, it is understood that India has not nominated observers to participate. If the initial participation is considered to be useful, India, in turn, could offer to host CERM exercises. Participation in such exercises would help build confidence in India about the intentions of the IEA, promote building relevant capacities in India to undertake similar response measures, and perhaps also yield adequate communications and systems of mutual monitoring. This would help ensure that the institutional capacities for coordinated action with the IEA would come into existence, should, at a moment of crisis, both sides actually agree to coordinate their actions.

Participation in IEA institutional structures

Russia and the IEA have already agreed on Russian participation in certain IEA structures.[34] Russia will participate as an observer in at least one meeting (during 2010) in the IEA Governing Board, and in at least one meeting of each of IEA's senior committees. Discussions in these forums would focus on issues of energy policy and strategy. In similar vein, as a measure of building the necessary confidence, before taking further steps to initiate actual collaboration during oil supply crises, if invited, India may participate as an observer in meetings of the IEA Governing Board and senior committees.

Collaboration in IEA's non-core activities

IEA has several non-core activities by way of policy analysis, data and information sharing, and policy dialogue (see below). While Indian institutions have participated in such collaboration in the past, these may be scaled up in the future, and cover a wider range of activities than in the past.

Participation in non-core functions of IEA

Apart from its core function of policy coordination in the event of global oil supply crises, the IEA also has a mission of lending its expertise to policy analysis and sharing data and information among its members. Since the IEA has considerable in-house professional expertise to fulfill its core mandate, and since oil crises are necessarily few and far between, its professional resources become available for policy analysis purposes.

IEA has valuable policy and technical reporting activities, but increasingly, its scope of work overlaps with those of others (e.g. International Renewable Energy Agency, IRENA). Three ways in which the IEA has made its expertise available are as follows:

1. Annual publications: *The World Energy Outlook*, now published annually. The WEO is considered to be a reliable guide to energy markets.
2. Reviews of individual member countries' energy policies (2–5 each year). This serves the purpose of 'educating' national policymakers about the strengths and weaknesses of their policies.
3. Dialogues with non-IEA members, including producer-consumer dialogue, and building technical capacity and sharing information. This also includes the IEA's participation in the JODI, created by IEF to provide comprehensive information on oil production and consumption. The IEA also exchanges assumptions and modeling methodologies for forecasting future oil and products demand, with other energy organizations, such as OPEC.

The overall policy perspective of the IEA revealed in its publications is similar to that of the World Bank and its sister organizations.

Conclusion

Membership of IEA is possible only after India is offered (and accepts) membership of the OECD, being a necessary precondition. Membership of the OECD is a separate question that is beyond the scope of this chapter.

Membership of the IEA carries with it two major costs: (1) upon membership, an incremental cost of c. $15.9 billion, together with proportionately increased O&M' costs, to bring India's strategic petroleum reserve up to the IEA norms; and (2) loss of control over national decision-making over petroleum policy *in times of emergency*, since decisions of the IEA regarding allocation of petroleum resources, including releases from the national strategic reserve, *are legally binding by treaty*. On the other hand, staying out of IEA membership allows India to benefit from the IEA's global oil stabilization measures, while retaining control over national petroleum policy.

The voting strengths of the IEA members is currently frozen on the basis of their respective net petroleum imports in 1973. Since India's petroleum imports at that time were extremely small in relation to the present level, allocation of India's vote in the event of membership on that basis would give it minimal power in the governing board. On the other hand, if India (and China) were to be admitted on a reallocation of votes based on current and projected future oil imports, and especially with a rescaling of the fixed votes assigned to IEA members, the voting strengths of currently dominant members of the IEA would fall substantially. In the absence of serious governance reforms, the costs of IEA membership to India clearly outweigh the benefits.

Short of membership, there are several ways to collaborate with the IEA and build mutual confidence. There may also be benefits in intensifying participation in the non-core activities of the IEA.

Appendix

Table 9.6: Votes of original 16 IEA members based on 1973 oil imports[35]

Country	General voting weigh ts	Oil consumption voting weights	Combine voting weights
Austria	3	1	4
Belgium	3	2	5
Canada	3	5	8
Denmark	3	1	4
Germany	3	8	11
Ireland	3	0	3
Italy	3	6	9
Japan	3	15	18

Country	General voting weigh ts	Oil consumption voting weights	Combine voting weights
Luxembourg	3	0	3
The Netherlands	3	2	5
Spain	3	2	5
Sweden	3	2	5
Switzerland	3	1	4
Turkey	3	1	4
United Kingdom	3	6	9
United States	3	48	51
Totals	**48**	**100**	**148**

Table 9.7: Voting strengths of 25 current IEA members[36]

Country	General voting weights	Oil consumption voting weights	Combined voting weights
Australia	3	1	4
Austria	3	1	4
Belgium	3	1	4
Canada	3	4	7
Czech Republic	3	1	4
Denmark	3	1	4
Finland	3	1	4
France	3	6	9
Germany	3	8	11
Grocco	3	0	3
Hungary	3	1	4
Ireland	3	0	3
Italy	3	5	8
Japan	3	14	17
Korea (Republic of)	3	1	4
Luxembourg	3	0	3
The Netherlands	3	1	4
New Zealand	3	0	3

Country	General voting weights	Oil consumption voting weights	Combined voting weights
Portgal	3	0	3
Spain	3	2	5
Sweden	3	2	5
Switzerland	3	1	4
Turkey	3	1	4
United Kingdom	3	5	8
United States	3	43	46
Totals	75	100	175
With Norway	3	0	3
Totals with Norway	78	100	178

Endnotes

1 However, this classification is not perfectly aligned to the participation of the members in the oil market, e.g. Canada and Norway, members of IEA, are significant oil exporters. Also, 'producers' is not congruent with 'exporters', e.g. US and China, both significant producers but not exporters. Other (regional) energy organizations include: Latin American Energy Organization (OLADE) formed in 1974; Asia–Pacific Economic Cooperation Energy Working Group, formed 1993; and the African Energy Commission, part of the African Union, formed in 2008.

2 Except perhaps the International Atomic Energy agency, whose mandate is limited to nuclear issues.

3 Recently there have been efforts to promote producer-consumer dialogue through the International Energy Forum (IEF), which have made little impact so far.

4 The moving spirit was Henry Kissinger, the then US Secretary of State.

5 Membership of OECD and IEA are not, however, congruent, since Mexico is a OECD, but not IEA member. Nevertheless, the two organizations are closely associated.

6 BP Statistical Review of World Energy, 2009.

7 Colgan, Jeff: 'The International Energy Agency – Challenges for the 21st Century,' GPPi Policy Chapter Series No. 6, 2009, Global Public Policy Institute, Berlin.

8 Originally G6 at its formation in 1975, later, with the addition of Canada in 1976, the G7, still later, with the formal admission of Russia, the G8.

9 In fact, the initial agenda of the G6 comprised energy and related economic problems, out of four principal issues.

10 The current list of IEA members include: Australia, Austria, Belgium and Luxembourg, Canada, Czech Republic, Denmark, Finland, France, Germany, Greece, Hungary, Ireland, Italy, Japan, Netherlands, New Zealand, Norway, Portugal, South Korea, Spain, Sweden, Switzerland, Turkey, UK and US (25 States).

11 Set out in the first five chapters of the agreement.

12 While the second may have been a natural disaster, the first was, apart from the merits of the US action (over which there were disagreements within the IEA/OECD itself, notably dissent by France), clearly a response to an essentially unilateral action by one influential member that holds a major share of voting rights in the IEA. This illustrates the potential of the IEA to act as a policy instrument for furthering the own objectives of influential members which may or may not be shared by other members. OECD: 'Becoming a member of the OECD', http://www.oecd.org.

13 Where voting is necessary, majority is found when 60 per cent of votes cast and 50 per cent of total votes of members are in favour.

14 Article 73: 'This Agreement may at any time be amended by the Governing Board, acting by unanimity. Such amendment shall come into force in a manner determined by the Governing Board, acting by unanimity and making provision for Participating Countries to comply with their respective constitutional procedures.'

15 The available official estimates of poverty following broadly the Expert Group (1993) method, based on calorie intake norms, and using the uniform reference period (URP) of 30 days indicate that below poverty line (BPL) population was 28.3 per cent of the rural population (described as headcount ratio or poverty ratio) and 25.7 per cent of the urban population in 2004–05. These official estimates released by the Planning Commission are based on (a) the 1973–74 rural and urban poverty line baskets originally at 1973–74 prices adjusted for price changes between 1973–74 and 2004–05 (b) a URP of 30 days for canvassing consumption of all items of current household consumption in NSS, and (c) rural and urban size distributions of per capita total consumer expenditure (PCTE for short) data collected during the 61st (quinquennial large sample) round (July 2004 to June 2005) on household consumer expenditure of the National Sample Surveys (NSS). *Source: Planning Commission.* Other estimates are: (i) Arjun Sengupta (estimated on 2004–05 data) based on monetary value of per capita daily consumption: 'Below Poverty Line' (₹ 11.6 pcpd): 21.8 per cent of total population; 'Poor and vulnerable' (c. $2 per day), 77 per cent of total population (i.e., 836 million). (ii) Tendulkar Committee (estimated on 2004–05 data): Based on urban poverty line basket for household goods and services consumed: 25.7 per cent urban and 41.8 per cent rural. (iii) World Bank: (for 2005) based on international poverty line of consumption levels of $1.25 pcpd (per capita consumption per day in US$ at purchasing power parity) and $2 pcpd: 456 million and 828 million respectively. These have been criticized by, among others, Surjit Bhalla.

16 This forecast does not consider the prospects of domestic shale gas.

17 Without considering the possibility of shale oil.

18 However, the US EIAs projection in the IEO 2010 shows a lower increase – from 2.5 in 2005 to 4.7 million barrels per day (mmbd) in 2035.

19 Percentages are derived from India's commercial energy balance, 2007–08, Table 9.2 above.

20 Hillary Clinton, US Secretary of State: '*...there needed to be 'formal links' created between the International Energy Agency and China and India*' Senate Confirmation Hearing, January 13, 2009.

21 Nobuo Tanaka, Executive Director, IEA: '*One of my priorities as the new IEA Executive Director is to step up our co–operation with both countries. In good time this could hopefully pave the way, with the support of all the governments concerned, to an ultimate objective of their future membership of the Agency.*', IEA Press Release, 07 November 2007.

22 Joint Statement of the Ministry of Energy, Russian Federation, and the International Energy Agency, October 14, 2009.

23 Source: Cogan, Jeff *ibid.*

24 Andhra Business Bureau, April 15, 2010.

25 Source: China Daily, May 10, 2010.

26 In a cartelized supply side market, all suppliers, and not only cartel members benefit from cartel behaviour. This is likewise true of cartelized demand side markets.

27 The loss of voting power would for some selected countries be as follows: US: 26.4 to 16.2 per cent, UK: 4.6 to 1.5 per cent, Germany: 6.3 to 5.2 per cent, Japan: 9.8 to8.9 per cent. India would have 5.8 per cent, and China 9.4 per cent upon entry on this basis.

28 Source: Cogan, Jeff: *Ibid.*

29 Source: Own calculations based on US Energy Information Administration 2010 data. Marginal adjustments have been made due to some cases of missing 2009 data; these do not materially alter the results.

30 China is likely to further take into account the OECD requirement that new members must demonstrate adherence to democracy, human rights, and an open market economy.

31 In fact, in respect of major international negotiations such as climate change, the EU negotiates as a single entity.

32 Source: International Energy Outlook, 2010, US EIA.

33 Recall that in terms of IEA procedures, majority is found when 60 per cent of votes cast representing at least 50 per cent of total votes is in favour.

34 Joint Statement of the Ministry of Energy, Russian Federation, and the International Energy Agency, Paris, October 14, 2009.

35 Source: Multilateral Agreement on International Energy Programmeme, 18 November 1974.

36 Source: History of the IEA Volume 4, P 50, OECD/IEA 2004.

Contributors

Parthasarathi Shome is Chairman (Minister of State) of the Tax Administration Reform Commission, Government of India. His experience spans international trade and finance and tax policy and administration, and includes the G20 and multilateralism. In his early career, he was Professor of Economics at The American University, Washington DC.

Rajesh Chakrabarti is Associate Professor at the Indian School of Business, Hyderabad.

Francis Xavier Rathinam is Evaluation Specialist, International Initiative for Impact Evaluation (3ie), New Delhi.

Vijay Kumar Varadi is Data Scientist, Global Analytics, Bengaluru.

Renu Kohli is an economist and consultant at various economic research organisations including at the Indian Council for Research on International Economic Relations (ICRIER), New Delhi.

D. K. Srivastava is Chief Policy Adviser, Tax & Regulatory Services, Ernst & Young Pvt. Ltd., Gurgaon.

Kirit S. Parikh is Chairman, Integrated Research and Action for Development (IRADe), New Delhi.

A. Damodaran is Professor at the Indian Institute of Management (IIM), Bangalore.

Amrita Goldar is Fellow at the Indian Council for Research on International Economic Relations (ICRIER), New Delhi.

Meeta Keswani Mehra is Associate Professor at the Centre for International Trade and Development, Jawaharlal Nehru University, New Delhi.

Divya Datt is Fellow at The Energy and Resources Institute (TERI), New Delhi.

Prodipto Ghosh is Distinguished Fellow at The Energy and Resources Institute (TERI), New Delhi.

Index